D0401072

PRAISE FOR
Savage Summit

"This inspiring book is highly recommended."

—*Library Journal*

"Jordan demonstrates how these women got swept up in their high-flying quests and gives us a sense of the rapture that comes from standing on top of the world's highest mountains." —*Los Angeles Times*

"For mountain-climbing enthusiasts and women's history buffs, Jordan's well-researched survey is worthwhile reading."

—*Publishers Weekly*

"Jordan highlights not only the dangers but also the sexism, disregard for basic decency, and narcissism that plague the world of high-altitude alpinism."

—*New York Times Book Review*

"*Savage Summit* fills an interesting and neglected place in mountaineering literature."

—*American Alpine Club* magazine

© Jeff Rhoads

About the Author

JENNIFER JORDAN has lived at the base of K2 twice while writing and producing the National Geographic documentary *The Women of K2*. She is a writer, producer, journalist, and news personality, having created, produced, and hosted her own public radio talk show. Jennifer lives with her husband, filmmaker and adventurer Jeff Rhoads, in Salt Lake City.

SAVAGE SUMMIT

JENNIFER JORDAN

SAVAGE SUMMIT

THE LIFE AND DEATH

OF THE FIRST WOMEN OF K2

Harper

An Imprint of HarperCollinsPublishers

A hardcover edition of this book was published by William Morrow, an imprint of HarperCollins Publishers.

SAVAGE SUMMIT. Copyright © 2005 by Jennifer Jordan. All rights reserved. Printed in the United States of America. No part of this book may be used or reproduced in any manner whatsoever without written permission except in the case of brief quotations embodied in critical articles and reviews. For information address HarperCollins Publishers, 10 East 53rd Street, New York, NY 10022.

HarperCollins books may be purchased for educational, business, or sales promotional use. For information please write: Special Markets Department, HarperCollins Publishers, 10 East 53rd Street, New York, NY 10022.

First Harper paperback published 2006.

Designed by Amy Hill

The Library of Congress has catalogued the hardcover edition as follows:

Jordan, Jennifer.
    Savage summit : the true stories of the first five women who climbed K2, the world's most feared mountain / Jennifer Jordan.
      p. cm.
    Includes bibliographical references.
    ISBN 0-06-058715-6 (hc : alk. paper)
      1. Women mountaineers—Biography. 2. Mountaineers—Biography. 3. Mountaineering—Pakistan—K2 (Mountain). 4. K2 (Pakistan : Mountain)—Description and travel.   I. Title.

GV199.9.J67 2005
796.52'2'0922—dc22
[B]   2004054658

ISBN-10: 0-06-058716-4 (pbk.)
ISBN-13: 978-0-06-058716-1 (pbk.)

07   08   09   10   ❖/RRD   10 9 8 7 6 5 4 3

*To Charlie Houston
and the women of K2,
my heroes of the Himalayan world*

76° 15'

Sarpo Lago Gl.

SINKIANG
CHINA

Muztagh
Pass

Sarpo Lago Pass
18520

35°
50'

MUZTAGH TOWER

17800

23860

LOBSANG

20420

Younghusband Gl.

Muztagh Gl.

TRANGO
TOWERS

Trango Gl.

Baltoro

Glacier

22160

Urdukas 13000

PAIYU

Mundi Gl.

Yermanendu Gl.

BIARCHED

21660

Lilipru
12000

22180

35°
40'

Paiyu

11000

MASHERBRUM

20510

25660

KASHMIR

PAKISTAN

Masherbrum Gl.

© 1978 D Molenaar

76° 30'   76° 45'

SKYANG
KANGRI
24750

Savoia
Pass   28250
K2

Windy
Gap
21300

Godwin-Austen Glacier

Sella
Pass
20207

22490

Savoia
Glacier

BROAD PK
26400

Marble Pk
20088

IV
26180   III   II   26360

Concordia
15000

Gasherbrum
V 24013
Group   HIDDEN PK
I • 26470

MITRE
19700

Upper

Vigne Gl.

VI •22976

Duke of Abruzzi Gl.

Baltoro

GOLDEN THRONE
• 23983

Glacier

0   1   2   3   4   5   Miles
0 1 2 3 4 5 6 7 8   Kilometers

22480

CHOGOLISA
(Bride Pk) 25110

BALTORO REGION
Karakoram Himalaya
Sinkiang China—Kashmir Pakistan

Shaksgam River

CONTENTS

WHY K2?

It's a logical question. K2 is not Everest, not many have climbed it, and almost no one knows where it is. And besides all that, why me? I'm a born and bred Yankee, worked most of my life reporting for Boston radio stations and magazines, and considered competing in ultra running trail races and the Ironman triathlon adventure enough. Not exactly your typical stepping-stones to the unspeakably dangerous and hypoxic world of 8,000-meter peaks that sit halfway around the world in Nepal, Tibet, and Pakistan. But that's exactly where I ended up.

My journey to K2, the second-highest mountain in the world, sitting weeks from civilization on the Pakistan-China border, began years earlier when I read *Into Thin Air*. Like millions of readers who learned the excruciating reality of high-altitude climbing through the story of Mount Everest's deadliest storm in 1996, I suddenly found myself fascinated with that exotic and ruthless world at 8,000 meters, or 26,000 feet, an altitude above which life begins to die. Who were these strange souls who sought to enter that so-called Death Zone, and why did they revel in the literally mind-blowing experience of having millions of brain cells die in minutes?

I also became fascinated by the roles that women played in this high-altitude game of life and death and wondered how their experience differed from that of their male teammates. In my reading of Jon Krakauer's brilliantly told story, I sensed a certain bias, an agenda, concerning the women on the mountain that year, particularly Sandy Hill Pittman, whose wealth and personality he spent a lot of ink chastising, as if being arrogant and rich somehow made her less of a climber. Further, while he seemed to point a finger of blame at Pittman for being a client who survived, he made heroes of the guides who died, and of one guide in particular who in my estimation made the worst errors of the day by climbing past his own turnaround time and pulling an exhausted client with him.

Why, I wondered, had Krakauer chosen to single out Pittman for vilification and not the men whose choices were, at the least, questionable, and did that bad air permeate the high-altitude experience for other women climbers?

So I kept digging, not knowing what I was looking for but somehow feeling I was missing the story. Then in 1998 I found it.

"Chantal Mauduit just died on Dhaulagiri. She's the last one," Charlotte Fox said.

We were sitting on Fox's back porch in Aspen, the afternoon summer sun hot on the terra-cotta tiles, sipping perfectly steeped ice tea and talking about her experience as a survivor of the 1996 disaster on Everest. She had been looking through a climbing magazine searching for an article I should read when she saw Mauduit's obituary.

"The last one what?" I asked, embarrassed to be so obviously clueless.

"The last woman who made it off K2 alive. She just died on Dhaulagiri in Nepal," Charlotte said, pausing to look at me to see if I had made the connection. "K2, the mountain? Now all of the five women who've climbed it are dead."

I didn't know who Mauduit was, or even where this K2 was, but I knew my mind and soul had had a sea change. My questions veered from women mountaineers in general to the women of K2. Why had so few women climbed it? Who were they? And most crucially, how could none of them have survived?

Soon I would learn that K2, at 28,268 feet (8,616 meters), is second out of the fourteen peaks in the world that rise above 8,000 meters, the height against which all other mountains are measured. Everest is, of course, first, but even though eight climbers had died there that one day in 1996, it seemed that toll was nothing compared to K2's track record. By the end of the 2003 climbing season, nearly 2,000 had climbed Everest, but fewer than 200 had climbed K2 in the same period. While Everest had suffered 180 deaths, K2 had seen 53—9.4 percent versus nearly 27 percent. Between K2's unrelenting 45- to 65-degree slopes, brutal weather, and general lack of high-altitude porters to carry oxygen and heavy loads high on the mountain, it suffered few fools and almost no clients. It simply didn't have the infrastructure for such hubris. As a result, it tended to attract the best climbers, and that made its death rate all the more remarkable. I had thought Everest was dangerous, but I was learning a whole new definition for the word *lethal*.

An early climber took one look at the far-off pyramid and declared it an unconquerable mountain of all "rock and ice and storm and abyss." In 1953 it was dubbed "the Savage Mountain" by a team of young American climbers after one of their friends perished high on the mountain, and it's continued to earn the distinction. At the beginning of the 2004 climbing season, nearly a half-century since an Italian team first made the summit in 1954, only five women had reached its summit (compared to ninety female ascents of Everest). Three of them died on their descent, and the two who made it off alive died shortly thereafter while climbing other 8,000-meter peaks. And in 1998 Mauduit became the last.

In the few years following that sunny Aspen afternoon, my research continued, and I came to know K2 as I knew few things in life. Over time I felt a love and tenderness for the five women who climbed it that journalists often gain for their research subjects. I learned that the first woman to climb K2 in 1986 remains unsurpassed with a climbing record of summiting eight—perhaps nine—8,000-meter peaks. I read that before another woman of K2 left Base Camp for her fatal summit bid, she had answered letters to her two young children eager for their "mummy" to return home—*couldn't she come home now?* I had spoken to another woman's brother and learned that his younger sister had a love for life that often made her jump without looking for a safety net, a carefree—and some charged careless—joie de vivre that defined her life. And I had learned that another woman of K2 had already seen six deaths on the mountain by the time she made her summit bid during the mountain's deadliest climbing season in 1986. Her death would be among the year's staggering toll of thirteen.

Who were these pioneering climbers, and why did they choose a life on the edge of death? Why did they die, and why did one mountain claim so many of them? How did they make the decision to leave family, husband, and children to venture into the world's highest and most deadly playground? Did their gender have a hand in their deaths? And while the mountain may not have cared that they were women, were there other forces at work that did?

Grim and gruesome, these questions haunted me, and I wanted to learn more than books and memoirs could provide. Plus, the books and memoirs were mostly about men; women mountaineers seemed to be a footnote in climbing history. I knew they deserved their own book and thought I might as well be the person to write it. And even though the very thought of it terrified me, I knew I had to travel to Pakistan and see the mountain for myself.

Less than two weeks before my departure in May 2000, I went to hear David Breashears, the filmmaker who became a hero when he helped save the survivors of the 1996 Everest disaster, deliver the commencement address at Sterling College in Craftsbury Common, Vermont. As we walked to the garden where the ceremonies were held, David gestured to an elderly man walking with him and said, "Jennifer, if you're on your way to K2, you have to meet this man."

We paused on the slate walkway, and the man turned to meet me. I found myself looking into blue eyes that positively danced with life. I didn't need any more of an introduction.

"Charlie Houston, I presume," I said, extending my hand. "I'm Jennifer Jordan, and I leave for K2 in two weeks. I'm honored to meet you."

Dr. Charles S. Houston led the 1938 and 1953 American expeditions to the mountain and has been called the grandfather of Himalayan mountaineering. Although it is a history often rife with ego, shame, and blame, Charlie remains universally loved and his expeditions heralded as "jewels in the crown of Himalayan climbing."

Not satisfied with formal introductions, he pushed my proffered hand aside and pulled me into a bear hug so tight I thought I could hear my ribs cracking.

"My dear girl," he said, "how lovely that you are going to my K2. Give that beautiful mountain my best, will you?"

I promised I would and walked to my seat beaming, not only at having met a piece of history but also over knowing instantly that he would be in my life for as long as time would allow. When I left for the mountain, I remembered that hug and his pure delight that I would be experiencing a place that he clearly loved with all his heart.

Unfortunately, my expedition was anything but delightful, lovely, or any other adjective that even suggests enjoyment. I traveled with a large American team to the mountain's North Ridge in China. I had hoped to find myself among a team of rare souls who understood that they were entering what some called "the Cathedral of the Mountain Gods," humbled to be among the world's most sacred peaks. Instead, it was a sad and disparate group of warring and unhappy egos, each with an opposing agenda and none with the ability to lead the group. We returned to the States after four wretched months in each other's company, the climbers without having achieved the summit, and I nowhere near having gotten my book. When I visited Charlie soon after my return, he looked at me with a devilish grin: "My dear, it really is your own fault for going to such a remote place with a group of strangers." He was right, of course, but it didn't help my sense of disappointment.

Then, two years later, I found myself again approaching the unbearably flawless mountain, this time with a small team of close friends, all talented climbers and gentle souls. When we turned for home nearly three months later, again not having achieved the summit, we were nonetheless better friends and more seasoned climbers than when we had left. I finally had my book.

Well, almost.

I've heard writers say that a book "just wrote itself." Well, not this one. If anything, it got harder to write as each day progressed, each new detail was learned, and each woman slowly became unveiled to me. In the beginning each was merely a cardboard cutout: climber, mother, daughter, lover. But as I found and interviewed their parents, spouses, children, siblings, friends, biographers, and rivals, their two-dimensional lives exploded with all the Technicolor and controversy in which we all live. Add to that tumultuous tableau the messy world of mountain climbing with its hypoxic and often self-serving memory of life and death at 8,000 meters and you have a recipe for tabloid trauma at its vivid best.

But it wasn't until I actually began to write down the stories of the five women of K2 that I realized just how tough a task I had undertaken. For one thing, they were all dead and their histories poorly recorded— so poorly recorded in fact that I was unable to find a single picture of any of them on the summit of K2. Either the cameras malfunctioned or the women were lost. In addition to scant and scattered information, I didn't become obsessed with these women with salacious intent, and so my job became even more difficult as I learned that each had hardly been a naive Girl Scout. Like most of us, they had ghosts and demons in some very crowded closets. Writing the lives of these complex, complicated women honestly and objectively, while maintaining a dignified distance from their very personal and often very troubled histories, became an arduous task.

I also wondered how I would comprehensively write about personalities that not only went to the edge of death but lived there, flirting with its oddly tantalizing edge for days, even months, at a time. I was near that edge of death when I fell into a deep crevasse on the north side of K2, and rather than stare in calm wonder at my very possible and imminent death, every fiber of my being screamed, "OHGODOHGODOHGOD! I CAN'T BELIEVE I'M GOING TO DIE HERE! NOT HERE, NOT NOW!" There was certainly no peace, no acquiescence, no gentle surrender. And when I watched other men and women on K2 dance on that edge, daring it and themselves to get closer with every step, I was paralyzed with fear, as if the panic they *should have* felt had somehow transplanted itself into my own heart, freezing it cold.

But I realized that even if I could not entirely understand their pleasure in almost courting death, I could at least hope to convey their sense of life. In doing so, I have employed a tactic used effectively by many historians, most notably Sebastian Junger in *The Perfect Storm,* and I did so for his same reason: re-creating the actual dialogue of the dead is often impossible with few or no living witnesses of the event. Therefore, in the pages that follow there are two forms of spoken word: one in quotes, which I gathered firsthand from journals, books, and witnesses, and the other in italics, representing thoughts and conversations that are based on fact but are not exact quotes.

Let me say at the beginning that this is not the end. As this book was going to press, a sixth woman, Edurne Pasabán of Spain, reached the summit of K2 and made it down alive, although barely. (See Author's Note.) While her accomplishment is enormous, my focus had been and remains the five who came before her as it is their stories, their lives, and their deaths which have consumed me for the better part of six years. So here you have my best attempt at bringing these women into your life. I hope my account is honest, straightforward, and compelling. But in no way do I claim to be the last word, the omniscient word, or the absolute truth about who they were, how they lived, and how they died. I aim simply to share with you the stories of five remarkable women who chose to live at the edge of death and all of whom ultimately died there.

This book is for them.

Wanda Rutkiewicz (1943–1992) summited K2 in 1986.
Liliane Barrard (1948–1986) died on her descent of K2 in 1986.
Julie Tullis (1939–1986) died on her descent of K2 in 1986.
Chantal Mauduit (1964–1998) summited K2 in 1992.
Alison Hargreaves (1962–1995) died on her descent of K2 in 1995.

SAVAGE SUMMIT

CHAPTER 1

A WOMEN'S HISTORY OF K2

The chief joy is the varied and perfect exercise, in the midst of noble scenery and exhilarating atmosphere. The peak utters a challenge. The climber responds by saying to himself, I can and I will conquer it.

—ANNIE SMITH PECK (1850–1935)

For most of the modern age, "woman climber" was an oxymoron. Women were almost without exception wives, widows, prostitutes, royalty, or slaves. But sometime during the late eighteenth century, when the first woman cinched a rope around her waist and lashed her boots into bear claw shaped steel crampons to climb up ice walls and steep snow slopes, war was declared on the status quo. From the time of those earliest rock and alpine pioneers, women have had to deal with their gender as well as the mountains in order to climb. Whether it has been climbing with the danger and annoyance of twenty-two-pound skirts and the inconvenience of monthly menses or negotiating the power struggles with their male teammates, porters, guides, and officials, women have had very different experiences than men in the climbing world.

Early explorers of the sea, desert, jungle, Arctic, and mountains were mostly men whose cultures and personal fortunes allowed them such freedom. The few women of the eighteenth, nineteenth, and early twentieth centuries who had the financial and societal independence to venture beyond the narrow confines of the day found getting to the mountains a difficult feat. Not only did men invite other men to attempt the then-unclimbed peaks around them, but many resented the intrusion of women into their very male pursuits, as if the presence of women some-how diluted the fun, the danger, and the escape of their adventures. If it had been possible, one can imagine those early men posting a "No Girls Allowed" sign above the mountains.

The early female mountaineers also faced resistance and umbrage from deep within the cultured societies of London, Paris, and Boston, which had difficulty embracing the display of women, in britches or skirts shortened to their calves, ropes pulled tight around their bodies, climbing and sleeping on mountains, *with men!* Further, it was one thing for men to risk death in their lofty pursuits, but for women who "belonged" safely at home caring for the children, it was practically blasphemous.

But the women pioneers of rock and ice persevered through their culture's indignation and scorn, first ascending Mont Blanc in 1808 (although barely, as Marie Paradis, exhausted and quite undone by her efforts, begged her companions to throw her into the nearest crevasse to put her out of her misery), the Matterhorn in 1871, and finally the world's mightiest peak, Mount Everest, in 1975. With every rope they suffered second-guessing, petty jealousy, and recrimination, not to mention the resentment of men who felt challenged when women achieved the same feats that they had heralded as pushing the limits of what the human body could endure. After all, if a mere woman could do it, how dangerous could it be?

Pretty damn dangerous, as it would turn out, particularly for those who set their sights on the world's highest mountains, the fourteen that stand above 8,000 meters, roughly the cruising altitude of a jetliner. Only a tiny fraction of the world's population will ever breathe the rar-efied thin air that veils the top of the world, and even fewer will survive the experience. High-altitude climbing is the most deadly of recre-ations, many times more lethal than skydiving, race-car driving, or base-jumping. On certain peaks the fatality rates are staggering, but on K2 they are mind-boggling. When a climber straps on his crampons with the intent of ascending K2, he knows he has a one-in-four chance of not making it off the mountain alive. One in four. And as bad as those odds are, they are even worse for women. Six women have reached the summit of K2, but five have died trying. (In addition to the three who died on descent, another two women died on ascent without reaching the summit.) For women the statistics are small but nonetheless powerful. The bottom line is that women have fared disastrously on K2.

Ironically, as bad as their experience on K2 has been, women actually die *less* often than men on the other 8,000-meter peaks. Although there has been almost no scientific research on the effects of high altitude on the female body, what little data there are actually indicate that women are *better* suited to the rigors of the Death Zone than their male colleagues. Recent studies suggest that as men and women climb higher, men's initial advantage of muscle mass and brute strength equalizes out against women's better endurance and ability to adapt to the thin air. Not only do women suffer high-altitude pulmonary edema less often, but they acclimatize *better,* they retain their basc body weight *better,* and their more efficient circulatory systems lead them to suffer less frostbite—the formation of ice crystals in the cells that destroys their structure and constricts the oxygen flow, leading to infection and, if untreated, quickly to gangrene, resulting finally in amputation. There is also early evidence that the female sex hormone helps to guard women against the deadly effects of high altitude, but further research needs to be done to make that theory conclusive.

Women have in fact survived their Himalayan ventures slightly better than men. In the entire Himalaya there have been thirty-one female deaths, or 4.7 percent of all fatalities. But women account for 5.4 percent of all the ascents. Women therefore have a 0.7 percent better survival rate than men in the Himalaya. An exception is on K2, where women represent almost 10 percent of the total deaths and only 2.5 percent of all ascents. Women are therefore four times more likely to get killed on K2 than nearly all the other 8,000-meter peaks.

So, given the fact that women, on average, perform physically better than men at altitude, why have they done so dreadfully on K2? If the mountain, weather, terrain, and equipment are treating the women with impartiality, what are the deciding factors in their staggering death rate? Some observers say the pool of women, six, is simply too small from which to draw concrete conclusions. Others point to the fact that four of these women died with men, so gender cannot be cited as a factor in their deaths. But many believe there is one quantifiable difference between women and men on K2: experience. And here, women do seem to tip the scales by pushing their experiential envelope and approaching the world's most infamous 8,000-meter peak too soon.

While male climbers tend to spend most of their youth climbing the rock and ice walls of America, Asia, and Europe and venture to the Himalayas only when experience and money allow, women often approach K2 early in their climbing career. Because there are so few women climbing the 8,000-meter peaks, they can cut sponsor deals, interest the media, and raise money for high-profile expeditions much more easily. With little or no experience, a woman can sell herself as a bona-fide contender for an 8,000-meter peak—and in the case of K2, as the first woman from America, Italy, Russia, or wherever to climb the mountain, cashing in on a slew of nationalistic pride and dollars. Once there, most women have found the mountain and its weather too much for their ability, strength, or experience, but it hasn't stopped them from trying.

By the time Italian climbers Lino Lacedelli and Achille Compagnoni placed the first flag on K2's summit in 1954, no fewer than seventeen reconnaissance, exploration, and climbing expeditions had traveled through the uncompromising landscape, and one of the first was led by a vanguard American explorer, Fanny Bullock Workman.

A solid plug of a woman, with a homely, round face and thick, commanding eyebrows, Fanny Bullock came from a prominent Massachusetts family, and her father served as a Republican governor of the state. Fanny was educated by private tutors before being sent to finishing schools in Paris and Dresden, where she became fluent in French and German, allowing her to travel without the language barriers many Americans still face. She returned home and at twenty-two married a retired physician twelve years her senior, William Workman. After raising a daughter, they together made it their late-in-life ambition to explore and map areas of the world that her relatives in Worcester never knew existed. And while Fanny eschewed the conventions that would have seen her at home attending social teas, she nonetheless chose to remain cloaked in their cumbersome clothing, touring temple ruins and tribal mud huts in neatly pressed white blouses, heavy skirts, thick leggings, and veiled hats.

Once they learned how to ride an early prototype of the mountain bike to come a century later, Fanny and William explored the Iberian Peninsula, bicycling through Morocco, then overland to Algeria, and from one end of the Indian subcontinent to the other. Then in 1899 they left their bicycles at the snouts of the great glaciers in the Karakoram Mountains and traveled from there by foot, reconnoitering the Biafo, Baltoro, Hispar, and Saichen Glaciers that snaked through the towering peaks. When they reached the Shigar Valley, Fanny and William climbed to the top of a 19,450-foot peak and promptly declared it Mount Bullock Workman. As they posed for pictures, they noticed a predominant frozen pyramid alone on the horizon.

"We had not expected to find the view so uninterruptedly beautiful and extensive as it proved," she wrote for the *British Alpine Journal.* "To the northeast, Mountain Godwin-Austin [sic] was seen grandly and without a cloud." (Early explorers gave K2 the name of the first European to get within twenty miles of the mountain, Sir H. H. Godwin-Austen in 1861. Thankfully, in some minds, its colonized appellation did not stick. Instead, the glacier at the base of the mountain bears his name, and K2 retains the simple designation of a cartographer's mark.)

It was the end of the nineteenth century, and a woman was admiring the world's second-highest mountain. Given the cultural norms of the times, she may have been the first. For centuries nomadic peoples traveled through the Nepalese and Tibetan Himalayan foothills of their godly mountains, and women were an obvious part of the human caravan. But to this day reaching K2 requires a treacherous seven-day walk on a fifty-mile glacier from the last village. Also, there were and still are cultural restrictions on that travel. For centuries Islamic—and before them Buddhist—peoples scratched out meager existences in the foothills of the Karakoram, painstakingly diverting the floodwaters to irrigate their fields. If those hardscrabble lives ever allowed for the leisure of climbing the lesser mountains from which one might get a glimpse of K2 far off in the distance, it is doubtful that such a luxury extended to women. Until large Western expeditions began exploring the area in the late nineteenth century and hiring local men to porter their loads during their explorations, there was simply no reason for the local farmers or nomadic tribesmen to travel anywhere near the mountain, a fact history bears out.

In 1856 Sir T. G. Montgomerie of the Great Trigonometric Survey of India sighted a vast and still unreachable colossus over a hundred miles away from his perch in Kashmir. He made a quick sketch of it and a nearby peak, dubbing them simply K1 and K2, "K" standing for the Karakoram Range in which they sat. Montgomerie made every effort to find out whether his "K1" and "K2" had local names; Everest, for instance, is known as Chomolungma by the Tibetans to the north and as Sagarmatha by the Nepalese to the south. While he discovered that K1 was called Masherbrum by the Baltistan people, he found that K2 had no such local nomenclature. K2, it seemed, was so secluded and so difficult to reach that the locals had no common name for it.

When Fanny Bullock Workman sat high above Shigar admiring "Mount Godwin-Austen" and penning her note for the *Alpine Journal*, she was making history for women and women explorers, and she knew it. Writing in one of her trip journals, she stated that she placed her name firmly in the expedition's legal dossier so that "it should be known to [future female adventurers] and stated in print that a woman was the initiator and special leader of this expedition."

While successful in fording new trails and mapping unforeseen wilds of the Karakoram, Fanny was not particularly liked. She was a suffragette who posed in 1917 with a newspaper headline "Votes for Women" on a mountaintop in the Karakoram, and her outspoken personality and success as an explorer irked many at home. Fanny also spent a lot of her time and a chunk of her money in a nasty and public battle with fellow New Englander Annie Peck Smith over who had in fact climbed the higher mountain. Hiring a team of French engineers to triangulate Huascarán in Peru, which Peck had climbed, Fanny proved that a 23,000-foot (7,000-meter) peak she had climbed with William near the Vale of Kashmir was indeed grander than Peck's 21,812-foot (6,648-meter) Huascarán.

In twenty-something years of exploring the wild and largely unknown world of ice, Fanny performed remarkably well, suffering only the usual effects of common altitude sickness and dehydration: headache, mild nausea, and shortness of breath. Her remedy was fast and sure—quarts of weak tea spiked with whiskey. But her stalwart good health and ability to adjust to the thin Himalayan air did not stay with her, and she died in 1925 at age sixty-six after a long and debilitating disease, leaving William a widower until his death twelve years later. In her obituary in the *Alpine Journal*, J. P. Farrar wrote:

> *She herself felt that she suffered from sex-antagonism and it is possible that some unconscious feeling, let us say of the novelty of a woman's intrusion into the domain of exploration so long reserved to men, may in some quarters have existed.*

That sense of a woman's "intrusion into the domain of men's exploration" was to plague Fanny and many of the women who followed her into the wilds of the Karakoram.

Regardless of the roadblocks, the next fifty years saw the forays of more and more women into the grandest mountain ranges of the world. In 1934 the 24,000-foot (7,300-meter) mark was broken by German climber Hettie Dyhrenfurth on Pakistan's 24,370-foot (7,422-meter) Sia Kangri (Queen Mary Peak), and in 1954 French climber Claude Kogan reached nearly 25,000 feet (7,600 meters) on her first attempt of 26,906-foot (8,201-meter) Cho Oyu in Nepal. In 1955 the first all-women team approached the Himalayas, successfully making a first ascent of 22,000-foot (6,700-meter) Gyalgen Peak.

By 1964 all of the 8,000-meter peaks had been climbed, but none of them by a woman. Finally, after years of trying, women broke the 8,000-meter mark in 1974 when a team of three Japanese women, Masako Uchida, Mieko Mori, and Naoko Nakaseko, climbed 8,156-meter

(26,758-foot) Manaslu, the world's eighth-highest peak. But the victory ended in tragedy when another of their teammates fell to her death descending the mountain, not having reached the summit. A year later Anna Okopinska and Halina Krüger-Syrokomska of Poland reached the summit of Pakistan's 8,035-meter (26,361-foot) Gasherbrum II without oxygen and on the first all-women rope, and on May 16, 1975, Junko Tabei of Japan became the first woman to reach the top of the world, 8,850-meter (29,035-foot) Mount Everest.

Only days after the highest point on Earth was finally visited by a woman, 800 miles (1,287 kilometers) north and west, a petite Canadian woman was taking her last footsteps toward the world's *second*-highest mountain, K2.

Dianne Roberts grew up in Calgary, Alberta, and spent her childhood hiking in the Canadian Rockies, but she never considered herself a mountaineer, at least not before she met and married one of America's finest climbers, Jim Whittaker, a man twenty-one years her senior. In 1963 Whittaker had succeeded in becoming the first American to climb Mount Everest. The picture of him on the summit, with one leg pitched high against the steep summit cone and the American and National Geographic Society flags flying from his ice ax triumphantly held above his head, is a classic featured on many mountaineering and museum walls. His subsequent invitation to the Rose Garden from President John F. Kennedy was the beginning of a lifelong friendship with the first family of American politics. In part because of those connections, Whittaker was asked in 1973 to help organize the first expedition into K2 since border wars between Pakistan and India had closed the area twelve years before. Whittaker called Washington for assistance in cutting through the red tape, and it was Senator Edward Kennedy who helped convince the new Pakistani government to issue the first climbing permit since that closure.

Whittaker's 1975 American K2 expedition has become legend, but mostly for the wrong reasons: crippling porter strikes, team dissension, leadership conflicts, and horrendous weather. Teammate Jim Wickwire said that the expedition was his greatest failure and that his "obsession to reach the summit helped doom our expedition to disappointment,

discord, and, for a time, disgrace." But along with the strife and turmoil they also made history in bringing the first woman to the base
of the mountain. Rather than celebrate their pioneering spirit, however,
the 1975 American K2 team allowed Roberts's very presence to tear the
team apart.

Whittaker said he never hesitated in including his twenty-six-year-
old bride on the team and was confident that she was capable of han-
dling the rigors of the trek as well as the mountain itself. "I knew her
capabilities," Whittaker said, "perhaps better than she did. I thought she
could do well, and she went very high. She did well. She's a good gal."

She also turned out to be a hell of a climber, but it wasn't enough for
her teammates. From the expedition's earliest steps up the wide Shigar
Valley out of Skardu, emotions and egos ran high, much of the turmoil
swirling around its only woman. Roberts said she never intended to go
for the summit; she wanted to take pictures and carry loads to the high
camps to support the team on the mountain. But the team felt her presence like a thorn.

Just as male soldiers have historically had trouble adjusting to a
female presence in combat, male climbers have often resisted the inclu-
sion of a woman on their very male expeditions to the high mountains.
Some blame the resistance on an almost biological imperative men feel
to protect women, a pressure with potentially fatal results in the perilous environments of battle and 8,000-meter peaks, places where soldiers or climbers can barely keep themselves alive.

Others say men just can't handle the sexual tension from having a
woman present during their three-month celibacy on an expedition. It's
fine, some have said, if the woman on the team is sharing your tent, but
if she's with another man, watch out. And a few men admit to simply
preferring the camaraderie of men; it's more fun, more safe, and less
complicated, they say. Most men admit that the problem is not with the
women, it's with men not being able to deal with them, but that doesn't
help the women who have to deal with the criticism, ridicule, and isolation for months on end.

There is also the fact that Roberts, like many women, was seen as not
having paid her dues as a climber to be on a mountain like K2, while

many of the men on the team had spent years, even decades, climbing, learning, and gaining experience. Roberts was seen not as a valued member of the climbing team but as a potential liability who would necessitate rescue, a rescue the men would risk their lives in performing.

Whatever the reasons for the tensions, the team festered while the weather kept them relatively low on the mountain, further adding to the pressure cooker of emotions, frustrations, and antagonism.

Roberts felt rejected and hurt after shouldering what she thought was more than her share of the load, and she told Wickwire that she felt "unwelcome and ostracized." It wasn't until years later that she learned that many of her teammates felt that she shouldn't have been there, most notably her new brother-in-law, Lou Whittaker, Jim's identical twin. "I think it was a twin thing, a brother thing, a jealousy thing. Who knows?" she said. "It was painful and I was pissed off, but I don't want to dwell on it."

Jim Whittaker said the only second thoughts he had about his team were those about having brought some of the men, but by the time the trouble started on the trek in, it was too late to send them home, "so we just had to live with it." The scars remained, and many on the team were still nursing their wounds decades later. The Whittaker twins, in the eyes of many, were never completely able to repair the damage. The team left the mountain in early July simmering in anger and resentment.

When Jim announced to Dianne his intention to return to the mountain in 1978 for another American try at the summit, she insisted on having more women on the team, hoping it would take some of the pressure off her. Besides, she hoped it would be more fun to have another woman to talk to during the months-long sequestering among the men.

The plan was less than successful when one of the three women included on the team, Cherie Bech, fell in love and began a very open affair with a handsome and charismatic climber named Chris Chandler, even though her husband, Terry Bech, was also on the team.

Rick Ridgeway, a climber from California and one of the four members to ascend the mountain in 1978, recalled his concern that their open affair would blow up into a nasty "life and death" fight between Terry Bech and Chandler.

"We actually talked about stuff like ice axes through people's heads. You never know. You're under duress at best at 8,000 meters."

Concerned, Ridgeway approached Bech to talk it over. He needn't have bothered. Bech told Ridgeway and some other teammates to mind their own business and said that Cherie had his consent to make her own decisions. An open marriage was one thing, but one on an 8,000-meter peak halfway around the world was more than most of the team could handle. Try as Ridgeway would to stay out of it, the affair nonetheless ended his friendship with Chris Chandler, who died high on Kangchenjunga in 1985 before any reconciliation could be made.

Apart from her affair with Chandler, Cherie's presence as a strong and capable climbing member seemed to affront many of her male teammates before the first rope was even anchored to the ice walls of K2. Ridgeway observed that Cherie often hauled enormous loads from base to the high camps, some as heavy as ninety pounds, nearly twice a typical "carry." Commenting that the loads were unnecessarily, even dangerously, large, Ridgeway thought that she seemed intent on impressing those around her.

For her part, Cherie said that rather than trying to prove something to her male teammates, she was only hoping for acceptance and appreciation for what she could contribute in helping supply the team's high camps. But she was fighting a losing battle. Another member of the team, John Roskelley, made a point of telling people that he had never met a woman climber "worth a damn." They lacked either the strength or the skill or both at high altitude. While few were as outspoken as the "redneck from Spokane," as Roskelley once proudly labeled himself, the undercurrent flowed throughout the team, and like 1975, the 1978 expedition was rent down the middle with tensions. In the words of one team member, each climber "bears their own scars of the experience."

Many have commented on the Peyton Place aspect of Himalayan expeditions, and in particular those to K2. Galen Rowell, the late author of *In the Throne Room of the Gods*, said, "Perhaps one of the biggest flaws in expedition mountaineering is that it can sometimes promote a ruthless brand of militant enthusiasm that runs roughshod over friendships, health, safety, and reason." Unlike Everest, where a soft bed and cold Coca-Cola are only a three-hour walk down a well-trod yak trail, the K2 Base Camp is a week's scramble over a rock-covered, crevasse-littered glacier to the nearest village. And even if you wanted to leave, Pakistani military regulations forbid unchaperoned travel through Pakistan's high-altitude war zone with India. That isolation weighs heavily on many psyches, particularly when problems begin.

In 1975 and again in '78, when trouble started brewing on Whittaker's K2 expeditions, there was no escape for the team's simmering emotions. But as fractious and ugly as the fighting got, it didn't stop four team members from successfully reaching the summit and being the first to place the American flag on the world's second-highest peak.

"It was a miracle we pulled it off," Ridgeway said years later. "We were as a team split right down the middle, split by difficulties that were introduced and caused by the fact that we had both men and women on the team."

The team's two women climbers, Cherie Bech and Dianne Roberts, were not among the summit celebrants.

"At Camp V it was absolutely clear to me that was it," Roberts said. "I couldn't breathe. I felt claustrophobic. I spent a horrible night in the tent feeling like I couldn't breathe. It was time to get off." Still, she was proud of her achievement. "I felt that I had done what I could do. I never had any ambitions to go for the summit on that mountain. I had said I wanted to go as high as I could go, I wanted to support the summit team, and I wanted to do the best job I could do at photography. I did all those things." Bech also made the decision to descend at Camp V; neither woman would ever return to the mountain.

The summer of 1978 also saw victory and defeat on two other 8,000-meter peaks, both of which changed women's Himalayan climbing history forever.

In mid-October the American Women's Himalayan Expedition to Annapurna, the tenth-highest mountain in the world, was celebrating having put the first women (and first Americans) on the summit when disaster struck. Shortly after the radio crackled at Base Camp with Vera Komarkova and Irene Miller's victorious message from the summit, the team received word that two other teammates had disappeared. After nearly a week of anguished waiting for them to miraculously appear, Arlene Blum and her team had to accept that Alison Chadwick-Onyszkiewicz and Vera Watson were dead in a fall or avalanche off of Annapurna's relentless slopes. To this day the tenth-highest mountain in the world remains its deadliest with nearly a 50 percent death to summit rate.

Further up the Himalayan chain, on October 16, most likely on the same day that Chadwick-Onyszkiewicz and Watson perished, a thirty-five-year-old Polish climber named Wanda Rutkiewicz became the first Pole and the first Western woman to climb Mount Everest. Her race to be the first woman to climb all fourteen 8,000-meter peaks had begun with number one, and soon she would turn her eyes to number two—K2.

While the first two times women were included on K2 expeditions were wrought with internecine battles, ego wars, and sexual tensions, the next would be exempt from most of those conflicts because of one simple omission: men.

CHAPTER 2

THE PERSISTENT
PIONEER

Once experienced, it becomes an obsession.

—ANONYMOUS

Five-year-old Wanda Blaszkiewicz sat crouched on the low chair, her legs and feet bare on the floor, peeling potatoes into a bowl. She was a pretty child with dark curly hair and slim arms and legs, more often at work than at play, feeding her younger siblings or helping her mother with the household chores. Only when all her daily duties were finished could she dry her hands, put on her shoes and socks, and run out of the family's ramshackle house into the ruins of World War II. Wroclaw, Poland, a historic city dating back to the tenth century and sitting closer to Dresden than Warsaw, was nearly destroyed by the retreating Russians and Nazis. Broken walls were all that remained of once-modest but comfortable homes and centuries-old buildings. Piles of rubble, some of it spent and ruined artillery, lay scattered in the damaged streets. For Wanda and the other neighborhood children, the wreckage provided a ghoulish playground.

Zbigniew Blaszkiewicz had been a weapons engineer in Radom, Poland, when the Germans invaded in 1939. Instead of moving to Western Europe, as many Poles chose to do, he went to Lithuania, where he met and married Maria Tyszkiewicz, an attractive woman who today might be called "new age" because of her penchant for the occult and Far Eastern religions. Theirs was an unlikely and largely unhappy alliance, although it produced four children. By the time Wanda was born in 1943, the conquering Russians had stolen or sold off anything that remained of Blaszkiewicz's land and property in Lithuania, so he took his young family to Wroclaw, in the southwest of Poland, where some of them remain to this day.

On an otherwise beautiful day in 1948, Wanda was rummaging through the wreckage of a bombed-out house with her older brother and his three friends when they found an unexploded artillery shell. The boys turned to Wanda and told her to go home; she was a *girl* and a *baby*, too young for their grown-up games. She ran home in tears through the dusty streets and told her mother how mean they were being. Wanda had spoken only a few words before Maria Blaszkiewicz began running in the direction of Wanda's small, outstretched arm. Wanda followed her down the street, trying desperately to keep up as her mother ran, her apron flapping out behind her and her hands still wet from the sink. As she neared the building, Maria was thrown to the ground by the blast that killed her son and his playmates. Years later Wanda would say, "I wouldn't be here if seven-year-old boys could stand to play with five-year-old girls."

Wanda became the older sister, calling the shots and dictating her younger siblings' behavior, particularly that of young Michal, her brother born shortly after the tragedy. Once when she was heading out the door to play cowboys and Indians with her friends, her mother said she had to run some errands and told Wanda to watch Michal. Wanda went to her room and emerged only after Maria had left the house. She was dressed like a wild sort of witch in one of her father's hats and an old dress that reminded Michal of his grandmother, all of it miles too big for the slim eleven-year-old girl.

"I am a magic fairy," she told her wild-eyed brother, "and even if you can't see me, I can see you! So you must stay in your room or else I will come back and punish you!" She gave her petrified brother a final, menacing shake of her finger so close to his bewildered face that he could have reached out and bitten it. He didn't.

With that, Wanda jumped out of the window and climbed up the skeletal walls of the nearby house with the ease of a rhesus monkey, dress and all. The ruse worked. While Michal knew the badly dressed goblin was his older sister, he nonetheless never moved from the edge of his bed until Wanda returned and told him that the fairy reported that he'd been a good boy. Looking back years later, Michal believed her early escape-artist moves were the kernel of her climbing career. Even then he recognized her joy as she moved with grace up the ragged walls.

As Wanda matured, the pretty, imaginative, and playful girl became a daydreamer often lost in her own silent thoughts. At mealtimes she would sit for long moments, eyes fixed on the air in front of her as the family around her hummed with conversation. One night, at a time when fresh eggs were a delicacy on any Polish dinner table, the Blaszkiewicz children watched in awe as Wanda left her prize egg uneaten and focused instead on an invisible point in front of her, lost in her private ruminations. Finally, as stealthy fingers itched to lift Wanda's forgotten egg, she suddenly came to and looked down at her plate.

"Ah, an egg," she said simply. The family erupted in laughter as Wanda slowly sectioned and ate the egg, oblivious to the scene she had created.

From an early age, Wanda was a natural athlete, whether jumping from building to building in her crumbling backyard or competing in the high jump, javelin, shot putt, discus, or volleyball, where she advanced to Poland's Olympic team. Academically she was also gifted and majored in mathematics, hoping its utter rationality would unlock some elusive key to the universe. She excelled, eventually earning an advanced mathematics degree from Warsaw Polytechnic, but she would find her life's passion far from the studied walls of science.

When Wanda was eighteen, she stood at the base of the climbing route and pulled the rope tight around her narrow waist. It was Saturday morning, and she had risen well before dawn to catch the first train out of Wroclaw, then jogged the last 15 kilometers (9.3 miles) from the station to the Sokole Góry (Hawk's Mountain), a climbing mecca several hours from her home in southwest Poland. She reached the cliffs as the first light flickered across their uneven ridges and waited for her friends from school to arrive.

She had never climbed and had to wait for them to finish their climbs to instruct her. But Wanda became impatient, and with the strength, balance, and arrogance of a natural athlete, she started up the rock alone. Her friends saw her inching up one of the wall's narrow chimneys and urged her to stop, put on a harness, and clip onto a safety rope. She refused. She wasn't going to fall, she assured them. She wasn't going to fail, she told herself.

Her first moves were tentative, but as she cleared the deck and the ground became more distant beneath her feet, she gained confidence and kept going. She learned immediately that the key to climbing was in the legs, not the arms or hands. With her toes finding bumps in the wall, some only the size of pimples on the skin of the rock, she pushed rather than pulled her 115-pound body higher. She found holds less than the width of a finger in the sharp rock and smaller and smaller cracks into which she jammed her hands for purchase, scraping off layers of skin as she climbed. But she barely registered the pain or the blood. She felt only joy. She reached the top of the rock and gazed down at the ground over 100 feet below, stunned at what she had done, alone, without safety, without help. Even though she returned to the Sokole Góry nearly every weekend for years, she was never able to repeat the route without being clipped onto a safety rope. By that time she had learned to respect the danger involved. Describing those first climbs as being "like an inner explosion," she knew she had found what would mark the rest of her life.

Wanda had discovered simple ecstasy. Her early climbing days were among the happiest of her life, and the stoic, serious girl peeling potatoes in a grim kitchen became a radiant, beautiful woman commanding the attention and respect of admirers who watched her ever-more-daring climbs. She descended from those intricate and dangerous routes laughing, her dark curly hair falling across her smiling face, biceps curled into Muhammad Ali's jubilant "I am the greatest!" pose, the climbing rope knotted around her slender waist.

After years spent learning the ropes and rocks of Poland, Czechoslovakia, and East Germany, she graduated to the more demanding Alps in

1964, when she was just twenty-one. For many climbers, and for Europeans in particular, the Alps are a necessary progression from their local rock and ice climbs to more challenging routes, but for Eastern Europeans in the midst of the Cold War, the Alps were an escape, and with relatively minor finagling climbers could flee the confines of their Communist system for some of the world's grandest peaks: Grandes Jorasses, the Matterhorn, the Eiger. For Wanda, these expeditions were pivotal, particularly her third trip, in 1966, which took her to the great Mont Blanc.

Standing at the base of the tram, Wanda watched the Aiguille du Midi Téléphérique as it pulled out of the tram terminal in Chamonix. At nearly the price of a night's lodging, she couldn't afford to take the scenic ride, the oldest and most beloved tourist Téléphérique in the Alps, which ascended 9,000 feet, two-thirds of the way up the rocky face of Mont Blanc. Turning from the station, she shouldered her backpack, laden with nearly forty pounds of climbing ropes, carabiners, pitons, her ice ax, crampons, food, clothing, stove, and tent, and climbed the mountain as the tram, filled to overflowing with laughing tourists and better-heeled alpinists, repeatedly passed overhead. That night she met other climbers at the top of the tram and with them climbed the last 3,500 feet to the summit in the morning. Although the climb to the summit was a mostly mixed terrain of rock and ice and technically not demanding for Wanda, it was nonetheless a frustrating and exhausting 12,500-foot ascent. She considered it as difficult as some of her later climbs in the Himalayas, and one that instilled in her a hatred of heavy loads.

When Wanda was twenty-four, she met fellow Polish climber Halina Krüger-Syrokomska and immediately liked the diminutive woman, known for her raunchy jokes, for her foul language, and for smoking a pipe, something only the rarest of Polish men enjoyed. At twenty-seven, Krüger was an esteemed journalist and already a popular and well-known climber in the Polish Alpine Club. In 1967 she asked Wanda to join her on a bold Mont Blanc route, as yet unclimbed by women. Wanda thrilled at the chance to do "what so many others were dreaming of."

With the Polish Alpine Club supporting the climb, Wanda was

finally able to ride the Téléphérique and watch the postcard-pretty Chamonix fall away from her feet as the tram rose nearly vertically up the mountain—a climb that had taken her all day the year before took less than ten minutes. After organizing their gear and shouldering their packs, the women first traversed Mont Blanc to ascend the mountain's Grepon East Face before attempting the infamous Bonatti Pillar, a 2,000-foot vertical face, considered one of the most difficult routes in the Alps, and one of the most treacherous to reach. At its base is the Dru Couloir (Death Couloir), and it is indeed a menacing, narrow runnel with unrelenting rock and ice fall. With one eye continuously fixed on the unsteady ice above them, Wanda and Halina climbed as quickly as they dared, their crampons and axes biting into the ice as they all but danced across the lethal slope, any minute expecting a bus-size chunk of ice or rock to break loose from the towers above them and come barreling down through the steep channel, a deadly, unstoppable force that had killed many before them. After nearly an hour of exposure, they made it through the couloir, but as they readied themselves and their gear to attack the rock pillar, bad weather descended, showering them in hail and lacing the black sky with flashes of lightning. Lightning can be dangerous anywhere, but on an exposed wall of rock it is lethal. They had no choice but to abort their climb; anything else would have been stupidly bold. They turned from the Bonatti and retraced their perilous steps across the couloir, before finally descending into the warmth and safety of the Chamonix Valley. They had not climbed their object, but they had survived the Dru, twice, and were exhilarated.

Two years later the pair successfully ascended the vertical mile wall of Norway's Trollryggen. Trying to save weight on the climb, they left their stove in their camp and were forced to drink cold water flavored with sickly sweet lemon powder. Climbing well but slowly, they realized they would have to spend not one but two nights anchored to the rock wall by their harnesses. Again, in order to save weight, they had left their sleeping bags and bivy sacks in camp, and so they sat huddled together, as close as two bodies can get, a jumble of arms and legs rubbing each other's hunched backs through the 10-degree night. Wanda nonetheless described the trip as "beautiful. Norway is so soft in July, the days are long and the darkness only lasts for four hours." Her elegant description is even more remarkable given that at the end of the trip she fell and broke her ankle. Undaunted, she continued traveling to the Sokole Góry cliffs, winching herself up and using her good leg to leverage against the rock and running on her crutches to catch the last train home after a long weekend of climbing.

Even with a cast on her leg, Wanda was an impressive, imposing figure. One day during her recovery she was riding a tram in Warsaw dressed impeccably, her fashionable jacket tailored to nip in at her waist and her skirt hemmed at the latest length, when Ewa Pankiewicz, riding the same tram, looked over and saw "this beautiful woman with a cast on her leg." She was struck by the effortless poise and power with which Wanda carried herself and felt a strange shyness as she snuck glimpses of a woman who looked like a movie star. A few days later the two women were introduced at the Alpine Club meeting. They would become lifelong friends and climbing partners.

In 1970 Wanda fell in love with and married a fellow mathematician whom she met climbing, Wojtek Rutkiewicz. A handsome, quiet man, Wojtek and she spent their courtship and early marriage exploring the different crags in the hills near Warsaw. Wanda felt happy and content that she had found a true partner to share her two passions—math and mountains. But as the young newlyweds settled into their life together, Wanda received an invitation to join her first expedition to a major peak, 7,134-meter (23,405-foot) Pik Lenin in the Russian Pamirs, and Wojtek was not invited. Unfortunately for the marriage, Wanda didn't hesitate before accepting. She loved Wojtek, but an invitation to travel outside of Poland to her first real mountain was irresistible. The Rutkiewiczes had an emotional good-bye in the airport, Wanda kissing Wojtek again and again and tearfully clutching him as her teammates boarded the flight. She kissed him a final time and was among the last of the climbers to get on the plane.

Once in her seat toward the back of the plane, Wanda sat alone, crying quietly. Andrzej Zawada, one of Poland's most revered climbers and a leader of the expedition, went back to where she sat and looked down at the damp but pretty woman whom he had been assured was a fearless climber and a talented alpinist. He shook his head gently.

"Either you stop crying, Wanda, and join the team properly, or I'll put you on the first flight home."

Wanda looked up. Andrzej was a handsome man with a shock of thick, brown hair bleached to a sandy color by the harsh sun at high altitude. His large, sculpted nose, prominent cheekbones, and deep-set eyes carved his angular face into sharp, distinct sections. Barely in his thirties, he was already beloved in the Polish climbing world, and Wanda couldn't help grinning back at him. She dried her tears, powdered her face, and with a large smile joined the team. She never again mentioned her husband on the expedition.

Wanda Rutkiewicz was hard to ignore. She was a beautiful woman in the almost exclusively male climbing world. She wore her thick, curly brown hair loose to her shoulders when not climbing, and she had large eyes the color of expensive dark chocolate, straight white teeth, and the characteristically strong jawline and prominent cheekbones of her Eastern European heritage. At five-foot-five, she was a woman of average height, but her figure was anything but average, with the long, shapely legs of a runway model, narrow hips and waist, and a full but not too full bosom. In the climbing world, however, her beauty was both a blessing and a curse. Although it provided her with an endless supply of eager assistants in the laborious work of load-carrying, camp-setting, and rope-fixing, those very aides de camp would retaliate when their help was not rewarded. Be it sexual favors or merely the soft friendship of a woman during the long, hard months of an expedition, many of Wanda's male helpers wanted something in return for their mentoring. But Wanda was there to learn, not to play or flirt, and once the lesson was learned she moved on to the next route, leaving a trail of men hopelessly in love with her and smarting at her rebuff. "None of us men realized that this gentle lass had an iron character, an enormous willpower," Zawada said.

Sitting at Base Camp in her cropped wool pants, a white boater's beanie, and silver bangle bracelets, Wanda looked more like a Girl Scout on her first adventure than a serious mountain climber. Surrounded by men many years older and more experienced, Wanda soon found that she was not permitted to lead the rope or contribute to the climbing decisions. The men, unaccustomed to seeing a woman on an expedition, never mind entrusting their lives on a rope to one, seemed unable to make the leap of faith that Wanda was a capable and gifted climber.

During a lazy evening in Base Camp, a group of French climbers from a nearby team approached her, strange smiles flickering at their lips.*

How about an arm wrestle, Wanda? Many of the men within earshot laughed, knowing they outweighed Wanda by at least twenty kilos, some thirty, and had been on some of the toughest routes the Alps had to offer. Wanda looked like a high school girl out for a picnic.

Wanda glanced around at the gathering crowd, some already rolling up their sleeves. If she had thought about it, she might have considered the offer insulting. Why should she have to prove her strength to these large and muscled men or be laughed at if they beat her, a woman barely reaching five-foot-five and weighing in at about 52 kilos (115 pounds)? Instead, she rubbed her calloused hands together slowly, pointed at the largest man, and said, *You.*

Andrzej Zawada, watching nearby, shook his head. He already knew what was coming.

Word spread through Base Camp like a bad smell, and men came running, eager for the show. Maybe now this little girl with the big ideas about her climbing would be put in her place. Wanda and the climber were pushed toward a table and two rickety chairs in the French mess tent.

Are you ready, little Wanda? he asked. Laughter roared from behind him.

Without a word, Wanda shook her right hand high in the air so that her silver bangle bracelets would fall higher on her forearm. She put her right elbow on the table and clasped his hand. It was moist and, like hers, rough with calluses.

---

*This anecdote was told to Ewa Matuszewska by Andrzej Zawada after Wanda's death. With Zawada now also deceased and Matuszewska unsure as to when exactly it occurred, the author apologizes for any unintentional error of time or place.

Ready, get set, go! The climbers shouted, still laughing.

Before the man had time to think about it, Wanda flattened his hand onto the table with a resounding *thwomp,* the silver bracelets jingling against the table.

The tent quieted so fast that it sounded like an H-bomb had sucked all the life out of it. Then, just as quickly, the place erupted with shouts of glee and ridicule.

You are no better than a girl! Putan! Little Wanda beat you! You pussy! How could you let her beat you?

The man knew better than to say he wasn't ready. Instead, he bet on not getting caught off guard next time and shouted above the din, *Best two out of three!*

Wanda smiled and nodded. *Sure, why not?* She put her arm back on the table and watched as he tore off his bulky sweater, then adjusted his shirtsleeve, rolling it back with painstaking care, folding it over and over and over in perfect two-inch sections until it wound tight and high around his bicep. Then he wiped his hand against his pant leg so furiously that sparks could have flown off the nylon. Still not ready, he got up from the wobbly steel and canvas chair and moved it back and forth until it was perfectly square on the ground. Wanda just watched. Finally, he put his elbow on the table and clasped Wanda's hand.

Ready, get set, go!

This time he was ready and held her hand at 90 degrees for several moments, their forearms quivering from the opposing efforts. Wanda watched as the man's mouth flattened against his teeth and his face turned the color of the borscht they had eaten for dinner. She slowly smiled. As she did, his eyes widened slightly. Wanda knew she had it.

Thwomp!

By now every climber, cook, military officer, and porter in camp was crowded around the tent. Several grabbed the tent's ground stakes and guy wires and folded the side flaps up so that more could see the action.

While the next man rolled up his sleeve, Andrzej whispered in Wanda's ear, *Take it easy! Please! Let them win at least one, otherwise we might not be invited to share their French wine.* Wanda just smiled as the next climber sat down. He too walked away rubbing his forearm from where it had been smacked onto the table.

After five or six men, the crowd of challengers had thinned, and by the time she flattened her last arm, she did so with no more effort than if she had been swatting flies.

Wanda had won the battle, but eventually she lost the war; rather than respect her strength, the men felt threatened and, worse, emasculated by it and left her shunned and embattled. It wasn't that Wanda didn't enjoy men—she did. But she was not about to boost their egos at the price of her pride. If men's egos needed to conquer or rescue or better a woman, she wanted no part of them. Through it all, she kept climbing, but it wasn't easy. It was her first exposure to the physical, emotional, and sometimes very personal rigors of an extended expedition, and she found even the most natural body functions a source of embarrassment, particularly when she had to add her feminine hygiene products to the regular trash-burning at camp. She also had never been above 15,000 feet (4,600 meters), and adjusting to the thinner air was grueling as her brain struggled with the decreased oxygen in her blood. She felt as if she were drunk and already suffering a terrible hangover; her stomach heaved, her head felt like an ax was three inches deep into her brain, and her body felt like it was carrying a lead suit of armor. The desire to lie down on the slope and stay there was overwhelming. When she could no longer stand, she fell to her knees and crawled, dragging her body, head down, concentrating only on the rock and ice between her hands as she scratched her way up. If she considered quitting, she never mentioned it. When she finally reached the 7,134-meter (23,405-foot) summit, rather than celebrate, she vomited. It was a miserable trip.

After the Pik Lenin expedition, Wanda sought other women as expedition and climbing partners, hoping to defuse the conflicts she encountered with men. "Climbing with all-women teams gives me the most satisfaction," she told writer and biographer Ewa Matuszewska, "because even the presence of a man on a rope sometimes subconsciously frees one from taking responsibility for a climbing action."

As troubled as the trip had been, after she returned home to Wojtek it was painfully obvious that her climbing had become her one, perhaps her only, passion. Her relationship with her husband never recovered from her decision to go on the expedition, and Wanda admitted that it "sealed the fate of my marriage. In effect I was taking myself on a honeymoon and Wojtek felt bitterly hurt." Another problem was that Wojtek wanted Wanda to settle down, something she flatly refused to do. The trip had been difficult, but Wanda was nevertheless addicted to something that demanded the full energies of her passion. It was her drug and nothing else mattered. There just wasn't room for a husband, a house, a routine. She was an unconventional woman in very conventional times, and by Polish standards she had it all. What could a man possibly add to her freedom and sense of thrill at each new conquest?

Three years later the couple divorced, childless. Although she never saw Wojtek again, she retained his name for the rest of her life.

Wanda continued to look for challenges, in particular those that no woman had achieved—or that she had been told no woman could ever achieve. In 1972 she joined an expedition to the second-highest mountain in the Hindu Kush Range, 7,492-meter (24,580-foot) Noshaq, which lies in the narrow Wakhan Corridor of Afghanistan separating Russia and China from Pakistan and India. With only $1,000 between them, Wanda and nine other climbers drove in jeeps from Poland to Afghanistan to save money. Wanda counted it as one of the most successful and enjoyable expeditions of her life, and one on which she finally felt like an equal partner. She sat in Base Camp and shared stories with the other women rather than having to suffer through the men's chatter, which focused on three things: what goes in, what goes out, and what goes in and out. Food, shit, and sex. In that order. Wanda also found herself in a group of intelligent women from around the world, among them her first bona-fide feminist, Arlene Blum of Berkeley, California, and Alison Chadwick-Onyszkiewicz, a British climber who had met and married one of Wanda's colleagues from the Polish Alpine Club.

"Until this expedition, women climbers had been added to groups more as ornaments than as full members," Wanda said. But this time, not only were there three women on the team, but each was a talented climber who proved that women could perform well in the demanding high altitude, often even better than their male teammates; they suffered fewer headaches and less shortness of breath as they acclimatized. The higher they climbed, the more men's initial advantage of brute strength seemed to even out against women's faster adaptation to the thin air.

As Wanda descended the mountain, she floated rather than climbed down the steep slopes. Had she ever been so happy? This world above 7,000 meters (23,000 feet) introduced her to a joy she hadn't felt since her first climbs in the Sokole Góry. Here she was able to put her strength, will, and talent to one single-minded purpose, a focus so strong that she felt she could turn around and do it all over again. As she continued down she saw a woman climbing toward her who was small and dark, with a wild mane of black curly hair barely restrained by her head scarf. It was Arlene. The two women embraced. It was a wonderful moment, the white-capped mountains and ochre-dry deserts of Afghanistan and Pakistan stretching out below them in every direction. While the world was debating whether women had the physical and mental tenacity to run a marathon, here they were standing on top of a 7,500-meter peak in Afghanistan. When Wanda, Arlene, and Alison reached the summit of Noshaq, they helped shatter many glass ceilings, not only in Himalayan climbing but in the minds of an entrenched world still hesitant to admit that women were capable, even talented athletes and adventurers.

"Now that we have climbed to 7,500 meters, why not 8,000?" Wanda asked Arlene, the view at their feet a magnificent sea of white-capped peaks bobbing in choppy waters. *Why not indeed?* Arlene thought, and the two women began discussing what would become Blum's triumphant and tragic 1978 expedition to put the first Americans and first women on the summit of Annapurna.

At Base Camp, Wanda also met Reinhold Messner, a handsome, burly climber, with a crow's nest of hair and beard, who was at the beginning of what would be his successful bid at becoming the first man to climb all fourteen of the world's 8,000-meter peaks, all without supplemental oxygen. Messner was fascinated by Wanda's team of strong Polish climbers; whereas his love of the mountains was born of pure ability and opportunity, the Poles seemed to approach climbing as a political activity, as an escape from their national prison. Indeed, along with the physical thrill Wanda and her countrymen found in the mountains was the pure escape from the grim world of Cold War Poland. In climbing they had found a relatively easy, if not exotic, way to gain exit visas, and often they even received support from a government eager to showcase the stamina and ability of its rising Communist stars. Watching them, Messner knew that, politics aside, they were strong, capable climbers as well, but he had no idea that they would become the leading high-altitude alpinists in the world.

Later that year Wanda was called home. Her younger brother Michal broke the shocking news to her: their father had been brutally murdered, dismembered, and buried in his garden by a couple who had rented out half his house. Wanda, as eldest, had the grim duty of officially identifying the mutilated body. It was a horrific scene. Wanda and Michal walked through his house, his blood still splattered on the walls. When they reached the morgue, the man on the cold slab was almost unrecognizable as their father; his face and torso had been slashed and crushed by scores of stab wounds and hammer blows. Zbigniew and Maria had divorced years before, and Wanda had struggled with what she considered her father's unkind treatment of her mother, but the loss was staggering. Years before her brother had died violently. Now her father lay before her in pieces. Wanda's pain, sadness, and anger simmered deep within her. She reached out and gave her baby brother's arm a soft caress. They didn't speak. Then she turned and left the morgue.

Her father's death forced Wanda to look at the dangers she faced nearly every day on her beloved rocks and snow slopes. "You don't appreciate the full flavor of life until you risk losing it. The perils of climbing fascinated me because they released so much joy and delight in simple things, like the feel of the wind, the scent of rock warmed by the sun, the sudden relaxation of tension, or the hot tea in the cup. By the end of my very first day's climbing, I knew that it surpassed anything I had ever experienced. The mountains have become the inner force of my life. There is no escape from a passion like climbing, even though it may be the path to death."

In 1973 Wanda and two other women, Danuta Wach and Stefania Egierszdorff, approached the North Face of the Eiger, one of climbing's most notorious and unforgiving ascents: nine climbers had died there before a first ascent was made. When Wanda stood at the base of the route, she didn't like what she saw. It wasn't the 6,000-foot wall of flaking limestone and falling rock so concave it had its own weather pattern that bothered her; it was the temperature. They needed it below freezing to keep the unstable rock and ice frozen firmly in place, but the temperature was well above freezing, and she could see that several key cruxes were running with water. *This is the way death comes to the Eiger,* she thought. She talked it over with Danuta and Stefania as they sat sipping coffee in the café at Kleine Scheidegg and looked up at the route. For generations, tourists, families, and other climbers had sat right where she was sitting watching history and horror unfold on the face in front of them. In a sport of epic legends, the North Face of the Eiger has a history all its own. In 1936 a four-man Austrian-German team all died as they attempted a first ascent. After his three teammates were swept off the face by an avalanche, the lone survivor, Toni Kurz, spent two frozen nights on a tiny ledge before he was able to marshal enough strength to lower himself toward the train tunnel's windows cut into the side of the mountain. But then a knot jammed in his carabiner. With fingers too frozen to free himself, Toni Kurz hung helpless on his rope while weeping rescuers called to him from the windows to keep trying. As night fell, the crowd dispersed and Kurz begged not to be left alone. Finally, in the morning, he muttered, "Ich kann nicht mehr" (I cannot go on) and collapsed and died on his rope, just beyond the reach of the outstretched arms. His body hung from the ropes for months in plain view of tourists on the train and café patio. Just where Wanda sat. Squinting up at the wall, she could see just where the man had hung until another team of climbers was able to go up and cut him down. She looked back at the women and suggested they try the North Pillar instead. They all agreed.

Sitting just to the left of the original and treacherous route, the North Pillar, or North Buttress, was a more terraced approach, with less exposure to falling rock from above, particularly given the hazardously warm temperature. As Wanda and the women climbed she found herself in belay after belay, forced to stand on perilously narrow ledges, holding onto the lives of her climbing partners, with frigid water running from the snow and ice above like waterfalls down her back, soaking her to the skin. But it wasn't the climbing that was the painful part. It was the nights, three of them one after the other, spent shivering in temperatures of 14 degrees Fahrenheit on tiny shale ledges. The gear they had been able to get from the Polish Alpine Club could have come from the Bolshevik Revolution, its threadbare jackets and broken zippers exposing them to every drop of water and degree of chill the mountain had to offer. They sat upright against the ice at their backs, their legs dangling over the cliff. Wanda would have loved to huddle closer to the women to steal a degree of warmth from their bodies, but there wasn't room on the narrow ledge. They sat in single file, only their arms touching. They spent the nights talking about the route, the cold, the dinner they would reward themselves with in Zermatt; the one thing they didn't talk about was quitting. After three nights in their too-small boots and sodden parkas, the women reached the summit. It was only the second time the route had been conquered, and the first time by women. (Peter Habeler and Reinhold Messner had made the first ascent in 1968.)

The women's victory was not without a price: Wanda nearly lost her toes to frostbite. She looked down at the blackened, peeling digits as the doctors told her they would probably have to come off. She should prepare herself for the almost inevitable amputations. *No,* she said. *I will wait. I will not cut them off if there is a chance they will survive. I know I risk gangrene if I wait. But I will wait,* she insisted. Within days, against all odds and medical opinion, the blood began to flow to her toes and the skin began to regenerate. Wanda's remarkable circulation and iron will had refused to bow, and won. It would not be the last time she retained all of her fingers and toes in the face of normally catastrophic frostbite.

Her ascent of the Eiger garnered a lot of publicity and helped put Wanda on the short list of the world's best climbers, male or female. The following year she was invited to join a Soviet-organized international expedition of 160 climbers to the Pamirs. Another woman on the trip was her friend Arlene Blum.

"We always seemed to meet under dramatic circumstances," Blum said. This trip to Pik Lenin would be no exception.

Wanda began to feel sick almost as soon as Base Camp was established. It began with a persistent headache, nausea, and sharp, painful cough. Instead of easing as her body struggled to acclimatize to the thin air, it worsened, and soon she could barely draw a breath without a bout of painful coughing. After one particularly bad fit, she looked down into her hand and saw pink foam: pulmonary edema. The capillaries in her lungs were filling with blood; if not treated, she would drown in her own fluids. A helicopter was called, and soon Wanda found herself being emergency-lifted off a mountain. She looked down as the scattered Base Camps of the different teams became smaller and smaller, eventually disappearing behind a ridge as the helicopter moved out of the mountains and toward the nearest hospital. She fell back against her seat, sick, defeated, and angry. She wondered whether her nonstop schedule had exacerbated this edema, or whether, as for so many, it was just bad luck. Edema was such a crapshoot disease. Some trips you'd climb higher and faster than you ever had without so much as a wheeze, and other times, like this one, you'd barely make it out of Base Camp before nearly dying from the altitude. She decided it had more to do with the crapshoot than her schedule and closed her eyes, trying to ease her labored breathing.

Wanda's second trip to Pik Lenin was over, but it would prove to be a fortuitous illness for her: fifteen other climbers perished on the expedition, eight of them Russian women who were trapped high on Pik Lenin by storms. Teammates, unable to reach or help the climbers, listened at Base Camp as Elvira Shataeva, the women's leader, radioed from their tents near the 23,400-foot (7,132-meter) summit as woman after woman died of exhaustion and exposure. Climbers at Base Camp, Americans Arlene Blum and Jeff Lowe among them, tried to insist that she and those still able to move descend as quickly as possible. But Elvira, in an eerie calm, insisted on staying. "Now there are only two of us who are functioning, and we are getting weaker. We would not, cannot leave our comrades after all they have done for us. We are Soviet women! We must stick together, no matter what happens!" After three days a weary voice crackled over the radio and spoke words that none who heard them would ever forget: "The others are all dead. I am too weak to push the button on the radio any longer. This is my last transmission. We tried but we could not. . . . Please forgive us. We love you. Good-bye." Vladimir Shataev, who was leading the women's team, had the gruesome task of climbing the mountain to identify the bodies and bring them down, among them that of his own wife, Elvira.

It was one of the worst tragedies in mountaineering history, and certainly one of the most devastating to the ranks of female alpinists. When Wanda heard of the tragedy, she bent her head and said a silent prayer, thankful that her friend Arlene hadn't been part of the summit team that day.

While 1974 marked one of women mountaineering's worst tragedies, it also marked one of its triumphs when a group of Japanese women became the first women to climb an 8,000-meter peak, Manaslu in Nepal, at 8,156 meters (26,758 feet), the world's eighth-highest mountain, as well as one of its deadliest. All of the world's 8,000-meter peaks had been conquered between 1950 and 1964, and all of them by men. Now women had entered their own race for the top.

Ever since Wanda had broken the 7,500-meter mark on Noshaq, she had been itching to join the 8,000-meter game, and she was looking for a suitable, worthy mountain. She looked all the way to Pakistan, where the world's highest still-unclimbed mountain stood: Gasherbrum III. Just shy of 8,000 meters at 7,952 meters (26,089 feet), GIII is tucked high and deep in the heart of Pakistan's Karakoram Range, and Wanda wanted it. Next to it are Gasherbrum I and Gasherbrum II, both bonafide 8,000-meter peaks. All three Gasherbrums sit in the shadow of K2, which towers over them a few miles up the glacier.

Wanda collected a group of ten women, including some of the world's strongest female climbers of their day—Halina Krüger, Anna

Okopinska, Ewa Pankiewicz, Anna Czerwinska, and Alison Chadwick-Onyszkiewicz. Calling it the Polish Women's Karakoram Expedition, the team joined forces with a team of seven Polish men led by Alison's husband, Janusz Onyszkiewicz. It was determined that each team, men and women, would climb on its own rope and thus enable the women to claim an "unsupported, all-female ascent." The distinction was an important one for Wanda.

"I was keen to climb with women because when I climb with [male] partners who always expect to lead and search out the routes, I lose all sense of responsibility. For me, climbing is not just getting there but how I got there. I don't feel I own a route unless I've had to conquer my fears and take my own risks. Worrying about my own decisions is an essential part of climbing. . . . How can we ever hope to distinguish the good climbers from the not so good, regardless of gender, until we have a solid representation of independent and self-sufficient women climbers on the mountains? Then there could be fair competition. I'm a competitor by nature, but I want equitable rules." She even insisted that "a genuine women's expedition has got to achieve its aims without help from [male] porters. A mixed expedition is obviously not a women's expedition."

Whether it was the mixture of men or the tincture of Wanda's obstinate leadership style, her team was rent by argument. Years later Alison Chadwick-Onyszkiewicz shared her frustration with Arlene Blum at Wanda's dogmatic approach to leading her team.

"I think she and Alison had their falling-outs," Blum said. "It was a time when women were not supposed to be dominant, and [Wanda] was pretty dominant. My experience with people from the Eastern Bloc countries is that to get out and do things you had to be a little stronger than the next person, and I'm sure she was. She was very single-purpose. She was probably so focused on her goals she probably didn't notice too much who was in the way. And that's not uncommon of guy climbers too, but I think when women exhibit those behaviors it draws more unfavorable attention than when guys do," Blum said.

If Wanda chose the climbing team, devised the schedule, or picked the meal, none of it was to be questioned. On Pik Lenin she had smarted at being excluded from the decisionmaking; now she was the intractable force. For her part, Wanda seemed baffled by the rising tensions and said that all parties were against her and she was against all parties. But she turned a blind eye to the tension and focused instead on the mountain as the problem, not her own autocratic leadership. She was defiant in her inflexibility. "I decided to be hard. . . . If people did not like me, it didn't matter." But it did matter, because at its root climbing is an exercise in trust, in putting your life in the hands of your climbing partners. Wanda seemed at a loss to explain why her teammates would rail against her.

"Surely—I thought—we would all subordinate our individual needs, private feelings, and any personal frictions to our larger, spectacular purpose. I assumed that everyone else would share those feelings. But unhappy conflicts developed between me, in my role as leader, and the rest of the group, who found my way of suggesting courses of action or solutions unacceptable."

Unacceptable or not, Wanda's team overcame their bickering to be the first team to climb Gasherbrum III. When Alison Chadwick-Onyszkiewicz took the final steps to the summit in August 1975 (quickly followed by Janusz, Wanda, and Krzysztof Zdzitowiecki), GIII became the world's highest peak first summited by a woman. Meanwhile, over on GII, Wanda's friends Halina Krüger and Anna Okopinska became the first women to climb an 8,000-meter peak on an all-female rope, and without supplemental oxygen. (At the time only two 8,000-meter peaks had been climbed by women, Manaslu in 1974 and Mount Everest in 1975, and both were achieved with supplemental oxygen.) Bickering and badmouthing aside, it was a wildly successful expedition by every objective measurement in mountaineering, and Wanda had planned a lion's share of it, not an easy task for a woman from Communist Poland.

"The Polish government helped certain figures like [Jerzy] Kukuczka, because they had interest in having the strongest climber in the world," according to Messner, "so they helped him with money and possibilities. But Wanda was not so helped." Or liked. Nevertheless, Messner had no doubt that she was fully in charge of her expedition.

Fresh from her victory on the Gasherbrums, she met Dr. Karl Maria

Herrligkoffer, a controversial German expedition leader famous for leading the first successful expedition to Nanga Parbat, another of Pakistan's deadly 8,215-meter peaks. Only Annapurna surpasses Nanga Parbat in being more fatal to climbers. By the time the towering "Killer Mountain" was finally climbed in 1953 by Hermann Buhl, thirty-one had already died trying, sixteen in a single avalanche. Soon after their introduction, Herrligkoffer invited Wanda to join his fifth expedition to the mountain in 1976, and she eagerly accepted. But their attempt on the mountain was abandoned after a climber from another expedition fell to his death. Wanda helped recover the body. It was a dangerous and emotionally agonizing job carrying the mutilated man, broken and smashed in his fall through rocks and ice, down thousands of feet of steel-plated ice and rock cliffs. She hadn't known the climber and hated the task, but she knew it was one of the costs of climbing. If you found a body, you dealt with it, either finding a nearby crevasse and pushing it in, burying it on the mountain under rocks and snow, or if at all possible bringing it off the mountain for a burial or to where a helicopter could come in and take it home. Even after this gruesome task, she did not want to desert the climb. "The death of a stranger on the mountain is like a motorway accident. You're aware of it, but you drive on. . . . I don't believe that any dead colleague would want the survivors robbed of their chances [at the summit]." Nevertheless, the expedition was over.

Ironically, Wanda's early retreat may have saved her life. When she returned home, she fell gravely ill and was diagnosed with a disease that would probably have killed her in the harsh and isolated environs of a Himalayan expedition: meningitis. If not treated quickly, meningitis can kill within hours and causes permanent brain damage in about 30 percent of those who survive. Soon after returning to Poland, Wanda was unable to walk and talk; in constant pain, she found that even shuffling around her tiny apartment took exhausting effort. Living on painkillers, antibiotics, and little else, when she did eat she needed her food cut up for her, and the fork carefully brought to her mouth. Her friends naturally assumed her climbing career was over. Hardly. After nearly three months spent painfully relearning the most basic motor skills, including walking unaided and holding a spoon and fork, Wanda was again planning a daring ascent: a first-female winter ascent of the Matterhorn's notorious North Face, an almost-mile-high climb of 60-degree ice slopes, vertical rock bands, and unstable faces that defy fixed protection. Only the finest technicians of ice and rock could even contemplate an ascent; a winter ascent demands the best of those. Even so, some of the finest had tried and failed, including Walter Bonatti and Toni Kinshofer, both of whom could claim first ascents on some of the Alps' and Himalayas' most defying routes. But the North Face of the Matterhorn in winter demands more.

In March 1978, Wanda, Anna Czerwinska, Irena Kesa, and Krystyna Palmowska, four of the world's strongest climbers and all of them Poles, began their ascent. Above them, a news helicopter roared, eager to capture the women's historic attempt or disastrous failure. Wanda could barely hear herself think or her ice ax and crampons making contact with the ice; communicating with her teammates below her was all but impossible. After several hours, with little to record, the noisy bird flew back to its base in Zermatt, and the women sunk their steel teeth into the wall. Wanda led most of the technical sections, with the other women following up behind her.

The days ran into each other as the women climbed 1,000 feet each day, their bodies pressed into the vertical rock, the teeth of their front-point crampons the only thing holding them to the wall. After four days of deteriorating weather, and with their faces pressed against the rock and ice—again wearing insufficient foul-weather gear and eating next to nothing—the women were in varying degrees of hypothermia. Finally, with the winds threatening to pluck them off the face and the smallest of the women unable to handle her climbing gear properly with frozen fingers and feet, Wanda dug the radio out of her rucksack to call for help.

She didn't want to make the call; in fact, admitting defeat was the last thing she wanted to do. She could almost taste it like bitter bile in her throat. But she had to think of tiny Irena. As she looked over at the woman Wanda's sense of dread deepened. Irena was unsteady, barely able to balance above the void, and mumbling little gibberish words. Wanda watched the wind and snow blowing horizontally by her face.

She picked up the radio but received only hissing static in reply. She told Irena, Anna, and Krystyna that she didn't think the message had transmitted and that they'd better keep climbing; going down was out of the question because gravity would be working against them, pulling them off the cliff. Perhaps above them they could find a suitable place to bivouac. Wanda stayed close to Irena while Anna and Krystyna continued to climb, but only Krystyna reached the summit.

As the women readied for a fourth miserable night on the rock and the storm roiled around them, Wanda heard a faint *thudder thudder thudder*. She called out to Anna and Krystyna, asking them if they heard something. The women struggled to hear against the wind. Suddenly the helicopter emerged from the clouds and roared above them, clearing the snow like a giant fan as it hovered for position. The pilot assessed the situation below him and how he would mount the rescue. Getting close enough to drop a rescue basket but not so close as to clip the rotors on the steep slope was a risky maneuver that had cost pilots before him their lives.

All Zermatt watched the spectacle unfold in front of them as one by one the women were lifted off the mountain and flown to safety. Wanda got each of the women secured in the rescue basket and carried off until she was left alone on the North Face of the Matterhorn. She looked out at the valley floor at her feet. The storm had lifted a bit so that she could see the lights of Zermatt begin to flicker on in the darkening twilight. She looked up at the summit; it seemed so close, but she knew it was a lifetime away. Her team had survived, but she had failed to get them all on the summit. She sat waiting, the chill of the night settling into her joints and feet. Ever since the Eiger she had suffered pain in her feet even when frostbite wasn't a concern. She shifted uncomfortably but calmly, waiting. Finally, she heard, then saw, the returning helicopter.

She watched as it hovered over her, the now-familiar basket being lowered a last time for her, the team's leader, the ship's captain, the last to go down in defeat. She wished she could wave them away, climb down under her own steam, not admit a total loss, but how could she? These men had risked their lives to rescue her and her team. She couldn't say, "Thanks, but no thanks, I'll walk," to the offered ride. The basket lowered and she hopped into it, almost casually, as if she were on an amusement park ride rather than on the edge of a cliff thousands of feet above the ground. But as she was being winched up she suddenly stopped, unable to move higher. She swung around and realized that her ice ax was stuck in the undercarriage of the helicopter. She tried to yell above the roar of the engines but failed, so she hung onto the basket with one hand and used her free arm to gesture wildly at the pilot. The pilot looked down and saw that she was caught, but his crew was powerless to help. They couldn't climb down the rope to free her ax without jeopardizing all their lives. And he knew that lingering at the edge of the cliff where a sudden gust of wind could send them crashing into the rock was the worst choice. After making sure that she was as secure as she would get, he pulled away from the cliff and began the descent into Zermatt.

Wanda couldn't believe it. She and her team had barely survived the climb, and now she was about to get killed in the rescue! But she knew she wasn't going to die. Of all the ways there were to die, she knew that falling off of a helicopter above the resort town of Zermatt was not going to be one of them. She actually was enjoying the view, and she knew she created quite a show for those watching below. She had to admit that she liked it.

When she rejoined her team, they were rushed to the hospital, where the nurses painfully peeled off her boots and socks, stiff with ice. Wanda looked down. Her toes were black, the skin already falling off in strips. Her stomach clenched with fear and nausea. She had seen enough frostbite to know hers was extreme, and she would probably lose at least some of her toes. But again she didn't; partly because of the expert mountaineering medicine in a climbing clinic in nearby Innsbruck, none of the women lost fingers or toes or suffered long-term disabilities owing to their exposure, and all were back in the mountains within weeks. And Wanda was among them, focusing her efforts on the crown jewel of Himalayan climbing, Mount Everest.

Karl Herrligkoffer, with French climber and politician Pierre Mazeaud, was now assembling a team of premier European alpinists to climb Mount Everest, and again he invited Wanda to join his expedition. She was thrilled: the expedition would give her the chance to become the first Pole, and the first Western woman, to climb the world's highest mountain. The Polish press, which had focused almost entirely on its strong male climbers, suddenly noticed the pretty brunette who looked like a Hollywood starlet but climbed like a comrade. Wanda happily left for Nepal but once on the mountain found herself again the target of scorn, criticism, and even hate on the team. Having hoped her credibility problems were behind her, the men's distrust and dislike was a bitter pill for her to swallow.

"The members made it very clear that woman's place was anywhere but on an alpine expedition," Wanda said. "But I'm my own person, and I'm never prepared to be treated as just any young woman." Whether she meant that she didn't want to be singled out as a woman on the team or that she *wanted* to be treated as an elite climber, she didn't say. Either way, as the only woman on the trip, Wanda again suffered. She told friends that the animosity was rooted in the men's fear that her climbing Everest would diminish their accomplishments in the eyes of the world. Part of the problem may also have been created when Herrligkoffer, hoping to honor her on the team, designated Wanda "second deputy leader," a title other teammates bridled at. In addition, Wanda planned to film the team's ascent. As any cameraperson or unwilling subject can attest, the constant presence of a camera can be off-putting in the extreme, particularly on long, difficult, and dangerous Himalayan expeditions. Wanda tried to brush off the insults and innuendos while at Base Camp, but once the climbing started she took the rebuffs personally.

Wanda looked around at the angry male faces and thought they were all against her, and had been from the beginning. Perhaps they had never encountered her kind of independence, or maybe they just couldn't stand the thought of a woman being an equal partner. Whatever it was, she was sick and tired of their fragile masculinity.

On September 6, there was a huge falling-out, with several men on the team and Wanda engaging in a loud shouting match. Having presented herself as a liberated woman and talented climber, the men were outraged when she refused to carry her own oxygen supply in addition to her heavy camera equipment.

Wanda was unrepentant, shouting back that they were assholes who didn't mind if women were on expeditions so long as they were in their tents and not actually climbing the mountain. *To hell with them,* she thought, *I will not sink to feminine wiles to get my way and be better liked by the bastards. I am here to climb a mountain!*

The team continued its ascent, but it was a bitter alliance, and Wanda climbed virtually alone and isolated from the team. When she reached the South Col, she rested in the tent, breathing deep of the bottled oxygen before it was time to leave for the summit. She gratefully accepted a cup of hot sweet tea from their climbing Sherpa, Mingma. Having slept in all of her clothes, hat, and mittens, she struggled in the frigid air to put on her boots and securely strap on her steel-toothed crampons, perhaps a climber's most crucial piece of equipment aside from an ice ax. The loss of a loose crampon has separated many climbers from the slope and sent them sailing to their deaths thousands of feet below. Checking that hers were firmly in place against the sole of her boots and the loose ends of the straps double-looped back around the clasps, Wanda stood up out of the tent doorway and set out from the South Col for the highest point on Earth. Her excitement was dulled only slightly by the numbing altitude.

When she, three teammates, and four Sherpas reached an equipment cache at 27,500 feet (8,382 meters), 1,500 feet (457 meters) below the actual summit, the expedition deputy leader, Sigi Hupfauer, told her that she had to carry her own oxygen bottle. Wanda protested that she couldn't possibly: she was already carrying all of her heavy camera equipment. Any more would be too much. Sigi was enraged and with the rest of the team walked away, leaving Wanda to search for the oxygen bottle, buried deep by recent snowfall.

"Please don't leave me," she shouted to her disappearing teammates. But they kept walking, soon fading into the high clouds. Her knees felt like they were going to give out, and she knelt on the slope so that she wouldn't fall. She was alone at the roof of the world, and the realization terrified her. If she fell, no one would know, or care. Despair filled her already throbbing head. *What is the point,* she wondered, *in conquering the mountain if it means unleashing such violent hatreds and aggressions?*

She looked around and saw Mingma Sherpa's kind face looking down at her. "Mem sahib, don't worry, I have your bottles." Wanda nodded in thanks and rose from the cold slope, checked her crampons, adjusted her pack, and continued up, each step measured against the exhausting effects of the increasingly thin air. She stopped below the Hillary Step to film the team as it climbed through the forty-foot section of vertical rock and ice, the most technical section of the entire two-mile climb from Base Camp.

Hours later she saw a ragtag collection of flags with nothing above them; she had reached it, the top of the world. She stood on the summit, the entire Earth at her feet in an endless reach of mountain peaks and clouds. She was above them all. She was above everything else. In an instant, all the hurt, all the hatred, all the insult were forgotten, and she embraced her teammates, tears of joy, relief, and pride filling her goggles. It was October 16, 1978, and she was the first Pole and the first European woman to summit Everest, following in the footsteps blazed by the Japanese climber Junko Tabei and Tibetan climber Phantog, both women who had reached the summit in May 1975.

Her success only seemed to increase the team's wrath. Sigi was incensed that she had relied on Mingma and fumed that without Sherpa support no woman would have a serious chance of reaching a summit this high, forgetting that he and his male teammates had much of the same help. When Wanda returned to Camp IV at the South Col to sleep for the night, she returned to the tent she had slept in before the summit. She looked around in the dim interior, but her sleeping bag was gone. She stumbled around camp asking her teammates whether someone had moved it or borrowed it. No one had seen it. No explanation was ever given as to why a sleeping bag, a critical piece of equipment, suddenly went missing, and none of her teammates, including Mazeaud's French climbers, who had made the summit the day before and had already rested a day, offered theirs. But Kurt Diemberger, an Austrian filmmaker and climbing legend, saw that Wanda was close to collapse. She stood in the middle of Camp IV paralyzed by her exhaustion, frustration, and emotion, not knowing what to do.

"Wanda, it is very important you rest," he said. "Take mine. There is more of me to keep me warm." That night a storm blasted Camp IV and the temperature dipped to −40 degrees Celsius. Diemberger, with a bearish body built for hibernation, hunkered down between her and her tentmate and had a remarkably comfortable night.

When she finally made it down to Base Camp two days later, Wanda wasted no time in packing her gear and ridding herself of the angry team. She trekked out of the Khumbu Glacier into Kathmandu, where Arlene Blum greeted her with the tragic news that Alison Chadwick-Onyszkiewicz (and American Vera Watson) had died while climbing Annapurna. After a three-year delay, Blum had finally been able to organize the American Women's Himalayan Expedition to Annapurna, and while the expedition succeeded in putting the first Americans and the first women on the summit, it failed in bringing them all home.

"We were all just totally shocked, saddened, blown away," Blum said. "You know when something happens like that, we were just shell-shocked, devastated. It was awful."

Wanda had little time to grieve. Not only was she the first Pole to climb Mount Everest, but her October 16 summit day was the same day Karol Wojtyla of Poland was elected Pope John Paul II, the first non-Italian pope since Adrian IV of Britain was elected in the tenth century. During his subsequent visit to Poland in July 1979, Wanda presented the new pope with a rock from Everest set in silver. He said to her, "It must have been God's will that we should both be set so high on one and the same day."

She and the Pope were instant icons for the struggling country. Like nothing else before it, her summit of Mount Everest defined her as a climber and a hero of Poland. A few weeks after her return to Warsaw she and a small group of friends gathered in her small apartment to celebrate her name day, June 23. Name day, a centuries-old Christian European tradition, celebrates a person's "rebirth in Christ" through their given name—usually that of a saint—as opposed to the day they were born. As Wanda was opening her modest gifts the doorbell rang. A teenage delivery boy stood nervously at the door holding a huge bouquet of flowers and a small, exquisitely wrapped gift. Wanda accepted the delivery and walked back into the living room with the flowers and the slender box. She quietly opened the thin box as conversation buzzed about what it could be. She suddenly froze: inside was a neat stack of 100,000 Polish zlotys, over $27,000 in 2003 dollars. In a time and place where an office or company director could expect to earn 2,000 to 3,000 zlotys a month, 100,000 was nearly three years' salary. Wanda read the attached note out loud to her friends: "Use this money for your next mountain adventure. Hopefully it will be in as good a style as your Everest ascent." The note was unsigned. Wanda nervously touched the clean stack of crisp bills; they seemed unreal. She had never seen or touched so much money. She insisted that she could not possibly keep the money; perhaps she could find the teenage courier and return it, or maybe she could give it away to charity? Meanwhile, her friends gaily played imaginary "if I had 100,000 zlotys I would . . ." games. Eventually she relaxed, agreed to keep the money, and in time put it toward the first all-women expedition to K2.

In June 1980, Wanda was invited by the Polish Olympic Committee to attend the Moscow games as a hero of Polish sports. Not only was the invitation a huge tribute for Wanda, but it provided another opportunity to escape, if briefly, from a country on the brink of martial law. She made the decision to go, but as she readied for the trip she found out that her beloved dog, Yeti, was pregnant. Wanda called her friends asking if they could take a puppy, but none could. When the puppies were finally born, only two survived the birth, and they were tiny and sick. Before Yeti could bond with her weak offspring, Wanda wrapped them up in old towels and took them to the vet. She told the attendant she couldn't care for the puppies, and they were destroyed.

Ewa Matuszewska was disgusted and told Wanda that she doubted if she would ever be able to forgive her cruelty. Ewa, who routinely called Wanda many times a day, didn't speak to her for nearly a week. When she finally did, she challenged Wanda's selfishness: how dare she kill innocent puppies because of her schedule? But Wanda was unapologetic. "What would you do in my place? Would you resign from the Olympic Games just to take care of *dogs*? This could be the only chance for me to be a part of such an event." Despite being heartsick, Matuszewska agreed that Wanda had different obligations and pressures, and the friendship survived the incident. Ewa feared it wouldn't be the last confrontation of "drama mixed with the grotesque, the warmest feeling mixed with coldest fury" of their fourteen-year friendship and collaboration. She was right.

A short time after the puppies were put to sleep, Wanda nearly killed herself and everyone else on the road saving Yeti's life. One day while playing in the park the dog was bitten by a bee and soon began frothing at the mouth and convulsing. Wanda swooped the eighty-pound dog into her arms, piled her into the front seat of her car, and stroked Yeti's panting chest with one hand while with the other she drove like a woman possessed, ignoring every stop sign, traffic light, crossing guard, and police siren to get Yeti across town to the vet. She nearly drove the car through the front door of the veterinarian's office, picked Yeti out of the car as easily as if she were a bag of groceries, and ran straight past reception and into the examining room demanding immediate care. She got it, and the doctor told her she would have lost Yeti if she had arrived fifteen minutes later.

Wanda tried to go about her life, but Poland's newest climbing star found that she was exposed as she never had been before to the harsh media limelight, a blinding glare she found increasingly intolerable. Time after time she opened her door to curious journalists "expecting to meet some happy summiteer. Instead they'd find a young woman who seemed to be incapable of dealing with her problems, or organizing her time, or even sorting the papers and photographs that were strewn around every room."

Wanda sat on the couch, answering the same questions to different faces while panic gripped invisibly at her throat, making the words hard to deliver. She felt like her world was collapsing. The more she told the same story, the less she owned it, until it seemed as if she were telling the story of a stranger: *Yes, I felt a wonderful joy on the summit of Everest. Yes, the view at the top of the world is beautiful. Yes, I feel a great pride climbing for the glory of Poland and all Poles everywhere.* She smiled nicely, served tea, showed some of her mountain photographs, and then finally closed the door and leaned against it once they were gone, exhausted at the effort of her performance.

With anxiety bordering on depression, Wanda considered giving up mountain climbing after her Everest triumph. When asked for written accounts of her historic climbs, she struggled, exclaiming, "Sometimes I think it was easier to reach the summit than to describe how it was done." But the same media glare that had blinded her also offered its shining rewards: publicity and popularity that led to more endorsements, financial backing, and the power to get through bureaucratic red tape. She was also able to garner a premier prize in Himalayan mountaineering: a permit for a women's team to attempt K2, the highest of Pakistan's five 8,000-meter peaks. She dug out her name day windfall and reserved the permit.

In February 1981, Wanda and a small group of friends went to Mount Elbrus in the Caucasus to do some winter training for the K2 expedition. It was a moderate climb, and they had enjoyed a spate of good weather. They ascended the mountain without a problem, but on descent Wanda heard a shout from above: someone, something was falling. Instinctively, she tried to duck closer into the slope, but she was on an exposed section with nothing to hide behind. It wouldn't have mattered: she was hit so fast that she wouldn't have had time to blink. It felt like a freight train when the other climber hit and took her clear off her feet. Before she could register what had happened, Wanda and her teammate were tumbling hundreds of feet down the icy and rocky slope, Wanda somersaulting between rocks, her arms and legs taking the worst of the blows. As suddenly as she had fallen, she stopped, but a blinding pain radiated from her leg through her body. She lay flat on the slope, unable to move. She knew she was alive, and she knew she was badly hurt, but she didn't know how bad. She didn't know that her left femur had fractured and was protruding from her skin, poking her nylon climbing pants away from her leg. Inside their waterproof shell, the blood soaked Wanda's underclothes. The largest and strongest bone in the human body, the femur with its bands of muscle, tendons, and ligaments provides the foundation of movement and support for the body, and a compound fracture of the femur is among the most painful and bloody breaks possible. Wanda lay on the slope in silent shock. Because she wasn't crying out, her friends thought her injuries weren't serious and gave her liquor to help with the pain. A rescue team was called, and within hours Wanda was loaded aboard an ambulance. With the immediate shock wearing off and the pain now blistering through her, she vomited on the floor. The emergency attendants, smelling the alcohol, thought she was drunk. She didn't have the strength to correct them.

After hours in surgery in a Russian hospital near Elbrus, a metal clamp was inserted in her leg and then it was set in plaster. When Wanda woke from the anesthesia, slightly nauseous and feeling the true brunt of the pain for the first time, she knew something was terribly wrong. She stared at her suspended leg, held high above the bed in traction, steel pins and supports poking out of the bandages around her thigh. She felt like she might vomit again. She knew, once broken, the femur was a difficult bone to mend. It was just too big and bore too much weight. Climbers who broke their femurs told terrible stories of long recovery and residual pain. To make it worse, she was sure she felt movement when she shifted her weight on the bed, a sharp, deep pain penetrating the drugs and anesthesia. When the doctors came into her room to check on her, she told them it wasn't set correctly and pled with them to reset the bone. They refused. It would prove a costly error.

When the doctors left her room, Wanda didn't think about the fall. She didn't think about her long recuperation. She looked at the institutional green walls with the same fixed stare her family had seen as she sat at her dinner table in Wroclaw. She stared off into space planning her K2 expedition, adjusting minor details in the logistics to accommodate the new reality. She never once considered canceling.

After she was released from the hospital, the pain persisted and she sought a surgeon to do the job of rebreaking and properly setting the bone. She turned to a friend of sixteen years, Dr. Helmut Scharfetter in Innsbruck, who offered not only the medical expertise she needed but emotional support as well. He was a large bear of a man, with a shock of reddish blond hair, and she found his gentle assuredness and calm control exactly what her fractured body and mind needed. While Poland now raged against the confines of martial law, which had been declared in December 1981, Wanda found she had nothing to return home to and retreated instead to Scharfetter's chateau in the Tyrolean Mountains to rest. A divorced father who was raising his two sons alone, Scharfetter wanted more than a lovely patient resting in his home, and when he shyly asked Wanda to be his wife, she accepted.

In January 1982, the clamps and plaster cast again were removed. Wanda was wheeled to the hospital door, but as she rose out of the wheelchair and took her first unassisted steps in weeks she heard a sickening *crack* as a familiar pain shot from her thigh upward through her body. As she fell forward she was able to catch herself on the handrail before tumbling down the cement stairs. She sat on the stairs and wept.

"I don't ever cry," she said, "but this time I lost my composure completely and burst into tears, crying loudly all the way through [the resetting of the leg]." Again in heavy plaster, Wanda was reinstructed not to put any weight on the damaged leg.

She returned to the chateau, glad for the surrounding beauty and Helmut's ever-present gentle strength. But the storybook romance soon dissolved. It didn't help that Helmut had a particular eccentricity: an aversion to all detergents, including soap and shampoo. Preferring plain hot water, the good doctor would occasionally acquiesce and allow a sharp-smelling bar of gray lye soap to be administered to the foulest offenses. Wanda, with her own eccentricity of loving crisp, white cotton shirts, wondered how she was ever going to get the collars to stand up without a lot of soap, bleach, and starch. When Scharfetter started calling Wanda "my frau" and Wanda responded with "my house commander," the marriage was over. "Wanda would never have gotten the Oscar for her performance as wife," Ewa Matuszewska said.

With her leg still in plaster and hobbling around on crutches, she refocused her energy on planning her 1982 all-women's expedition to K2. But the pain in her thigh was constant, and she began taking handfuls of painkillers. The pain and drugs combined with the lack of exercise killed her appetite and her gaunt appearance shocked friends who hadn't seen her since before the latest surgery. She coolly dismissed their concern: "The less weight I have to carry to get to K2, the better for me."

With a twisted sort of logic, she made some sense.

CHAPTER 3

A SPECTACULAR SUMMIT

You never conquer a mountain, you conquer yourself.

—ANONYMOUS

The approach to K2 was infamous, and Wanda knew what she was in for: a grueling two weeks of travel, most of it on foot. Under the best of circumstances, it would demand a level of peak physical fitness. On crutches, it would be excruciating, but she was determined to be part of the expedition she'd so painstakingly planned.

Before climbers learned anything about the so-called Savage Mountain they first heard about the journey necessary to get there, beginning with the notorious Karakoram Highway. From its start just outside of Islamabad in Rawalpindi, the KKH was a perilous strip of crumbling asphalt, rock, and dirt dug into the cliffs hundreds of feet above the churning Indus River. Rusted bus and truck carcasses lay at the bottom. After twenty-four hours of hairpin turns and countless mud- and landslide detours, Wanda and her team arrived in the northern town of Skardu, slightly bruised and already exhausted before they were even close to the mountain they'd come so far to climb.

Skardu, in the heart of Baltistan, was Pakistan's northern climbing capital and served as the last staging ground before teams headed into the true wilderness of the Karakoram Range. Here they bought their final food stores and supplies and organized them into carefully weighed loads for the porters. Lodging ranged from grim cold-water hostels to four-star hotels, like the remarkably clean K2 Motel and its lovely gardens that

overlooked the Indus River. First built in the 1960s for UN observers touring the troubled Kashmir region, Wanda chose it for her team and sat happily on the patio watching the lazy river roll by, elevating her leg and
gratefully accepting bags of precious ice from the white-clad waiters.
After a day of logistics planning, they left the city's asphalt streets, crossed
the Indus, and held on and didn't let go during the full day's journey over
more crumbling, rut-filled roads, many washed out by the annual floods
of the mountains' melt-off. Many of the women wished they'd worn more
supportive bras as the jeeps lurched and jumped over the rocks and ruts
and teetered on the edge of the raging Braldu River where its waters came
flooding out of the mountains. With every jump on the rutted road, Wanda
winced in pain while marveling at the landscape. It was like nothing that
she had ever seen before. Unlike her approach to Everest through the lush
jungles of Nepal, northern Pakistan was a high desert at the bottom of
spectacular, distant mountains, and the women kept their eyes squinted
nearly shut and wore scarves around their mouths against the sand and
dust billowing around through their open jeeps. The day's journey wan-
dered through a handful of villages where the only evidence of the twentieth century was the occasional electric fan or neon store sign. It was like
driving through a time warp. It was also a picture window into a world
where women lived for one purpose: work. This was a world where
women were not only not heard but not seen. In village after village, as the
exotic jeeps of a foreign culture and their mysterious passengers rumbled
through, dogs, chickens, and children scurried away from the tires, and
men lifted their heads in only mild curiosity as they sat in storefronts and
by the side of the road smoking cigarettes and drinking tea, but the
women were absent. Invisible. Occasionally, if she looked hard enough
and quickly enough before they had a chance to pull their shawls over
their heads, Wanda could see women and girls far off in distant fields,
babies strapped to their backs, tending the crops, carrying water, leading
oxen, bathing children.

   When the team finally stumbled out of their jeeps at the end of the
road, more bruised and now nauseated after their day of bone-rattling
driving, their relief at having the jeep travel behind them was tempered

by the reality of what was ahead: eleven days of sunup to sundown trekking through some of the roughest landscape on Earth.

Getting out of the jeep at Dasso, Wanda and the women were greeted by hundreds of Balti men and boys, ranging from twelve to sixty years old, who were eager for the backbreaking work of carrying 25-kilo loads (55 pounds) of team gear, plus their own food, shelter, and clothing, to Base Camp 150 kilometers (93 miles) away. For their trouble, they would earn only a few dollars a day, but it was nonetheless a gold-mine sum, equal to a year's earnings working the fields and farms of their villages. Looking out over the sea of dark, dirty faces, Wanda saw a handful of goats wandering through the outpost. Meals on wheels, they were called. They would provide some well-needed protein and flavor along the way.

Wanda and her Pakistani *sirdar* (expedition foreman) chose over 260 porters out of the hundreds gathered; once hired, they immediately strapped on their loads and started out on the trek. Soon they stretched out for miles along the narrow trail above the river, bobbing rhythmically, only their legs visible beneath their enormous loads and their light, quick steps belying the weight on their backs. If the women had been climbing with oxygen, they would have needed even more porters, not only to carry the extra weight into Base Camp but then to get it high on the mountain. As strong as they were, carrying twenty-pound canisters for a maximum of six hours of supplemental oxygen wasn't worth the effort of getting it there.

Unable to carry any extra weight because of her leg, Wanda chose one of the porters to assume her private pack and asked that he stay with her in case she needed clothing or gear during the long day ahead. Then she looked up the deep cavern of the Braldu River gorge to where it disappeared in a riot of rock, river, and cliff. It was a sobering sight for anyone; for someone on crutches it must have been heart-stopping. The journey from there to Askole, the last village before they climbed onto the glacier, would take three days of trekking along a thin ribbon of trail cut into the cliff side above the roiling waters, a crumbling trail so narrow at points that Wanda's shoulders and crutches scraped along the rock wall next to her as she hugged the edge. The days were hot and cloudless, and the sun not only burned down from above but was reflected up from the water and sand. If she wasn't careful, the reflected sunlight would burn the insides of her nostrils, causing painful nose-bleeds before the blood congealed and peeled off in large, unsightly slabs. And getting from Dasso to Askole was the easy part.

After days in the blustery heat and dust, the team was instantly charmed by the garden oasis of Askole and the sheer lushness of the green, terraced fields and colorfully dressed hill people quietly farming their fields of rice, potatoes, and alfalfa and their fruit trees. Painstak-ingly irrigated by the diverted floodwaters from the mountains, Askole sat tucked into the harsh landscape like a perfect emerald in a world of stone. This felt like Eden, and the women lingered in the cool shade while their sirdar bought the last of their fruits, vegetables, flour, and rice for the expedition. Wanda tried to elevate her throbbing leg while they rested, but that didn't help the pain.

On the glacier the porters forded a new trail up and over the ever-changing, churning, grinding, cracking river of ice, skirting the crevasses and luge-like runnels cut into the ice by the powerfully rushing water. When the porters first reached the prominent snout of the glacier, sitting at the head of the river like a rock and ice dam, Wanda watched them pause in prayer. As she passed where they had prayed she saw that it was a makeshift graveyard built over the years for porters who had perished in glacial crevasses, avalanches, and raging streams or from the cold. She had known that people died on the approach, but seeing the crudely fash-ioned gravestones and markers made her clutch her crutches.

Glaciers are as old as the Ice Age itself, and in the pictures Wanda had seen of the great glaciers of the Karakoram taken from far above by previous climbers, she was reminded of highways: dark, dirty ribbons winding through the mountains. But the ribbons were actually rocks, some as small as pebbles and some as large as houses, that broke off from the mountains above, creating a frozen boulder field slowly rolling toward the river many miles below. Climbing up and over and through the boulders was an exercise in fear, frustration, and determination made all the more so as the sun rose and melted the surface layer of rocks out of the ice, so that every footfall was a potential slip and tumble as the rocks gave way to the sheet of ice beneath. Many climbers have called the glacier as challenging as the mountain itself. But only one of them did it with a broken leg.

Gritting her teeth against the pain, Wanda wore through several pairs of crutches on the onerous eleven-day journey but was nonetheless nonchalant. She was determined not to slow the team down and not to feel sorry for herself. Looking down at the goats sharing the path with her, she thought, *Hell, if these walking pieces of porters' meat can get through here, so can I.* With a skill bordering on the acrobatic, she used her crutches to propel herself from rock to rock and over to the increasingly wild floodwaters of the Baltoro and Godwin-Austen Glaciers. Many of the water crossings were no more than rocks slashed together with hairy rope—and sometimes not even that—but she barely got her feet wet on the long trek.

The trek was designed to proceed about six miles and gain 1,000 feet of elevation a day; going farther would risk harm to the laden porters as well as to the team members who were beginning their weeks-long acclimatization process, which would allow them to eventually climb to an altitude that sat two miles above where life ceased to exist. If the process was rushed, the women risked an assortment of illnesses, ranging from mild but persistent headaches to potentially fatal high-altitude sickness and edemas in which the brain and/or lungs are flooded with fluids. Wanda was asked why she didn't just helicopter into Base Camp, but she knew a gain of nearly 7,000 feet in little over an hour would cause nausea, vomiting, a migraine, pleurisy, and dizziness for three days. That is, if it didn't kill her first.

After three days of exhausting but exhilarating trekking through some of the most spectacular landscape imaginable, an ever-changing canvas of mile-high granite walls and towering snowcapped peaks on either side of the undulating frozen river of rock and ice at her feet, Wanda reached Concordia, the confluence of the Baltoro and Godwin-Austen Glaciers. Nearly three weeks after she left home, she got her first real look at the colossus of K2, still ten miles and a final day's trek away. Within a short radius of ten miles stand forty-one peaks over 6,500 meters (21,000 feet), including four above 8,000 meters (26,000 feet). Their beauty inspired her to pause in prayer to the Mountain Gods who were believed to live in their cathedral. She had grown up Catholic but rarely found solace in the Church's ritual. Standing in the presence of such majestic grandeur, however, she couldn't help but mutter an emotional thanks for the gift of getting there. Her arms ached and her hands were blistered from navigating the crutches through 150 kilometers of unrelenting rocks and ice, but she had made it.

She continued walking and looked up often from the rocks to gaze at the mountain in front of her. She had seen pictures, but nothing had prepared her for its magnificence, its power, its uninterrupted rise from the glacier to the cobalt-blue sky above. Everest had been hidden from view behind adjoining peaks, obscuring a "floor-to-ceiling" view of the mountain. But K2 was different. K2 commanded respect. It demanded notice. And she gave it. Like so many mountaineers before her, Wanda was instantly captivated by K2's sheer power and beauty. Resting often, she kept one eye trained on her destination, as if wishing it could meet her halfway. Her leg had begun to feel as if she were walking on the exposed, broken bone rather than her boots.

When she was still a few hours from Base Camp, she collapsed onto the rocks and ice, tears silently running down her cheeks as she gently massaged her throbbing leg. *Perhaps I have come too far after all.* Her friends and fellow Poles Wojtek Kurtyka and Jerzy "Jurek" Kukuczka came upon her on the trail. When Kukuczka saw her sitting on the rock, rubbing her thigh, the tears sliding down her cheeks from behind her sunglasses, his heart felt like it would crack in two. He loved this woman. He loved her strength and her will and her beauty, but this was too much. In the years that they had known each other and climbed together, he had never seen her cry, and his heart broke at how much pain she must have suffered to allow him to see her weakness. *We're almost there, let me carry you the rest of the way,* he told her and knelt down so that she could climb onto his back. She hesitated: taking such pitiful help, even from Jurek, insulted everything she had worked so hard to gain. But her pain was blurring her vision, upsetting her stomach, making even water taste like vinegar. She placed her hands on his ropey shoulders, hopped up on a small rock to boost herself, and with a swift, easy jump that belied her pain landed squarely on his back. Careful to avoid holding her by her damaged leg, Jerzy made a basket of his fingers behind his back and instead cradled her bottom the remaining miles to K2 Base Camp.

Watching the spectacle, her teammates were appalled, saying that her coming on the trip was absolute folly.

"But she was determined to do it, independent of all the circumstances and obstacles; she was this kind of person. Once she decided something, she was determined to do it and she did it, but it was of course at the cost of her own health and the leg, which never really recovered," Krystyna Palmowska said.

In analyzing the mistakes she had made as leader of the Gasherbrum III expedition, Wanda realized that the 1975 team had felt as if she were in it for herself, not for them. They had been wrong. She had respected them, but somehow she hadn't been able to communicate that admiration or connect with her team. This K2 trip would be different. This year she would not let her team down as leader, even if it meant taking a million painful steps to get there, even if her leg prevented her from even touching the mountain, never mind climbing up its dangerous and demanding slopes. But her teammates questioned that devotion, some charging that she was there merely to scope the mountain for a subsequent attempt.

Regardless of their skepticism, Wanda's team was there to climb the mountain. They comprised eleven of the world's finest female alpinists, then or since, and after only twelve days two of the climbers were able to establish Camp II at 6,700 meters. Halina Krüger-Syrokomska, the now forty-three-year-old journalist, editor, and mother who had first teamed with Wanda in 1967 for their epic attempt on Mont Blanc, was climbing with her partner Anna Okopinska. She and Anna had reached the summit of Gasherbrum II in 1975, setting a woman's team record, but they found K2 a different ball game. After crossing a difficult, overhanging section of the route above Camp I, Halina turned to Anna and said, "These are not the Gasherbrums, Mrs. Anna. Here we need to climb." After reaching Camp II, Halina radioed Base Camp to update the team on their progress on the mountain.

From base, Wanda asked her what the weather looked like.

Halina smiled over at Anna as she spoke into the radio: "I'll have to ask God what he intends for our weather." After signing off, she suddenly slumped over.

Anna reached over and felt Halina: she had no pulse, her breath had stopped, and her eyes were fixed and dilated. Anna yelled for two Austrians also in their tent at Camp II to help her. She grabbed the radio out of Halina's hands and shouted down to Base Camp that Halina had stopped breathing.

Wanda grabbed her crutches and scrambled down the moraine to get another team's doctor in a nearby camp. With the preternatural calm of a 911 operator, they talked Anna through the one-breath-five-pumps procedure, telling her how to locate Halina's heart under her breastbone, how to check for any pulse, any breath, any sign that she was still alive. For an hour and a half, Anna and the Austrian men took turns pounding and pumping and trying to breathe life back into Halina. Exhausted, Anna finally sat back on her heels and wept. Then she called Wanda at Base Camp. Halina was dead. Because she died so far from any opportunity to make a real diagnosis or do an autopsy, Wanda and the other women believed for years that Halina had died of a heart attack. But the suddenness and apparent painlessness of her collapse indicate that she more likely was killed by a brain embolism.

K2 had claimed its first woman.

Halina had needed a lot of urging to come on the expedition; she eventually agreed because many of the women, already familiar with Wanda's doctrinaire leadership style, said they wouldn't go if she didn't. She promised her husband and daughter that it would be her last Himalayan trip. From the start she had suffered physically but refused medical attention and isolated herself at Base Camp. Even Anna Okopinska felt something was different when the normally agnostic Halina brought a Bible on the expedition.

After Halina's death, Wanda told the women they had to get her body off the mountain, something rarely done because of the danger to other climbers involved in lowering a body down an already treacherous slope. Wanda told her grim-faced teammates that they had to give Halina a real grave, a place her daughter could come and visit. They could not leave her to become prey to the birds and to be stepped over by future climbers. She deserved more. They agreed.

Nowhere does bad news travel faster than through Himalayan mountains, and climbers from up and down the glacier raced to K2 Base Camp to help, among them Kukuczka, Reinhold Messner, and climbers from Austrian and Mexican teams on the mountain. Moving with agonizing care, fearful of dropping the lifeless body and watching it fall down the sheer face, as well as for their own safety, the climbers inched the trussed bundle down 5,000 feet from Camp II to the glacier. Wanda, unable to climb up to assist, monitored their progress from the base of the route. When they reached the bottom, she helped them put the body on a crude stretcher made of old tent poles and fabric and carried it down the glacier for burial at the Gilkey Memorial.

Built in 1953 for American climber Art Gilkey, the rock cairn became an instant shrine for those lost on K2. A handsome, gentle man from Iowa, Gilkey was a geologist who went on the expedition as much to collect his beloved rocks as to climb the mountain. He and his team climbed well but found themselves trapped high at 25,000 feet in a relentless ten-day storm. When the climbers were finally able to leave their tents, Art stood up and quickly collapsed back onto the snow. Team doctor Charlie Houston made a wrenching diagnosis: thrombophlebitis. After days of lying in his tent, inactive and not able to keep up with his body's voracious need for liquids, Art's blood had slowed to molasses-like treacle, forming clots in his legs. At any moment those clots could break free and travel to his lungs, heart, or brain, killing him instantly; Art would surely die before his team could get him off the mountain, if indeed they could rescue a non-ambulatory man from that high on the mountain. In one of mountaineering's most heroic rescue attempts, teammate Pete Schoening saved the lives of six men with a Herculean ice belay, including Gilkey in his sleeping-bag sling. But moments later, as the team struggled to establish camp on a steep ice slope, an avalanche swept Gilkey clean from the slope. The next day the surviving men descended through his blood-stained path down the mountain in silence. At Base Camp they collected as many colors, shapes, and sizes as they could find of the rocks that had so fascinated Gilkey, and with them built him a fitting monument.

Twenty-nine years later Wanda and her team readied themselves for a service at the Memorial. On a cloudless day without a breath of wind, the women climbed up a ridge overlooking Base Camp where they found a small hillock of beautiful tiny white flowers that, amazingly, were growing nearly a mile higher than the last blade of grass they'd seen on the trek in. The flowers were a poignant, delicate reminder that living, breathing things awaited them at the other end of their frozen, dead wasteland. They picked every one and took them to the Memorial. Gilkey's 1953 team had built it ten meters above the glacier so that it would be safe from the constantly churning tumult of the ice, and they had lashed it together with bailing wire. When Wanda and her team climbed to the Memorial, they found a forlorn tomb that held the crudely hammered plaques of two more climbers who had died on the mountain after Gilkey, Mario Puchoz in 1954 and Nick Estcourt in 1978. Wanda knew that nine men had actually perished, but five of them were either Nepalese or Pakistani high-altitude porters, and their memorials sat at the snout of the glacier many miles below them. The first to die, Dudley Wolfe in 1939, had been left for dead high on the mountain, his body not yet found, and no one had bothered to make a plaque for the long-lost man. Watching the sun set behind Chogolisa Peak, the women spoke solemn words of good-bye and then quietly laid their white flowers on Halina's rock grave.

Halina's funeral was Wanda's first at the Gilkey, but it would not be her last.

The women turned from the Memorial and looked up at the spot on the mountain where Halina had died. They walked silently back to camp as the last light faded behind the mountains, leaving the sky a blue-black sprinkled with stars so bright that they could have been ten-karat diamonds.

Halina's death cast a pall over the expedition, but not for long. Anna Okopinska, grieving bitterly, was repulsed by the women's almost jovial return to business as usual only days after Halina's funeral; loud music once again rocked from their mess tent, a steady stream of climbers from other camps visited for tea and coffee, and flirtatious laughter floated down the glacier. She had lost her best friend and climbing partner, and these women behaved as if they had lost nothing more important than a piece of equipment.

But organizing the expedition had taken Wanda years and cost her thousands of dollars of her own money, and she was not about to give it up without a fight. The team returned to the mountain for another six weeks, but ferocious winds continued to blow and never broke long enough for them to get higher than Camp II. Frustrated, they finally packed their barrels and turned south for home on September 26. It was Anna's last Himalayan expedition, and Wanda's last as leader. Enough was enough; she didn't need the hassle and responsibility of leadership. She would concentrate her energies on climbing, not on organizing.

When she returned from K2, Wanda's leg ached, and she realized, finally, that she would have to give it ample time to heal. In her downtime from climbing she decided to pursue a passion far from the pristine mountains above 8,000 meters: car racing. She loved both sports equally, both of them among the most dangerous sports imaginable and both dominated by men. She joined the Polish rally circuit for the sheer joy of learning something new and was soon equally confident behind the wheel as she was scaling walls of ice and rock at 27,000 feet. Like climbing 8,000-meter peaks, racing cars filled her with the adrenaline of risk and adventure.

Whether sitting behind the wheel of an expensive, high performance machine or her two-cylinder jalopy, Wanda drove with a wild abandon, speeding through narrow streets, weaving around other cars, and ignoring the traditional rules of the road. She drove like a teenager, with all the confidence and arrogance of youth. But she was in her thirties, and when stopped by police, as she often was, she would turn on the charm, smiling sweetly and asking the officer if perhaps he had seen her recently in the newspapers? Had he heard of her? She was a famous Polish climber. Sometimes he had and she'd drive off with a warning; sometimes he hadn't and she'd stuff the ticket into her already crammed glove box. Once, when spiriting the French climbing writer Christine Grosjean around Warsaw, Wanda flipped the car she was driving. "She got out laughing," Grosjean said. "She was like a child that way, she wasn't afraid of anything."

By early 1984, Wanda could finally walk on her leg without pain, and she trained with a vengeance for a return to K2. The leg and the mountain had defeated her in 1982, but she was determined neither would this time. As her departure day approached she drove to her mother's house to say good-bye. Since her divorce from Zbigniew and then his violent murder, Maria had found a greater and greater measure of peace from her mystical beliefs. When Maria opened the door to Wanda, she insisted that her daughter join her in prayer. Wanda, the ultimate pragmatist, resisted, but seeing how important it was for her mother, she finally agreed, and the two women knelt before a small shrine built in the corner of Maria's modest living room.

Maria intoned to her God to please bring her daughter safely back to her. Wanda reached over and held her mother's hand. *Don't worry*, she told her, *I will always come back to you.*

Wanda's 1984 K2 team included two of her 1982 teammates, Anna Czerwinska and Krystyna Palmowska, as well as a third new climber, Dobroslawa Miodowicz-Wolf, a popular woman whose tiny stature and tireless work had earned her the affectionate nickname Mrowka, "the Ant." But again, bad weather and terrible conditions on the mountain prevented them from climbing much beyond Camp III at 7,300 meters. Still, it was a victory for Wanda. She had climbed like a machine, never feeling fatigue or pain; she was finally healed.

In 1985 Wanda climbed South America's highest peak, Aconcagua (6,959 meters, 22,831 feet), in Argentina before heading to Nanga Parbat for another attempt at the Killer Mountain. As in 1984, Czerwinska, Palmowska, and Wolf were her climbing partners, and when she and Mrowka entered their hotel in Islamabad, every head turned. Wanda was wearing one of her best summer dresses, with fashionable pumps, and she had carefully applied her lipstick. Mexican climber Carlos Carsolio watched them walk through the lobby, their heels clicking on the cool marble floor, and followed their every step until they disappeared up the stairs. Later he saw them return from their appointment with the Minister of Tourism and Climbing, waving a piece of paper happily at him. *What?* he asked. *You got your permit already?* He and his team had been waiting ten days for the same piece of paper and would wait another seven before it came through.

Although Wanda struggled with her place as a woman in the male climbing world, she was a pro in dealing with the patriarchy of Pakistan and its restrictive mantel. Rather than fall victim to its age-old chauvinism, Wanda became a master at the game. She entered the land of Islam with respect, and she knew when and where to play the woman card. On one approach to the Baltoro, she discovered a small but nonetheless disgusting mite in her thick hair. She bounded out of her tent, her stocking feet creating little pockets of dust as she stamped around camp shrieking like a Hollywood starlet having spied a mouse. Finally, a few men on a British team came to her rescue and carefully combed through every strand until they had found the offending bug. Some saw it as an endearing demonstration of her vulnerability. But others, having lived through her dogmatic tantrums over control, scoffed at her use of feminine wiles.

As she approached Nanga Parbat in 1985 Wanda once again found herself isolated and challenged. She also felt exploited, complaining that her partners weren't pulling their own weight toward the common goal. Nevertheless, the first all-women team of Czerwińska, Palmowska, and Wanda reached the summit of Nanga Parbat, with Wolf turning back just shy of the top. Although their success was a landmark for female alpinism, referred to by some as a greater achievement than Wanda's summit of Everest, it would be the last time the four women climbed together. Palmowska said simply that Wanda had become too ambitious for her increasing limitations: age, the persistently painful leg, and, always, financial concerns that forced her to spend more time raising money than training for her high-risk climbs. "She was not as good as before, so the gap was widening, simply," Palmowska said. "Her determination was even greater, so we couldn't understand or agree; we tried to explain to her she shouldn't continue in such a way, but she wouldn't listen to us. After Nanga Parbat, our ways parted somehow."

Many of Wanda's problems were due to her strong personality, the personality of all great people. But great people tend to make poor friends because there's very little downtime in their high-octane lives; and there's too much rivalry and competition.

Ironically, the very image of a mountaineer is one of resilience, iron will, and dogged determination. Climbers tell stories about their various team leaders with a mixture of awe and whimsy when discussing particularly tough personalities, like the late, great Vladimir Balyberdin, famous for standing over a teammate high on K2 while the stricken climber vomited, yelling at the "pussy" to "get up!!" Climbing to 8,000 meters in chest-deep snow and demonstrating the first signs of high-altitude sickness were evidently no excuse in Balyberdin's Prussian mind.

But Wanda did not garner such bemused commentary about her take-no-prisoners personality. Instead, she found her former friends and colleagues less and less willing to join her in the mountains. In 1986, when she was planning her third assault on K2, her old climbing friends Anna Czerwinska, Krystyna Palmowska, and Mrowka Wolf were all scheduled to go to the mountain with a large Polish team that Wanda was not invited to join. Instead, Wanda chose a small French team that was scheduled to reach the mountain weeks before the Polish team. In her former climbing partners' minds, her choice to join the French was strategic rather than merely opportunistic.

"I know she was very determined to be the first [woman] on K2, and she joined the French team because it was the first expedition operating on K2 that year," Krystyna Palmowska said. "She wanted to be first, simply, and this French expedition gave her more chance to be the first, and she did it."

The team was led by Maurice and Liliane Barrard, a husband-and-wife team billing themselves as "the World's Highest Couple"—Wanda had met them on Broad Peak the year before—and a Parisian journalist, Michel Parmentier. Wanda knew that in 1984 Liliane had become the first woman to climb the deadly Nanga Parbat; given the severity of that climb and the relative ease of Liliane's ascent, Wanda was aware that she had a challenger for K2, but she wasn't worried. Wanda had seen Liliane climb and felt she was stronger than the diminutive French woman and had years more experience. But if Liliane made it high on the mountain, Wanda was going to be right there with her.

The women's race for the mountain had begun in earnest.

As Wanda was making the final preparations in late April she noticed a strange greenish tint to the clouds above Warsaw, but she didn't think anything of it. A few weeks later she walked through the airport security scanner on her way to Islamabad.

Beep beep beep. The alarm confused her: she had taken her climbing knife out of her pocket and removed her trademark silver bracelets.

"I'm sorry, miss," the technician said, "you'll have to step through again."

Wanda backed up and tried again.

Beep beep beep. The alarm was beginning to annoy her.

The technician called over his supervisor while Wanda, now impatient to get to her plane, tried again. But again the alarm sounded, and the security guards began surrounding her.

"Your shoes, take off your shoes."

She did and once again walked under the metal bridge. *Beep beep beep.*

The technicians looked at each other, then at Wanda, and then they motioned to a large Slavic woman standing nearby.

"I'm sorry, but you'll have to step this way."

Wanda was led into a cordoned-off area of the departure terminal where the robust woman led her into a curtained stall and told her to spread her legs and hold out her arms "like this!" She then firmly but professionally poked, prodded, and squeezed every inch of Wanda's body until she was convinced that Wanda was concealing nothing under her clothes besides her bra and panties. She was ushered back to the security checkpoint, where a group of officials scratched their heads.

It seemed that Wanda herself was setting off the detector.

On April 26, a nuclear reactor in the Soviet Union had overheated and blown up in the small town of Chernobyl. The explosion sent radioactive debris one mile into the atmosphere and around the world in a lethal cloud. Desperate to hide their technological failure from the world, the Soviet government did not release official notification of the disaster until Swiss officials recorded 10,000 times the normal reading of radioactive Cesium 137 in their air nearly 1,000 miles away. Then, and only then, did the Soviets recommend that residents in Chernobyl consider relocating until the crisis passed. Citizens did not learn that they were living in a toxic environment until their May Day parade was abruptly canceled. Still, children played in the green rain and rolled in the radioactive fields. Wanda, happy to steer clear of the ugly political world around her, knew nothing of the disaster 500 miles east of her until she found herself unable to get through the airport scanners. Her body was radioactive from the fallout. After much discussion and head-shaking, Wanda was allowed through the security station and then escorted to her plane, just to make sure nothing had been missed.

Wanda and her team arrived at Base Camp on May 22, weeks earlier than most expeditions make it to the mountain; only an Italian husband-and-wife team, Renato and Goretta Casarotto, had beaten them in. Renato was attempting the South Southwest Pillar, so Wanda and her French teammates were alone on the Abruzzi Ridge. A month later they would be joined by eight expeditions from all over the world. Wanda, having climbed to 7,350 meters (24,100 feet) on the Abruzzi in 1984, knew it better than any of them. She hoped it would give her the edge she needed to outperform her Polish friends who would also be attempting the SSW Pillar, which for them was a new and alien route.

Wanda, Parmentier, and the Barrards planned to climb the mountain virtually alpine—without the aid and safety of fixed ropes and with only a few caches of gear above 7,000 meters, rather than by establishing high camps. This kind of climbing was new to Wanda, but she was attracted immediately to its less encumbered style. If you had the skill and strength, she knew, you could reduce the time spent exposed to the mountain's objective dangers of avalanche, rockfall, equipment failure, and severe weather and therefore increase your odds of survival.

As the team readied itself for its first foray up the mountain Wanda announced that she wasn't going. Her throat felt like she had swallowed acid, and she was running a fever. She walked down the glacier to the British team, which had arrived shortly after them, and asked their doctor for medicine. For nearly a week she lay curled up in her tent, reading and drinking her favorite sweet Nepalese tea as her teammates carried loads to and established their Camp I at 6,200 meters (20,300 feet). Sick or not sick, her lack of help on the mountain couldn't have gone over well with her French comrades.

By May 31, Wanda was feeling better and left Base Camp early to help the team stock Camp I and establish Camp II, their last planned camp on the mountain. Without the weight of ropes, the team climbed fast and light, carrying one stove between them. Maurice and Liliane shared one tent while Wanda and Michel shared another. By June 4, they had established Camp II at 7,000 meters before strong gusting winds that nearly flattened their tents forced them back to Base Camp. So far they were right on schedule, if not a bit ahead. They had been at the mountain less than two weeks and had already established themselves halfway up it.

After several days resting at Base Camp, chatting with the ever-growing number of climbers arriving at the mountain, and checking and rechecking their high-altitude gear, they were ready for another ascent. Again rising before daybreak on June 8, Wanda and her team started out of Base Camp and spent nights in Advance Base at the base of the Abruzzi, at Camp I, and at Camp II. As they lay in their Camp II tents the night of June 10, Wanda tried to keep up with the rapid French discussion buzzing between the tents. It sounded like they were planning on a summit push already! She couldn't believe it. *Isn't it too soon?* she asked. *We've only been acclimatizing a couple of weeks; shouldn't we give it at least another week before heading for the summit?* No one seemed to have heard her, and the conversation continued between the tents and between the men. Wanda lay in her sleeping bag, Michel's body uncomfortably close as he and Maurice shouted back and forth over the increasing din of the wind. Soon the wind became too loud, and they gave up trying to talk to each other. As the tent vibrated in the increasing storm Wanda finally fell into a fitful sleep. Two days later the team decided that the wind had won that round, and they descended to Base Camp. Back in camp, Wanda immediately trudged down to the British team's camp where it sat below the Gilkey Memorial and approached Adrian "Aid" Burgess. She had met Aid and his identical twin brother, Alan, years before while climbing in the Tatra Mountains. Aid could see that she was carrying a tent rolled tightly in a stuff sack.

"Do you have a small tent I might trade with you for this one? This one is too large for the mountain, but it's a good tent, yes?"

Aid looked at the striking and somewhat formidable woman standing on the rocks, her legs set wide and her hands firmly planted on her hips, and asked her why she needed another tent. He knew that she was sharing a tent with Parmentier on the mountain.

She hesitated before she answered. "I need my *own* tent." She looked at the handsome Briton, his infamously impish smile begging for an explanation. "I simply cannot share a tent with Michel." As much as Parmentier disgusted her, it was too undignified to share that disgust with other climbers. She knew all too well how words traveled on a glacier, particularly harsh or profane words.

Aid didn't need the explanation. He was well aware that expeditions could bring out the worst in people and make living together in close confines next to impossible. He had seen more than one expedition falter and fail because climbers just couldn't manage to trust their lives on the same rope with the guy who was driving them crazy. Aid rooted around in the gear tent and then handed her a small, barely two-man tent. He and Al had been unable to sleep shoulder to shoulder in it, it was that small. She thanked him, rewarded him with one of her truly gorgeous smiles, and turned to walk back to her tent farther up the glacier.

As she started back she saw Michel sitting outside their mess tent, smoking a cigarette and laughing with Maurice.

Kurwa, she uttered to no one but the wind. It was the foulest word she could say in Polish, so foul she could only bear to say it to people who didn't speak the language; it was just too vulgar. She used it like English speakers used "fuck," but kurwa was a much better word. Depending on whom she was talking to and how pleased or pissed off she was at the time, it could mean "whore," "your mother is a whore," "bitch," "bastard," "cunt," "prick," "fuck you," "fuck off," "fucker," or merely "fuck!" Sometimes she said it with a smile on her face to a flirtatious but arrogant climber who didn't know if she was coming on to him or telling him to get stuffed. She liked that. Keep them wondering.

But sometimes she said it in pure disgust to a particular jerk or bastard in her way, like now. *Michel, now he is a real kurwa.* And tent or no tent, she still had to live with him for the next month.

When Wanda signed on to the team, she thought that the Barrards were a loving, competent couple and that the notion of their small, four-person team was romantic. But she had never met Michel Parmentier. After their first prolonged shut-in on the mountain, she knew her idea of a tight-knit team was in trouble.

Parmentier was an award-winning journalist who had, among other dangerous assignments, covered the war in Beirut. He was a small man with sad, dark eyes, a perpetual cigarette hanging from his lips, and a shock of unkempt hair that he covered with an English-style hat. He had paid half of the expedition costs in the hope of writing the story of Liliane's triumph as the first woman to climb K2; one can only imagine his fury when he learned that Maurice and Liliane had invited Rutkiewicz to join the team.

Wanda thought him the most narcissistic man she had ever met. The thought of one more night in a small tent lying face to face with his stale cigarette breath was more than she could handle. The antagonism would cost the team dearly in morale and logistical nightmares. As Maurice was dividing up the team gear for their next ascent Wanda announced that she would no longer be sharing a tent with Michel; she had her own. Claiming it was the price of her independence, Wanda shouldered the extra tent along with her share of the team food, gas, and stove, but the extra weight was born by the entire team.

As climbers continued to arrive at Base Camp they watched the growing tensions in alarm. Kurt Diemberger was among them. Not only was Wanda behaving too emotionally in regard to Michel, but he worried that his good friend had become too ambitious, too determined, as if K2 were just one mountain on a laundry list of 8,000ers she would pick off that summer. Having lost his friend and climbing partner Hermann Buhl on Chogolisa many years before, Diemberger knew all too well the price of such ambition. He also noted that she seemed lonely and less happy than on earlier occasions; she was no longer part of her Polish women's team but a free agent, jumping from team to team when opportunity presented itself. Entering the harshest landscape on Earth in the company of strangers was to risk finding yourself trapped, unhappy, and on your own. But Wanda believed it was a necessary evil: "People who climb mountains are lonely people; loneliness is needed. Acquaintances and friends are great things, but climbers need defined mental space that is untouched and unbothered by anyone."

On June 18, Wanda woke to a calm, cloudless morning; the sun was still hours away from peeking over the ridge of Broad Peak, but the sky was already fading from jet black to gray. She took care, as she always did, to make sure she had packed her checklist of essential gear. Particularly today. Today they were going for the summit. Barely three weeks on the mountain, Maurice and Michel felt they were ready, and Wanda just wanted to get it over with and say good-bye forever to her hated team-mate. As Wanda, Michel, Maurice, and Liliane walked up the glacier in the predawn darkness, Wanda watched the rocks and ice at her feet that were illuminated by the small circle of light from her headlamp. Their crampons crunched across the glacial rime toward Advance Base. It was the only sound the team made. There was no happy, excited chatter about heading toward their goal, the summit of the world's second-highest peak where only thirty-nine men had ever gone, and not one woman. Neither their mood nor their pace improved. They were moving devastatingly slowly, and what should have taken three days of climbing took six.

On day four of their ascent they approached an overhanging serac at about 7,700 meters (25,660 feet). Michel went first while Maurice, Liliane, and Wanda waited below for him to clear the most dangerous section before proceeding. Suddenly his boots broke through a fragile snow bridge at the edge of a crevasse, widening it too much for anyone else to be able to climb across it without a rope. Liliane shrank back from the abyss at her feet, insisting that she could not cross it without a rope. Maurice called ahead to Michel to throw back the team's only length of rope, but he had already moved too far ahead and refused to turn back. They watched him disappear over the edge of the ice barrier. Wanda couldn't believe it. *Bastard!* she thought, *his selfishness will force the three of us to find another route around the crevasse.* It also meant soloing through a perilous overhang, which Maurice had to pull the women over bodily, his gloved hands desperately grasping theirs as they climbed up the ice with their crampons. Wanda had never climbed an overhang at this altitude, and while exhilarating, it was exhausting for them all and forced yet another bivouac at 7,900 meters. When they rose the next morning, they hoped it would be their summit day, but increasing winds, their exhaustion, and the route above them thwarted those plans.

One of the many treacherous aspects of K2's topography sits just above 8,300 meters (27,250 feet)—a narrow gulley of 60–80-degree ice, rock, and unstable snow called "the Bottleneck" and above it an exposed, 50-degree wall of ice called "the Traverse." For many climbers, it is the crux of K2, and most will wait until large teams with high-altitude porters and oxygen have come and fixed the route with safety rope. But Wanda, Michel, and the Barrards were not going to wait. After caching all of their gear except for one small stove and one tent above their last bivy at 7,900 meters, they soloed through both sections, careful to place their ice axes firmly before they moved each foot, again making sure the teeth of their crampons were firmly embedded in the ice before pulling their axes out of their pinches and moving on. One false move, one false hold, one bad chunk of ice, and they would lose their purchase on the steep terrain and tumble backward down the face of K2. Littered throughout the ice slope were rocks covered by a thin and deadly layer of ice; handholds were impossible, and planting an ax in the thin ice was perilous. Instead, they had to "friction-climb," using only their crampons below and pressing their hands as hard as they could into the glassy rocks to increase their connection to the slope. It took a terrifying and exhausting effort and was so emotionally and physically draining that they were forced to suffer yet another bivouac, their third in a row. On a −30-degree Fahrenheit night without a single sleeping bag between them, all four crammed into a tent built for two and waited for the first light of day for their summit bid.

June 23, Wanda's name day, dawned clear and calm, and Wanda felt it was finally her moment. Michel and Maurice broke trail through deep snow for most of the morning, then stopped to rest and make soup only a few hundred feet below the summit. Wanda thought it so strange that they were resting that close to the summit that she wondered whether it had been a hallucination until climbers later told her they found one-minute soup packets on the trail. The lunch break gave Wanda the opportunity she had been looking for, and she went for the summit alone, leaving the three to their soup.

At 10:00 Wanda took the last, labored steps toward the summit. Unlike Everest's small tabletop, K2's summit stretched broadly and gently out above her. It was almost the size of a good-sized living room, large enough to dance around, which she was tempted to do when at 10:15 she became the first woman and the first Pole to place a boot on the summit of the world's second-highest mountain.

When she could go no higher, she knelt on the hardpacked snow, thanked God for her safe ascent, and prayed to be delivered back down safely. Then she cried. She was so glad to be alone, not to have to share this moment of unparalleled happiness and peace. It was perfectly quiet and still, with not a breath of wind; she thanked God for giving her such an ideal summit day and weather. Everything had gone right, and here she was. Not only the first woman but the first Pole. *How some of the men will hate that,* she laughed.

She looked around her at the sea of peaks below; the other 8,000-meter giants, Broad Peak, Gasherbrums I and II, and far-off Nanga Parbat, looked small in comparison. She got up from her knees and twirled around slowly, carefully, on the summit precipice, her crampons crunching the wind-blasted snow, her arms outstretched, trying to embrace the scene, to make a mental image she could never forget. Her smile was so broad that her teeth began to hurt in the sharp cold. She had done it. After three attempts, two lost lives, and four years of trying, she had made it, and no one could ever take it away: Wanda Rutkiewicz was the first woman to stand atop the great K2.

"It was sheer ecstasy being on the summit," she said. "K2 had been my mountain of dreams for so many years."

It would be a short-lived ecstasy.

CHAPTER 4

THE BLACK SUMMER

Unlike any sport, it demands that its players die.

—BRUCE BORCOTT

On June 21, 1986, as Wanda Rutkiewicz, Michel Parmentier, and Liliane and Maurice Barrard climbed between Camps II and III on their way to the summit of K2, below them on the mountain two American climbers were swept to their deaths. John Smolich and Al Pennington had been traversing a steep snow slope on the South Southwest Ridge when a catastrophic avalanche broke loose above, burying them in tons of snow and rock in its thunderous 125-mile-per-hour path.

The Black Summer of 1986 had begun. In the end, twenty-seven climbers would make it to the summit of K2, but a staggering thirteen would die in the process. Smolich and Pennington were the first.

When she reached the summit two days later, Wanda busied herself writing a note to commemorate her achievement. "Wanda Rutkiewicz, June 21, 1986, 10:15 A.M., and Women's First Ascent," she wrote. Below her name she wrote "Liliane Barrard," but left the time of Liliane's ascent blank. She wanted to be correct, to have her record taken seriously, and an estimate wouldn't be good enough. It wouldn't be accurate. Besides, what if Liliane turned back below the summit? Wanda put the partially finished note and a small Polish flag in a plastic bag, along with a rock from her childhood climbing crag in the Skalki, closed it up, and anchored in on the summit. Increasingly anxious about spending too much time too high, Wanda climbed down a few meters, hoping for a glimpse of Liliane, Maurice, and Michel. At last she saw them, still over thirty minutes away, appearing as black specks against the sea of white around them. *Why are they taking so long? How can minute soup take an hour, for heaven's sake?* she thought. The altitude made the moments seem like hours, and her patience quickly wore as thin as the air.

Finally, at around 11:15 A.M., they arrived over the last cornice and joined her on the summit. K2 had not only its first but its second female summiteer, all in the course of an hour. Liliane was hidden behind her dark glacier glasses, a bright pink hat with an attached neck gaiter, and an oversized noseguard, an unsightly but effective method she had of keeping her nose from burning in the thin air from exposure to strong UV rays over five miles closer to the sun than at home in France. She and Maurice fell into each other's arms. It was more of a collapse than a hug. Michel and Wanda had worried about Maurice's flagging strength on ascent, and now came the hard part—getting both himself and his wife down.

Liliane and Maurice were an oddly matched couple. She was shy and small, only four-foot-eleven, with long, thick, dark brown hair that she often wore loose, and at thirty-seven she retained the hourglass figure of a woman years younger. She spoke no English and filled the void of language with enormous, friendly smiles. Maurice was over six feet tall, thin to the point of gangly, and he wore his graying hair long to his shoulders, with thick sideburns and a bushy mustache that could almost be described as handlebar. He looked like he'd just arrived from central casting for an American Western movie, not from a quiet farm in rural France. But odd or not, the Barrards had begun to bill themselves as "the World's Highest Couple," having already reached the summit of two other 8,000-meter peaks, among them the notorious Nanga Parbat.

When she was in her early twenties, Liliane Bontemps sat in a Paris clinic and reached up to tenderly touch her painful shoulder. She had fallen during a routine gymnastics practice and dislocated it. She didn't think she had broken her collarbone; it wasn't that painful. She had always wanted to be, not a gymnast, but a teacher of gymnastics, the fabulous sport that allowed her such freedom and movement and joy of spirit. She wanted to watch other girls learn how to throw their bodies meters into the air and across a mat, only to land as gently as a heron on a still lake. She had wanted to watch her love of the sport reflected in their young eyes and bodies. But feeling the throbbing pain in her shoulder, she knew it would never again have the strength necessary to support her body weight. She knew she had better find something else to do.

Later, with her shoulder stabilized with an arm sling, she rode home to Montmartre thinking about the other things she enjoyed doing as much as gymnastics. Each was a mountain activity: skiing, hiking, and climbing. She and her brother Alain had been introduced to the Alps early by their father, who had skied on the legendary Pierre Allain's Chamonix team. At every opportunity she joined Alain on climbs in the mountains of Peru, Norway, the Russian Pamirs, even Greenland. But she doubted whether she was big enough, or strong enough, to make a career in the mountains. Besides, in all the years she traipsed through the mountains she had never met a female guide. *Well,* she thought, *no matter what I do, I know it can't be a normal office job. I need the freedom to travel, to spend time in the mountains, to breathe the air high above the crowded streets of Paris.*

Liliane chose physical therapy and soon had her license to practice. She loved her work, but when she was twenty-four, she found her future.

Liliane sat at the base of 22,205-foot (6,768-meter) Huascarán, writing in her journal and taking frequent peeks at Peru's highest mountain. She thought the mountain one of the most beautiful she'd ever seen. While she loved the Alps, Huascarán's Base Camp was at 13,700 feet (4,175 meters), almost as high as the summit of Mont Blanc, and the summit towered nearly another 9,000 feet (2,700 meters) above that. She had had few challenges as demanding, and she loved testing herself against such a formidable mountain. Two years before, when she was just twenty-two, she and Alain had been on their first expedition traveling to the Caucasus Mountains, but getting into the closed Soviet system through a carefully planned network of secret meeting points and passwords proved more exciting than the mountains themselves. Here, looking up at this beautiful white-crowned peak rising straight out of the South American forest, she felt like she was finally a mountaineer.

As usual, she was the only woman on the expedition, but with her protective brother close by, it was never much of an issue. She had worked hard to develop her climbing skills to compensate for her lack of height and strength, and so far that strategy had worked. The men around her seemed to accept her as one of the team.

She breathed deeply of the air around her; even though she sat at 15,500 feet, she barely noticed that the air had only half the oxygen. She smiled. Everything seemed exotic and wild. She was trying to get it all down in words when suddenly a shadow fell across her tablet. She looked up and saw that a man, a very tall man, was standing in front of her, but with the sun behind him, she couldn't make out his features. She held her hand over her squinted eyes, hoping to separate the sun from this man's outline, but it didn't help. He remained obscured.

Bonjour, je suis Maurice Barrard, he said. It surprised her that the first person she should meet on this trip halfway around the world was French, and she smiled back up at him as she introduced herself, extending her hand to clasp his.

In some ways Liliane never let go.

Over the course of the expedition Liliane and Maurice spent long hours together deep into most nights, telling each other of their lives until that moment. Maurice told her that he had left his first marriage for the mountains; climbing was that important to him. He said that he had spent the better part of the sixties and seventies climbing all the major routes that the French Alps had to offer, and now he was turning his sights toward the greater mountains of the Andes and then the Himalayas. He too loved teaching and had found he had a gift with special needs children, but as much as he loved it, teaching was only a means to the end—mountains.

She sat rapt, watching his eyes light up as he told her where he'd been and where he wanted to go. She found herself nodding in agreement and smiling in understanding, reaching out often, at first shyly but then with growing confidence, to touch his arm as he spoke.

When the two left Peru, they returned to Paris a couple and immediately moved in together. Maurice's children from his first marriage welcomed Liliane and were glad that she shared their father's passion for the most beautiful mountains in the world.

They came at their passion with a simple, pragmatic approach: live simply to simply live. Working only part-time and earning as little as 2,000 francs ($260) a month, Liliane and Maurice geared their entire lives toward the mountains. And once there, they aimed to climb the mountain on its terms—no supplemental oxygen, no high-altitude porters, a minimal amount of rope, and as few high camps on the mountain as possible. Not only was the austere style more affordable, but it was preferable. Maurice had joined a French national team of eighteen climbers attempting K2 in 1979, and forever after swore off the size, hassle, and bureaucracy of enormous Himalayan expeditions.

Merde, Maurice had thought, looking at the serpentine line of 1,400 porters, cameramen, climbers, and even a man who planned to hang-glide off the summit, *this is worse than the army! It's just another huge bureaucratic waste of time, money, and efficiency.* But K2 had impressed him, and although the team wasn't able to make much progress on the mountain, Maurice thought it a worthy goal.

Maurice returned to the Karakoram in 1980, climbing Hidden Peak (Gasherbrum I) with his friend and mentor, Georges Narbaud. It would not be until 1982 that Maurice and Liliane traveled together to an 8,000-meter peak, and again, it would be one in the Karakoram—Gasherbrum II.

Maurice told Liliane in careful detail of the blistering heat that would greet them in Islamabad, the harrowing two-day bus ride to Skardu, the eleven-day trek into Base Camp, and the two-month stay on the mountain. He gave her lists of everything they would need, and she carefully shopped and packed for each segment of the trip, happy to finally be going with him rather than sending him off at Charles de

Gaulle International Airport, never knowing when or even if he would be coming home. The months she spent without him, often enduring weeks without any word, had been torture, and she smiled as she carefully folded long underwear shirts and pants and placed them in piles on the floor for packing. She was going to climb higher than she ever had, but she wasn't even nervous. *Why should I be? I'm going with Maurice; he has always taken care of me and always known the exact right thing to do in the mountains. He is one of France's best climbers, and at forty-one only getting stronger.* They had also convinced Alain to come along and film the expedition; she was going to the ends of the Earth with her two favorite men in the world. She thought herself the luckiest woman alive.

The alarm rang. It was 5:00 A.M. and finally happening. Alain knocked gently on their door. *Reveillez-vous?* he asked. *Yes, we're up!* Liliane answered as she heard others in the Skardu motel waking for the break-of-dawn departure for Dasso, a day's trip by four-wheel jeep up the Shigar River, almost to where it met the Braldu. There the road stopped and the walking began.

Liliane got up first, putting the covers back over Maurice so he could have a few more moments of rest, and pulled on her carefully laid-out clothes: white T-shirt, khaki pants, a small-rimmed fisherman's hat, thick socks, and sturdy hiking boots. She stood in the dingy bathroom, tiptoeing to inspect herself in the cracked mirror over the sink. She smiled at her reflection, not because her outfit pleased her but because she was finally going to see an 8,000-meter peak. And she was going to see it with Maurice.

Later, as the jeep bounced along the narrow, rutted road on its way to Dasso, she looked over at Alain. *Mon Dieu! Give it a rest,* she laughed as her brother clicked through the colorful Rubik's Cube for the umpteenth time. He considered himself something of a Rubik's Cube genius and had decided he would complete the world's highest Rubik's Cube on the top of Gasherbrum II. Who knew, maybe the scientific community would be interested in his results, hypoxia notwithstanding. The cube had barely been out of his hands since they left Paris. She shook her head and went back to watching the dry desert fade behind them as they rose up the Shigar Valley, each village more lush than the last, with the carefully irrigated runoff from the mountains feeding farmlands and fruit trees.

After a long, dusty day, the jeeps left them and their gear at the desolate army barracks in Dasso where the road ended. Maurice and Alain carefully walked among the Baltistan men and boys, hoping to find porters to take their loads to Base Camp. Even with scores milling about waiting to be hired, they seemed older and less capable than Maurice remembered from past years. Then he was told that a huge team of Polish and French women, led by "Mr. Wanda," had been through only weeks before. Liliane smiled at the gender confusion of the porters who relayed the information. She knew that they would address her as "Sir" or "Mister," without rancor or guile; they simply didn't understand the language subtlety between "Mister" and "Miss," let alone "Monsieur" and "Mademoiselle."

In the morning she was finally walking toward GII, and as she scrambled across the rocks to keep pace with Maurice she felt the burning stares of the porters, men unaccustomed to seeing even their own wives' skin, let alone that of a beautiful, shapely Frenchwoman. With her long hair swinging beneath the brim of the hat and her snug T-shirt, she was easily recognizable on the team. She found herself hunching over and pulling at her T-shirt, hoping to loosen its grip on her breasts. Maurice seemed so at ease with the odd, dark people, but she was not so comfortable with them or they with her. She hung back, hoping their fascination with her would fade, letting Maurice do all the communicating. In their first camp on the trail she found a perfect place to sit and stare up at the 6,000- and 7,000-meter peaks around her while she wrote in her journal. She looked up from her writing to see a circle of curious but cold eyes watching her. Judging her. *They don't like me,* she thought. *The mere presence of a woman upsets their routines, their habits. Maybe they don't like a woman to be their boss.* She climbed in the tent and pulled the flap closed after her, happy to be out of their harsh stare.

While many Western women have felt compelled to confront the often obnoxious curiosity of the Balti porters, Liliane retreated. And once she realized that her form-fitting shirts and pants were part of their fascination, she changed to less revealing clothes and tied her long hair up under her floppy sun hat. Aware but not upset or defiant, Liliane merely faded quietly into the fold of the expedition, emerging only when they were firmly established at Base Camp and the porters had disappeared back down the glacier toward their villages.

Her only apprehension of the porters was their left hands. In place of toilet paper, porters traditionally used their left hand and stream water to cleanse their bottoms after defecating, reserving their right hand for eating and greeting each other. She just hoped their cook had been instructed that nothing replaced soap and hot water. She knew from Maurice that many teams had had their expeditions end at Base Camp in dysentery and other illnesses.

At Base Camp she played the role of team caretaker, almost maternally so, gently chiding the men when their language became foul or their personal hygiene less than hygienic. She spent her days doing laundry, writing, and posing for sponsor photos, cheerfully laughing into the camera as Maurice asked for more and more angles. Most nights Maurice would hold court, talking about the mountain, their planned route, its obvious hazards and subtle dangers, while teammates listened, particularly Liliane. On the rare occasion when she would offer her comments, Maurice most often finished the thought for her as she smiled in agreement. And always, Alain sat clicking through the Rubik's Cube as the conversations buzzed around him. She had to admit, *he is damned good*. He could solve the puzzle in a matter of minutes, his hands a blur and the colorful squares blending their primary colors into purple, green, and orange.

Gasherbrum II, while a challenge for any climber, is seen by many as "the easiest" 8,000-meter mountain, and it is indeed the most climbed next to Everest and Cho Oyu, where commercial expeditions bring hundreds of clients to their well-roped and -supported routes every year. Even with Gasherbrum II's larger numbers, Pakistan in general and the harsher climbing environment in particular have kept most commercial outfits off of the region's five 8,000-meter peaks. Climbers who venture into the unforgiving Karakoram are usually those who crave the wilderness experience and find personal merit in pushing beyond all measures of comfort and care.

Like most Karakoram expeditions, the Barrards' small team climbed without any high-altitude porters to carry their loads above Base Camp or to help establish fixed lines or camps to the summit. Wanting nothing to do with commercial expeditions, Maurice happily climbed with his tight team, setting only small sections of rope through the worst sections and stopping only to bivouac for the night rather than set and stock camps. They climbed strongly and efficiently, and within weeks of their arrival Liliane stood on the summit of Gasherbrum II, her first 8,000-meter peak. Standing just a few kilometers from two of the most beautiful mountains in the world, K2 and Gasherbrum IV, the view from GII was stunning. But Liliane saw nothing as she looked around in mock disgust, her heavily mittened hands sitting on her hips.

"Here I am on the top, and I can't see anything with all these fucking clouds," she laughed as Maurice shot yet another sponsor photo. "Mon amour, this is not the moment to doll myself up in the middle of all this rotten snow," she told him, but nonetheless she "dolled up" as best she could standing close to the top of the world and swathed in her hat, neck gaitor, glacier glasses, noseguard, and billows of down. She looked like a colorful and trussed bundle of climbing gear, the tiny speck of her unprotected cheeks the only visible sign that a human lived beneath the layers.

As they descended back into Base Camp, Liliane heard a cry of anguish from Alain's tent. She looked over at where he was unpacking from their climb, and when she saw him she burst out laughing so hard she doubled over, holding on to her ski pole for balance. Alain stood on the glacier looking like a boy who'd missed Christmas. In his hand was the Rubik's Cube. He had forgotten to get it out of his sack on the summit.

Mon cherie! Now you know firsthand how the high altitude affects your brain! Liliane called over, still chuckling.

So much for science, he thought, and threw the cube into his pack.

Liliane assumed the challenge and risk of the mountains with a certain cheerful resignation, but she didn't demonstrate any real exuberance or joy, apart from being with Maurice. In fact, the mountains seemed like a means to an end: Maurice. Unlike many climbers, she did not narrow her focus to the mountain; instead, she thought mostly of Maurice and dreamed of the cherry trees in their garden at home in La Beauce and how "they must be in bloom" even as she climbed the ice walls at her feet.

They returned to France and began their two-person publicity campaign as "the World's Highest Couple" (Le couple le plus haut du monde), airing the footage that Alain had shot and telling talk-show audiences of their feats. While they were home, they worked sporadically at their careers, Maurice teaching special needs children and Liliane working as a physical therapist, but mostly they focused on getting to their next 8,000-er.

Many women struggle with choosing between their life's passion and their biological imperative to have children, but Liliane had little or no maternal instinct and usually demurred when asked about motherhood, "Not now, not now." She wanted to be free, free for the mountains and free for Maurice. He filled her life with everything she needed. Maurice, already a father from a previous marriage, put no pressure on her to have a child, and they didn't.

After the relatively benign GII, Liliane and Maurice decided that they would return to Pakistan and climb its notorious Nanga Parbat. Sitting 120 miles south-southwest of K2, Nanga Parbat was known for decades as the "Killer Mountain" because thirty-one men had died trying to climb it before the first climber—Hermann Buhl—reached the top in 1953. Much of that deadly reputation was earned in 1934 when nine members of a German team died of exposure, and again in 1937 when seven more Germans and their nine Sherpas were lost in a single avalanche. Not only were the Germans untrained and unprepared for a mountain of Nanga Parbat's size and weather, but they had been told in no uncertain terms that if they didn't reach the summit for the glory of the burgeoning Third Reich, they shouldn't bother coming home at all. So perhaps the inclination to reduce risk was lost on the already doomed team. After Buhl reached the summit in 1953, it would be thirty-one more years before a woman reached those heights. And that woman was Liliane Barrard.

Unlike the other Karakoram peaks, Nanga Parbat's Base Camp was at an unusually low altitude, and Liliane relished being surrounded by green fields and poplar trees. At night the air was resplendent with sweet wood smoke, an impossibly delicious smell in the ice worlds of the Karakoram. Again operating as a small, self-sufficient team, with Alain acting as cameraman, they acclimatized quickly and went for their summit bid after only a few weeks at the mountain.

On June 27, 1984, Liliane became the first woman to climb the infamous mountain. Suddenly she was a star of the French climbing world and came home to a flurry of media requests for interviews. She sat through them stiffly, deferring to Maurice to answer most questions, although they had been put to her. If she hesitated just long enough, he would fill in the blank air, and she could sit back and relax until the next one. Her preference to remain in Maurice's shadow worked: today there are no books and no articles that focus solely on Liliane and her accomplishments, and in a world eager to bestow fame on the noteworthy, there are almost no people who remember the woman beyond her smile and her shyness.

In rare outspokenness, Liliane showed uncommon emotion in an interview when she disdained the climbing style of a woman she had yet to meet, Wanda Rutkiewicz.

"I have no desire to enter competition with Wanda Rutkiewicz, who goes to the Himalaya with a very different mind-set than mine. I have always disliked the spirit of competition; this creates aggressiveness and meanness. Simply, I like to go and see."

Partly fueled by their success on Nanga Parbat and the resulting media attention, the Barrards looked higher than they ever had. After only two 8,000-meter peaks and four years' experience in the Himalayas, Maurice set their sights on K2, hoping Liliane would be the first woman, and they the first couple, to climb its demanding slopes. Then, they announced, they would head to the rarely climbed and treacherous Kangshung Face of Everest. But before they tested their limits on the two highest mountains in the world, they needed one more mountain.

Although number five in height, Nepal's Makalu was deceptively difficult for Liliane. She suffered from the brittle cold, her toes becoming so painful that kicking her front points into the ice became more and more difficult. Then, at 8,440 meters, with their goal in spitting distance on the mountain's long 100-meter summit ridge, they decided it would be risking too much to continue in the driving wind and relentless cold. Only twenty vertical meters from the summit, they turned back. French record-keepers tried to award them the summit, but Liliane and Maurice refused to accept it. "No, we did not make the summit. Twenty meters away is not the top. We failed." In a time when an 8,000-meter summit meant much-needed sponsorship dollars and support, theirs was a stoic climbing ethic rarely matched in the high-stakes world of mountaineering.

They returned from Makalu beaten and broke but undeterred in facing their next objective: K2.

Film footage from the expedition's approach march to K2 shows Maurice playing chess with Michel Parmentier in the natural hot springs above Askole and jokingly nodding to the music on his headphones as Liliane and Wanda wash their hair in the steaming water nearby. But appearances were deceiving; the expedition was anything but fun.

Before Maurice and Liliane left for K2, many friends and family members had a bad feeling about the trip. They were under too much stress, money problems had continued to plague them, and the endless logistics of such an enormous undertaking had exhausted Maurice, who assumed almost full control of the details. Alain tried to help where he could, but he was busy applying for their next permit—the Kang-shung Face of Everest—where they would go directly after K2, so the lion's share of the work was done by Maurice, shuttling between Paris and the tiny farmhouse.

Their arrival in Pakistan in early May didn't ease the constant worry. Soon after landing, Maurice discovered that he had left 100,000 French francs (about $13,000 at 1986 exchange rates, $22,000 in 2004), his expedition's entire purse, in the back of a Rawalpindi taxicab. For the impecunious French couple, it was a devastating loss. Having worked with the French Federation of Mountain Climbing (FFME) office of Himalayan climbing, Maurice called Paris and convinced the federation to loan them tens of thousands of francs. They were able to continue with the expedition, but they knew they would return home to a crushing debt.

For many at Base Camp, Liliane and Maurice Barrard were the first husband-and-wife climbing team they had witnessed in the Himalayas, and some felt it was not necessarily a good trend in the sport. Jim Curran, a member of the British expedition, commented that "whatever you might think, to have a very close, intimate relationship going on like that did seem to put an extraordinary external pressure on their performance and reliability. It's difficult enough when you're just climbing with a mate, but when you're married to them, it must be almost impossible for one or the other not to dominate and bring an extra tension. I suppose it could work brilliantly," he added, but nonetheless, he watched both of them with growing concern.

Theirs was a passionate relationship, both emotionally and sexually. Even though she was constantly in his presence, Liliane was breathless in her desire for Maurice and wrote of "having my entire body pressed against you, to be back in our safe nest, each centimeter of my body pressed against yours." At night her dreams were graphic and troubling and repeatedly ended in longing, not satisfaction. "When I come home, you are already sleeping; when I awake you are already up and busy."

Other climbers at Base Camp watched her bent over her journal, frantically writing, her brow creased with concentration and strain and her pen clenched so tightly that her fingers were white. A few would approach and ask her why she looked so sad, so forlorn. Reflexively hiding her written words, she would slap her hand over the page and look up into the worried face.

"Oh really? What makes you say that?" she would laugh, hoping it sounded genuine. But she knew why they would say that—she was just surprised that they would notice or care about her mood. And her mood was indeed dark. She was heavy with ominous forewarnings, in her dreams and her waking thoughts, and she wrote furiously to keep up with the troubling visions.

"Why must we [always] be doing something? I just want to be together with you, simply doing nothing but being with you." But even this uncomplicated desire filled her with angst: she was with him, she should have been happy, but she was not. "Perhaps only those who sleep are really happy." She thought a lot about sleep, deep undisturbed sleep. She had been to three other 8,000-meter peaks and knew that even Base Camp altitude can affect sleep, but never had she had such restless nights, waking only to be exhausted from her tossing and turning, her worry and fear. Beneath her head, the glacier cracked and moaned as it shifted position. Sometimes the rumblings were so loud and forceful that she could feel it in her teeth. It was an unsettling feeling, to sense the glacier's movement and wonder whether it would suddenly split wide open and swallow you whole. And it didn't help with her unease and anxiety. She didn't know why she felt so unraveled. She looked up at K2 and shuddered at the sheer power of the mountain. Unlike the other mountains she had climbed, this one kept her mind gloomy and disturbed, and she counted the days until they would start back down the glacier to their little farmhouse.

Meanwhile, Michel Parmentier watched the Barrards with increasing alarm. He thought the team was shaky from the start, with Liliane depending on Maurice and Wanda depending on them all, and things were only getting worse. Maurice wasn't moving with his regular robust strength, and Liliane was always at him, complaining about something. *Ball-buster,* he thought, watching her fuss and fumble around Base Camp. *If Maurice didn't have to worry about her, he'd be fine.* Michel approached Maurice and urged him to rope with him, claiming that the two things needed for a Himalayan summit were "autonomy and speed," neither of which was possible when roping up with slower, less experienced women. Maurice refused, in Michel's mind because he was looking for the greater payout of "the World's Highest Couple" ascent. Many expeditions were laden with internecine fighting and unbridled ego, but theirs seemed particularly fractious.

Others at Base Camp also noted that Maurice seemed exhausted before he started. "Liliane appears calm and strong, but Maurice is only a shadow of himself," Diemberger wrote. As the team came back to camp after depositing a load of supplies at Advanced Base Camp (directly at the base of the route) Liliane and Wanda almost skipped along the rocks and ice compared to Maurice, who, bent and exhausted, trailed behind them like an old man.

They were the second team to arrive at the mountain, and they planned to climb the Abruzzi route alpine-style. For the Barrards, alpine style meant climbing light and fast with only the bare necessities of tent or light bivy sack, stove, fuel, food, and sleeping bag, not setting any fixed rope on the route, establishing only one or two high camps on the mountain, and not using supplemental oxygen. Once they had acclimatized to the thin air, they would go for the summit in one push, Base Camp to the top, carrying only essential items with them. It demanded a level of physical strength and experience rare among high-altitude climbers and necessitated their ability to ascend in pairs, occasionally roped to each other but not to the mountain. Each climber had to be experienced on technical ice and rock and capable of climbing without the safety of a fixed rope. And that was just the getting up. Descent was where the lack of supplemental oxygen, inadequate fuel supplies to melt snow and cook food, and little or no shelter in sudden storms could get them into trouble. Maurice knew that few had attempted and no one had yet succeeded in ascending K2 in a true alpine style, but he was determined to try.

In the typical French style of "fast and light" alpinism, the team spent the minimum amount of time acclimatizing. Also, they stocked tents only at 6,200 meters and 7,000 meters, only halfway to the 8,616-meter summit. As a result, they had no erected tents or supplies above 7,000 meters to support the traditionally weeklong summit bid. They wanted to come in, conquer, and leave the mountain as soon as possible. The theory was that the less time they spent exposed to the objective dangers of an 8,000-meter peak, the better. Also, shorter expeditions are, if not always safer, cheaper. And the Barrards were watching every centime. After only two weeks on the mountain, they made their first summit bid, climbing for four days before bad weather turned them back.

Wanda, concerned about her lack of acclimatization, was glad for the retreat, although Base Camp was less and less a refuge as she and Michel became open combatants in a fishbowl war. Base Camp, on a good day, is a hotbed of ego, frustration, aggression, and envy, and climbers, eager for any distraction from their own dysfunction, find great sport in picking the bones of other, even more unhappy expeditions. And the small

French team was easy fodder for the rumor gristmill: Wanda gave the impression that she was too good for her team, while Michel let it be known that he thought Liliane was wearing the pants in the marriage, and everybody worried about Maurice and his increasingly haggard demeanor.

Liliane ignored it all, focusing exclusively on Maurice, doing laundry for him and happily sitting on a rock while he cut off huge chunks of her hair so that it wouldn't get in the way during the summit bid. *Soon, she thought, we will be going home, where we can be alone together in our little farmhouse and rest, and Maurice will become his old, strong self again.*

Early on the morning of June 18 they left Base Camp for their second, and last, bid for the summit of K2, four disparate minds each struggling to survive.

Their progress was slow but steady as they climbed the first 1,000 meters of the route up a deceptively easy scree hill of loose rock. Maurice and Michel led the way, their footfalls loosening small and not so small rocks that clattered down the slope, bouncing off Wanda's and Liliane's helmets. Thankfully, they got away with minor dings and dents. It was not a section of the route where they could spend much time gazing up at the beauty around them; instead, they kept their faces down and as close to the mountain as possible. Without ropes to jumar up, Maurice and Michel made deep and clean stairs for the women to draft up. The only tricky section of their first day was the 50-meter rock wall called House's Chimney, named in 1938 for American climber Bill House, who first figured out how to pass through it after decades of climbers before him had been turned back. Liliane and her team found a jumble of old ropes, some of them frayed to strings over the years of rockfall, wind, and sun eating at their fibers, and clipped onto as many of them as they could fit in their ascending device, hoping at least one of the ropes would hold.

They stopped where they had established tents at 6,200 meters the first night but skipped over their tents at 7,000 meters the following night, choosing instead to stop at 7,100 meters below the Black Pyramid, an imposing 400-meter wall of dark, vertical rock and ice, one of the most technically challenging aspects of the 12,000-foot ascent. Like many before them, they decided to cache some gear to lighten their loads at the base of the Pyramid for their perilous ascent over the snow slopes above 24,000 feet. Between the hurricane-force winds blowing between K2 and Broad Peak and the 30-degree angle of the snow-heavy slope, the climb above the Black Pyramid to the Shoulder has turned many climbers back, and killed some who didn't. The faster and lighter they could climb to get over and above its danger, the better.

Finally, on their third night, June 20, they set their tents at 7,700 meters, just below a serac band that Wanda thought looked "only a little dangerous" from the threat of falling snow and ice. They hoped it would take just one more night before their summit bid on the 22nd.

As the team hunkered down for another cramped, cold night in their small bivy tents, Liliane pulled out her tablet and pen. In what would be her last journal entry, she never mentioned the mountain.

"Maurice, my love, there are times when you ask me what I feel like doing, and I respond, whatever *you* feel like doing. Whatever. When I say that I really don't care at all. I'm there with you and happy."

By their fourth day of ascent, they knew they were in trouble. They had reduced their slow pace to a crawl, and instead of making it high above the Shoulder for their last bivy before the summit, they didn't even make it *onto* the Shoulder; they set up their tents near 7,900 meters.

Michel had had enough. *Maurice!* he yelled at the haggard man, *for God's sake, you can't put one foot in front of the other. Enough! Go down!* Maurice barely registered the assault. *No, no way. I'm fine*, he whispered, and he slumped into the slope.

Maurice wasn't fine. The next day Michel tried to get the team up for an early start, hoping to make the summit and spare them another enervating night in the debilitating air. But he couldn't rouse the Barrards. When they finally managed to get out of their sleeping bags and drink some of the offered sweet tea, the sun was already beating down on them, making hydration a critical necessity. If they couldn't keep up their fluid intake, it would start a downward spiral toward pulmonary and cerebral edemas, fast. Finally, Maurice and Liliane strapped on their crampons and continued their now painful ascent. With every extra ounce a critical factor, they pared down from three tents to one bivouac tent, one stove, and no sleeping bags, the plan being to make the summit and return to their tents at 7,900 meters. But after climbing up the sloping Shoulder and then soloing through the Bottleneck and Traverse, the Barrards collapsed, crawling into the one tiny bivy tent, refusing to climb another foot. They had gained only 450 meters.

Stopping to rest at 8,400 meters was a fatal mistake. Without even one sleeping bag between them and crammed in the bivy, sleep was out of the question. At those altitudes, their blood was running like molasses and their lungs were panting as they tried to capture more and more oxygen in the emaciated air. Their digestive systems were no longer processing food, and their hearts were beating frantically trying to get their brains the blood they so desperately needed. But nothing worked. Filmmaker David Breashears has likened breathing at this altitude to "running on a treadmill while breathing through a straw." And the team had already been close to this altitude for two days without reaching the summit.

Finally, on June 23, they did. After another slow start in the morning, they left their miserable bivy at 7:30 A.M., with Michel and Maurice breaking the trail. After a few hours they stopped to have soup, but Wanda kept going alone, eager for the window of opportunity to be the first woman on the summit. An hour later Liliane, Maurice, and Michel joined her on the top of K2 at 11:15 A.M.

Liliane hugged Wanda and told her that she had never had such good weather on any of her other summits. For the moment the team forgot all their animosities and exhaustion, took pictures, and drank in the scenery for over an hour. Because today there are no survivors of their heralding achievement, the facts and exact conversation will never be known. But given the state they were in on the ascent and the length of time they had been in the Death Zone, their conversation was most likely far from scintillating.

In 1978 Rick Ridgeway had climbed K2 in mid-September after three months of trying. As he stood on the summit his one dim thought was that he "should really try to remember this moment, because some-day it's going to matter to me." But it didn't matter then. Then, his only thought was a dull but persistent alarm: how am I ever going to get back down alive? He survived, but had to reach down into the bottom of his reserves, using every last scrap of wits and will to do so.

Prolonged exposure to the thin air above 25,000 feet is a deadly game of roulette, and the next decision of the Barrard team would load another bullet in their already crowded chamber. When they finally reached the summit, Wanda, who'd been waiting an hour, urged them to descend quickly, knowing that every second spent at that altitude was costing all of them dearly. But they lingered over an hour, and when they finally made it back to their bivouac at 8,400 meters, once again the Barrards collapsed in the meager shelter. Michel said later he implored them to continue descending (while Wanda wrote that it was Michel who wanted to stop and rest), but Maurice refused to budge, and the entire team hunkered down for a third night above 26,000 feet.

For Maurice Barrard, even the thought of survival seemed like too much effort. When two Basque climbers on their descent from the summit passed the Barrards, Liliane turned to Maurice: "I hear the living; they're climbing down." "I don't give a shit about the living," Maurice replied, barely moving.

It was a bad night, and another bad decision for the team. Wanda took two sleeping pills, hoping to find a few moments of rest and escape from her intolerance of Michel; "his body touching mine became unbearable." Instead, the pills further dulled her already numb senses, making her limbs feel "distant and leaden while my mind stayed all too active." In the morning there was no more cooking gas. Without gas, there was no water, no food, no hope of replenishing their severely depleted reserves. Michel rose first, choked down an aspirin without water, and, professing to be going ahead to make tea for the others with the gas at their tents on the Shoulder, fled down the mountain. Wanda watched his back disappear down the slope. *What a coward,* she thought. *He says he wants to help, but all he wants to do is get his own ass off this mountain as fast as he can.* Turning back to her gear, she struggled to put on her crampons and harness for the descent, her brain struggling with the altitude, exhaustion, and sleeping pills. Maurice and Liliane said nothing to Wanda or to each other as they helped strike the tent and pack up the meager camp.

Fighting not only the effects of high altitude but now starvation, dehydration, and the ever-constant threat of edema, the three finally started their long descent. If Maurice's fried brain was still filtering cognitive thought, he must have realized that he had spent every ounce of his reserves on the ascent and that he simply didn't have the strength, or will, to get himself and his wife 11,000 feet back down to safety.

Wanda concentrated on herself. The Barrards had each other; she was alone. She knew that without fixed lines she had to depend on her own wits, her own strength, her own instinct to survive to get her down alive. She turned from the Barrards and didn't look back until she was through the worst of the summit pyramid. She knew they were tired, but they were on their own. Climbing at that level demanded narcissism, and she never questioned that her priority was her own life.

After seven days on the mountain, five of them at or above 8,000 meters, traversing 50- and 60-degree slopes that yawned over 10,000-foot drops to the glacier beneath, with crampons and ice axes that bounced off the bulletproof ice and no safety rope or partner, Wanda talked out loud as she made agonizingly slow progress down the mountain.

Careful, Wanda, careful! . . . You can't afford the slightest slip . . . no one can help you here, no one can get you down . . . you are alone . . . she chanted, methodically, as she made sure that each crampon was wedged in the ice, her ax another connection to the wall in front of her, before she took a step.

As she cleared the open traverse and entered the relatively easier Bottleneck, with its cushion of snow, she heard a cry and turned in time to see Michel Parmentier somersaulting down the narrow couloir below her. Like a character in a cartoon, after a final flip, he bounced back up on his feet and trotted to the nearby Basque tents.

Turning her attention back to the ice and rocks in front of her, she inched down the Bottleneck, muttering to herself. Only when she had reached the flat of the Shoulder did she look back up behind her. What she saw 300 meters above puzzled her. "Way up there in the Bottleneck I saw Liliane and Maurice, and I wondered, why are they proceeding so slowly with all that long descending ahead of them?"

In an odd foreshadowing, Maurice had spoken of this very spot in the climb months before in Paris. "I have serious misgivings about the serac wall on that hanging glacier," he told Diemberger as they considered the route and its ever-changing conditions. Global warming had changed the landscape of the high mountains with dangerous results; broken cornices, enormous rocks melting out of the snow, high glaciers suddenly breaking off in huge, catastrophic avalanches. Maurice, having climbed on the mountain in 1979, didn't like what he saw as he surveyed photos before the trip in 1986. "It is definitely worse than it was in 1979," he said. "Look at this latest shot: the fracture zone along this great balcony bit looks to have more cracks than ever. Heaven knows how much will come off and funnel down through the Bottleneck." Even so, the Abruzzi and its Bottleneck offered the most straightforward approach to the summit, and Maurice had chosen it.

Wanda, watching from below, thought them out of danger. But she was wrong. "I didn't know it then, but it would be the last time I saw my friends. They never returned."

Wanda caught up with Michel at their tents low on the Shoulder, but with dwindling supplies of gas and food and ominous weather moving in, he urged her to continue down with the Basques while he waited for the Barrards. She looked over at the tent Aid Burgess had given her, debating whether to take it down with her. She had taken everything she needed out of it. She shook her head; it was just too much trouble. She turned and started down the mountain but soon became separated from the other climbers and was alone in a growing storm, searching for the top of the fixed lines. The world around her was without features—it had no boundaries, no edges. The lingering sleeping pills in her system further fogged her brain, and she struggled for something, anything that would ground her. She looked down the slope, and there sat the green tent. She shook her head, trying to clear it. But there it sat. *Impossible*, she muttered, *I know I didn't take it down*. She walked down to where it sat empty but intact, as if waiting for her. She looked back up and realized that it must have been blown off the Shoulder and rolled down the slope.

"Well, I guess you want to come with me," she said to the tent, the hypoxia softening her reality and her fear being glad for the diversion. Taking off her gloves in the cold, she struggled against the increasing wind but managed to pack up the tent and stuff it in her pack.

Resuming her descent, she found the start of the fixed lines within a few meters and eagerly clipped onto them. On ascent she had been afraid to use them, but now, with her reserves all but empty, she was glad for any safety they could lend, old, frayed, or otherwise. It was a sinister day, the worst she'd spent on K2 in her three attempts to climb its forbidding terrain. She finally made it to their tent at Camp II on the night of June 25, falling into her sleeping bag in grateful exhaustion. She wasn't safe, but she was a mile closer. In the morning she rose late, hoping to find three small figures moving down the mountain toward her. But the storm made it difficult to see clearly. As the clouds moved across the slope above her she could get intermittent glimpses of the route, but it was clear. Nothing on it moved. The Barrards and Michel were still up there somewhere. She brewed tea and soup and waited a day for her teammates. She wished she was a better writer: she wanted to capture the emotion, the overwhelming joy and pride she felt, but it had always been a chore. Instead, she slept and tried to drink as much fluid as she could melt, a shovelful of snow at a time. By the morning of the 27th, Michel and the Barrards still hadn't descended, and she knew something had gone terribly wrong. Was she the only survivor of the team? Having taken off her gloves to pack up her wandering tent, her fingers were showing the first signs of frostbite, and she decided to continue down alone. As she retreated she met Benoit Chamoux on his way up to help Michel. *Wanda! he exclaimed, you are alive! We spoke with Michel on the mountain, and he said you'd descended days ago! We thought you had died.*

She hugged the handsome Frenchman and laughed, assuring him she was very much alive, although she was worried about the Barrards. Benoit said he would do what he could, and he continued up the slope. She turned and continued down. Soon she saw two more climbers ascending toward her. When she saw it was Wojciech Wroz and Przemyslaw Piasecki, she started to cry. Her Polish friends had come to help her, to make sure she was okay. They cared about her. They loved her, and she loved them. After so many lonely and angry expeditions, she was overwhelmed by feeling such concern and affection from her fellow climbers. Then and only then did she know she was finally safe.

After receiving medical attention at Advance Base Camp for her frostbitten hands, she continued down the glacier to base on June 28. Jim Curran watched her approach, horrified. It had been only ten days since she left on her summit bid, but she had aged ten years, looking "gaunt and drawn like a ghost."

But she made it back. The Barrards did not. At Base Camp she told Kurt Diemberger that it had never occurred to her that she could be so close to death. "All of us go up there without ever thinking, next it could be I to remain on the mountains. Perhaps that's the way it has to be. And this mountain, so dangerous, haunting, and beautiful."

After three days of waiting in a storm, Michel Parmentier gave up all hope that the Barrards could have survived the conditions or the terrain without food, drink, or shelter and started his descent. Unable to find his way off the broad, flat Shoulder, he radioed Base Camp, desperate for help as the blizzard roiled around him. Benoit Chamoux, who had turned back from his rescue bid in the worsening weather, manned the radio with the cool calm of "an air traffic controller talking to the pilot of a stricken airliner." As Michel's panic reached the boiling point Benoit told him to keep right, away from the abyss to his left, and asked him whether he could see anything, any characteristic that would indicate where he was on the Shoulder and how near he was to one of its two sides, which fell off into 1,000-foot cliffs. Panting with exhaustion, frantic with terror, and his mind numb from spending more than a week above 26,000 feet, Parmentier walked in circles, mumbling into the radio and praying that his feet wouldn't touch the void of thin air. Finally, he saw a patch of urine where previous descending climbers had left their mark.

"That's it!" Chamoux shouted, relief flooding his body. "I remember that spot! Go left about three meters—you'll find the top of the fixed ropes there!" Those gathered around the radio in Base Camp whooped with joy and embraced in emotional bear hugs. In an awful irony, several years later Chamoux would be in a similar position on Kangchenjunga, lost at 8,400 meters and looking for the descent route, but there would be no one there to give him the direction he needed, and he would never be seen again.

When Parmentier finally made it into Base Camp—like Wanda, a shadow of himself, wrecked and wretched—Jim Curran offered solace on the loss of his friends. Parmentier refused to admit that Maurice Barrard was gone. "He is strong, he will come down; I am sure."

But he didn't make it down. About a month later, a team of Koreans were descending the glacier back to Base Camp when they saw something incongruous in the field of white. Off to the edge of the glacier, near the base of the mountain, lay something impossibly pink. As they neared, they saw that it was a body. *It is Miss Liliane*, one of the climbers said. It was, although barely recognizable. After falling 10,000 feet from where she was last seen, Liliane's beautiful, girlish body and smart pink climbing suit were a ruin of blood and dismemberment. The Koreans sent word down to Base Camp and soon Austrian climbers Alfred Imitzer and Hannes Wieser arrived with skis to help move the body. The Korean team took pictures as Imitzer bent down on one knee and cut off her swollen finger to get her gold wedding ring. Perhaps he wanted to give the ring to her family. Perhaps he thought the insurance company would need proof of their finding her body. Perhaps he thought burying gold was a waste. Whatever his reasons, the ghoulish images were later released and published in the press. They are not images her brother Alain can even discuss.

When word reached Wanda, she immediately ran up to help bring Liliane back to camp. Wanda had stayed in Base Camp after her climb, part of her unwilling to leave until she knew what happened to her teammates, part of her also hoping for a chance to summit Broad Peak. She had thought it might help her cleanse her mind of the disaster on K2, but the haunting image of her friends stayed with her. She was able to climb high on Broad, but her already frostbitten fingers and toes progressed dangerously toward infection, and she readied herself to finally leave Base Camp. Then Liliane was found.

With Liliane's body wrapped in a tent and lashed to the makeshift ski stretcher, it began the sad march to the Gilkey Memorial. As the solemn cortege made its way down the glacier, other climbers silently joined the procession. For at least one afternoon in the fractious Base Camp, there were no arguments, no nationalities, no egos. There was just overwhelming grief in the thin line of men and women who walked with heads bowed to bury a fellow climber. Jim Curran thought the caravan would make a remarkable photograph but he kept his camera at his side. As the group neared the tents of a team who had recently lost a member, they hurriedly decided to veer around the camp, hoping to spare them any more pain.

Wanda asked Austrian climber Michael Messner to fashion the Barrards a memorial plaque out of an aluminum dinner plate to hang with the seven or eight others already buried at the mountain's Memorial; four years after she buried Halina there, she was returning to the Gilkey. Two of the plates were shinier than those hanging on the stone cairn; John Smolich and Al Pennington, killed only a month before. For the second time that summer, climbers gathered to bury a body at the Memorial. They placed Liliane in a cradle of rocks, and then covered her with flat stones so others who came to the stoic grave would be able to sit and gather on her tombstone. When the last rock was placed and people began drifting back to Base Camp, Wanda sat down, put her head on her knees, and wept.

The film footage shot at Liliane's funeral is a sad testament to the horrific toll of high-altitude mountaineering. Michel Parmentier and Peter Bozik, who both survived the storm the Barrards did not, would disappear two years later on Everest. Benoit Chamoux, who would make a record twenty-three-hour ascent of K2 later that summer, would die on Kangchenjunga in 1995. Renato Casarotto, Al Rouse, Mrowka Wolf, and Wojciech Wroz would become four more victims in the Black Summer's terrible toll. Jerzy Kukuczka, who carried Wanda into Base Camp in 1982 and had gone on to become the second man to summit all fourteen 8,000-meter peaks, would die on Lhotse after clipping onto a bad rope. And every year the list gets longer.

Wanda sat near the Gilkey's newest grave. She was so tired. Two of her trips to K2 had been marred by death. She had realized her greatest achievement only a month before but she would never be able to celebrate it without the heavy weight of grief. As the climbers began their solemn march back to Base Camp, she and Michel Parmentier found they couldn't look at each other, both simmering in their own blame, shame, and sorrow.

One evening in late June 1986, Alain Bontemps's phone rang in Paris. It was Madame Barrard, Maurice's mother. Her son and Liliane were both missing on K2, she told him, her voice breaking with the news. They were presumed dead.

"Oh God, not now," Alain sobbed. He had been busy readying their trip from K2 to Everest, so consumed with the details and logistics that he had forgotten the mortal danger they faced. He had become accustomed to their strength, a combined force of will and talent that he just assumed would keep them safe and successful. But he had forgotten that above 8,000 meters nothing can be assumed or assured.

When Alain received Liliane's journals from K2, he read her last thoughts and learned of her many anguished dreams on K2. In one she returns home but feels terrible emptiness in the house and locks the door behind her because she knows Maurice "will not open the door; no one will be coming home." In another recurrent dream she looks for Maurice in a long, narrow meadow between the dark rows of trees, a metaphor eerily resembling the path of snow and ice and the dark corridor of the Bottleneck, and in fact she used an odd combination of words—"summit" and "meadow"—to describe her dark forest: "I looked for you in the meadow, and you weren't there. Then I went back up to the summit of the meadow and looked for you, everywhere." *Partout*. But he was gone.

Years later American climber Heidi Howkins looked across the wide expanse of the glacier and thought she saw something dark poking out of it. Moving closer, she saw that it was a tattered shirt. A shirt that was still heavy with a human torso.

She knelt down and saw a name sewn in neat, white block letters into the jersey. MAURICE. After her teammates took pictures of her posing with the body, they buried him near Liliane in the Gilkey Memorial.

It was 1998. After twelve years, Liliane had finally found him in the meadow.

CHAPTER 5

OUR MOUNTAIN OF DESTINY

Seeing one's peak is like seeing one's existence.

—MIGUEL C. LOPEZ

Julie Tullis sat in the delicious warmth of a sunny Base Camp afternoon writing a long-overdue letter home. "Dear Terry, Chris, and Lindsay, I'm coming home," she started. She looked up at the mountain. It seemed to taunt her. It was so damn arrogant, but she still loved it. And she still wanted it. But it would have to wait. She turned back to the page. "We buried another climber yesterday. I've had enough for one year. I simply haven't the heart for another try at the summit." There was one more month in the regular climbing season, but she was calling it quits.

She and her climbing and filmmaking partner Kurt Diemberger had arrived at Base Camp in early June 1986 to film the Italian team "Quota 8000." But that was perhaps a bit ingenuous. Having been to K2's North Ridge in 1983 and its south side in 1984 during their successful ascent of nearby Broad Peak, Tullis and Diemberger were themselves intent on finally conquering their "mountain of mountains."

But not this year. This Black Summer had claimed enough lives. She had a family to get back to who were more important than this damned mountain. She looked up at K2 and shook her head. It never ceased to amaze her how far she was from her quiet, almost prosaic existence thousands of miles and another lifetime away. And yet, as she thought about it, she realized that even her so-called ordinary life in England had never really been that ordinary.

. . .

Forty-three years earlier, four-year-old Julie watched the steam billow out of the train's huge engine in great white gasps as it pulled away from the station, the warmth of the steam going with it, leaving her and her older sister Zita shivering in the damp cold of the Norfolk night. She tried to pull her thin woolen coat tighter around her, but it didn't help her chill. Her name tag was pinned to her collar, and her gas mask hung around her neck awkwardly, hitting against her jaw and making it difficult to turn her head. Its huge bug eyes made her think of a space alien, and she almost giggled, but didn't. She knew Zita would haul off and give her a smack if she so much as opened her mouth. She'd been warned. She looked around at the crowd on the platform and saw that most of the other children had similar masks, so she didn't feel too self-conscious, but they also held firmly to their parents' hands. She and Zita were alone. The last time they had seen their mother she had been waving at the London station as the train, packed with evacuees, slowly chugged out of the glass and steel tunnel. Her mother's trim silhouette became smaller and smaller until she blended into those around her and all they could see was the tiny white flag of her handkerchief desperately waving to her little girls.

It was 1943, and Julie and seven-year-old Zita were already war veterans, having survived air raids that demolished houses in their neighborhood and flooded their basement. But as the bombs fell closer and closer to their house Julie developed asthma and began wetting the bed. Erica and Francis Palau decided it was time to get their girls safely north, far away from ground zero in the air war with Germany.

When their mother had taken them to the Liverpool Street station, she hadn't told the girls that they were going away, or that she and their father might never see them again. Julie had thought it was all very exciting, until she saw the postcards in Erica's hand.

"Zita, you're the older sister." Their mother's voice sounded very stern, her German accent even more pronounced. "You must be sure to take care of Julie. Do not, under any circumstance, allow yourselves to get separated! No matter what, you'll stay together. Promise me, Zita. Promise!"

Zita nodded solemnly; she gave Julie a threatening glare. Julie had suffered greatly at the hands of Zita's pranks and had often been punished for the sin of being the little sister, but Julie knew Zita would never let them get pulled apart.

When Julie was born in 1939, her father's first comment upon seeing his second daughter was, "But she's such an ugly baby!" and Julie herself was not much kinder, admitting that her "tiny, screwed-up face was totally dominated by an enormous nose. My sister had been a pretty baby and grew into a small-boned graceful child who loved ballet dancing, while I grew tall and awkward with over-size feet." But Julie grew into her nose, and her wide-set, dark eyes became the center of her young face. As she matured those eyes were often scrunched into happy laughter, and her good looks were better described as strong grace than as delicate beauty.

Erica and Francis worked in the restaurant trade, the long hours often keeping them too busy to care for their young daughters, so the girls were sent to a boarding school in Cambridgeshire. But it didn't last long. The mischievous Zita time and again lured her meek little sister into various and ultimately expensive dares, from pushing buttons up her nose that necessitated surgical removal to Zita jumping suddenly off her end of the seesaw, causing Julie to fall and break her wrist. After the broken wrist, the school said, enough, and the girls were sent home. But home was now in the heart of war-torn London.

If people had the means to leave their work and homes, they would evacuate as a family, but the Palaus did not have that luxury: they remained in London to work and sent their daughters away without them.

Before their final hugs at the station, Erica gave Zita two postcards with careful instructions. On one was written "yes" and on the other "no." Each had Erica and Francis's address in London on it. Once the girls were in their new home with their foster parents, they were to send the yes card if they had been chosen by good people. If they sent the no postcard, Erica promised she would be on the next train to fetch them, war or no war.

"Do you understand, Zita? Julie? You promise you will do this on your first day there so I will know if you are happy?"

The girls promised their mother they would. Julie looked at the cards clenched in Zita's small hand and knew that this was not an ordinary adventure. This was something much much more.

The train arrived in Norfolk's tiny Ellingham Station at 1:30 in the morning. Local families, who had been told to gather if they could take in evacuees from London, milled about in the chilly darkness awaiting their charges. The two tired, dusty girls stood alone and apart from the crowd. Whenever anyone would look their way, Zita shouted, "We must stay together!" and the interested party would look away. Julie watched as child after child and family after family got chosen and went off to their new homes. She and Zita were alone on the platform when George Burcham, who had been waiting for two boys to bring home to try to fill the void left by the sons he had already lost in the war, approached the scared, hungry girls. "Well, I'd better take you home with me then," he said. Relieved at being picked but nervous about their new home, the girls diligently followed the strange man into the dark. After being greeted by George's wife Mary and fed, bathed, and shown their room, the last thing the two sisters did before they finally collapsed into the double bed they would share for the next several years was to pick the yes postcard and put it in the mailbox for the morning pickup.

Their lives with George and Mary Burcham were a happy respite from the dark terrors of war-torn London, and they came to love their "Paunt and Punk" deeply.

As the girls flourished, so did Zita's pranks. Time after time Zita would lure Julie into a dare or a "game," only to have it end painfully for Julie. Once, as Julie stretched to her limits to hold up her end of a steel pipe as instructed, Zita dropped her end. The pipe smashed directly into Julie's upturned and open mouth, breaking a front tooth. The pain exploded in Julie's head, and she cried out. Zita rushed to her side.

"Don't you dare show that tooth to Paunt and Puck," she threatened, scared that Julie's injury would be her punishment.

At dinner, when Paunt gently urged Julie to drink her hot milk, the liquid felt like a drill on the exposed nerve of the broken tooth, but still she kept her screams silent and her mouth shut. After all, she didn't want to get Zita into trouble. Julie never considered the dares, pranks, pushes, or shoves anything more than normal big sister behavior. Julie insisted they were each other's best advocates, never allowing a negative word to be said about the other. Several years later Zita would push her into a schoolyard wall, breaking the other front tooth. Still, Julie insisted it was inadvertent and cheerfully accepted that she now had *two* broken front teeth, which she never had repaired.

The sisters more than survived their evacuation and their mishaps and returned to London after the war, trading trees and pastures for "bombed-out houses and debris-filled water tanks." While Julie remembered returning to London immediately, Zita said they remained in Ellingham another two years after the war because their parents still had no home to which the girls could return. When they finally managed to get a proper house near Kensington, Erica took the train up and retrieved her now eight- and eleven-year-old girls. Although Julie had stopped wetting the bed, her asthma continued to plague her, and night after night Erica would sit on the edge of her bed begging her to *breathe, breathe*. Julie felt like a fish out of water, gasping desperately for breath, looking up into her worried mother's face as her labored wheezing filled the still night hours.

Like children all over Europe, Julie and Zita found a new, endlessly fascinating playground in the bombed-out buildings of their neighborhood. Julie's early timidity was replaced with an eager fearlessness as she joined older girls and boys in jumping from beam to beam, swinging on old electrical cables shouting Tarzan calls, and playing cops and robbers in rubble-filled cellars. Being the smallest and lightest, Julie's favorite game was riding the tiny food lifts in the bombed-out buildings while the other children pulled the ropes sending her up and down the shaft.

As soon as she was old enough Julie began working in an office, and as soon as she had saved enough she purchased her first true, unadulterated love: a Vespa scooter, a common sight on the narrow streets and lanes of Europe. She was so excited when she handed over the thirty pounds for her deposit and received the keys from the dealer that she forgot to ask how to run the damn thing. As she saw the approaching four-way stop she had a choice: keep going and risk being run over by an oncoming lorry or hit the pavement. Luckily she had worn long pants and a jacket, and so she made the latter choice, watching the wheels of the oncoming traffic screech to a halt as she slid through the intersection beneath them. With the adrenaline rushing, she jumped up, waved at the horrified drivers, pulled up the Vespa in one clean jerk, and pushed it off the road, running with it around the corner so she could practice properly. After a few more dives and slides, she mastered the brakes and clutch and happily drove through the streets, the cold wind squinting her eyes into slits and reminding her to wear gloves.

One day in November 1956, Zita invited her to go rock climbing with a group of boys forty miles south of London at a popular crag, High Rocks, outside of Tunbridge Wells. Zita was the more natural athlete, and Julie worried; she had always felt so awkward and gangly next to Zita. But Zita convinced her to go. She left London after work on her beloved Vespa, but the drive was longer and chillier than she had anticipated, and when she finally walked into the High Rocks Hotel in her light cotton pants and wool sweater, her teeth were chattering and her hands were cramped with the cold. She had forgotten her gloves again.

"You look cold," said a friendly man with sparkling blue eyes and a full, dark beard.

She told him she was there to meet her sister, but she didn't think she'd arrived yet. "I think you better come with me," the man said and led her out the door into the dark night. "You better hold my hand or you're bound to fall over." When she hesitated, he assured her, "My name is Terry. Don't worry. I'll see that you don't come to any harm." As they rounded a corner behind the inn, Julie was greeted by a welcome sight: a roaring bonfire surrounded by cheerful boys, a tangle of ropes near them on the ground. She smiled, instantly happy, and settled into the warm group, excited at her new adventure.

Then Zita arrived.

Letting loose with a string of expletives for Julie, she then turned on Terry and let him have it. She had found Julie's Vespa but no Julie, and for a few terrible moments thought her sister was dead and knew she would be blamed. When she saw Julie sitting around a hot fire and sipping cocoa, surrounded by handsome, attentive boys, her concern instantly flamed into rage.

Julie held firmly to her cup, still luxuriating in its warm comfort, and let her sister rail. For once she was happy and content, and Zita's anger felt as threatening as a puppy's nip at her ankles. More nuisance than danger. Terry chuckled good-naturedly and was able to calm Zita down, but there had been a sea change in the sisters' relationship; Julie felt a new autonomy, and she liked it.

Over the next three years Julie worked her office job during the week, then escaped to the sandstone walls in Tunbridge most weekends. If Julie's early years had been insecure, her young adult ones were anything but. As she watched Terry and the others ascend narrow cracks in the wall called "chimneys" and then wrap the rope around their shoulders for friction and jump off the sandstone walls and into the air, she itched to try it. With a minimal amount of instruction, she soon was climbing the chimneys and jumping off the top edge, thrilling at the sensation of the semicontrolled freefall. She spent nearly every weekend climbing all day and sleeping under the stars with Terry and his friends, relishing her new outdoor and very physical life, her childhood asthma forgotten so long as she stayed clear of cigarette smoke. She excelled fast: progressing from relatively easy climbs on belay, she quickly found her way up ever more challenging faces, often without a safety rope from above.

Like many Britons, Terry Tullis had been climbing all his life on the readily available and wildly diverse offerings of rock faces in the Peak District, and he enjoyed sharing his passion with his new young protégée. But theirs was not a relationship born of passion or even immediate attraction, Julie going so far as to admit that they didn't even like each other that much at the beginning, particularly since she suspected his weekday visits to her house were to see Zita. But she was wrong, and on November 7, 1959, she and Terry Tullis were married.

Their early marriage was an eclectic adventure of odd jobs variously offering financial security followed by penury followed by a brief respite of security again, finally settling down a bit in the early sixties when they bought a tiny general store near the climbing rocks. Soon Julie and Terry became four; a son, Christopher, was born in 1962, and a daughter, Lindsay, in 1964. Julie instantly adored motherhood and reveled in the little moments: watching and feeling them suckle her breast, helping make huge batches of Christmas cookies, and showing them how to find holds in the sandstone, their tiny fingers able to hang on the littlest of ledges. Her contentment was palpable, but as the children grew Julie tired of the long, grueling hours running the shop. Finally, it was more grind than reward, and they decided to sell the business and try their fortunes as professional climbing instructors, a plan that required finding cheap housing. They got a tip that a local farm's outbuildings might be available, and Julie drove over to take a look.

When Julie first drove up to "the Bothy" in 1967, she knew immediately they could make a life in its odd confines. A peculiar shoebox of a structure, the Bothy was long and narrow, low and deep, more of a railroad car than a cottage. Measuring 10 feet wide and 100 feet long, and originally built as one of many utility buildings on a large estate, the Bothy was a blood-spattered turkey slaughterhouse when Julie first walked into it. Still, she fell in love at first sight. So did Terry, and after scrubbing the walls and floors of blood and body parts, painting as many of the surfaces as they could, and covering the rest with drapes, they began filling their boxcar of a house with an assortment of old, comfortable, lumpy furniture and an ever-changing cast of boxers. There was a certain charm to living in such confined space, even for Terry, whose strong body was becoming a tad rounder with each year.

For ten years they lived simply, running a climbing shop and café, teaching various clients and special needs children how to climb, and finding the occasional odd jobs to supplement their income. Julie had never been happier. It was an idyllic time, and she relished her new-found time for herself, her home, and her children, spending her days in the gardens around the house, planting and playing with the children. But one day when she and Terry went to the Rocks for a routine climb, she knew something was different. Terry climbed first and had some trouble getting through the crux. Finally through it, he awaited her on the top of the first pitch. She climbed confidently as she started up the familiar wall, her harness snug and the rope tied expertly around her waist, but when she reached the troublesome transition that Terry had struggled through, she froze. She told him she couldn't do it; something deep and dark was preventing her from taking the literal leap of faith to the next hold. He tried to talk her through it, but couldn't. Then, when it was he who struggled to follow her through the dangerous transition, they knew their climbing as a team was over. The risk of Christopher and Lindsay losing both of them in a climbing accident weighed too heavily. They had seen a lot of death already in their young lives in the climbing community around them, and they knew all too well that the dangers were real and ever-present. No amount of skill could overcome bad luck, and they were unwilling to make Chris and Lindsay victims.

Ironically, it would be an accident quite apart from climbing that nearly cost Terry his life. While he was working as a day laborer on a nearby farm, a "rotavator," used to churn up the land for planting, overturned, and one of the tines impaled Terry's leg below the knee. With the tines still churning, it took Terry several agonizing attempts before he finally was able to reach the off switch; then he lay in a pool of gathering blood and fuel, waiting for help.

Hours later Julie sat by his hospital bed, horrified to see her always cheerful, virile husband a semiconscious heap of pain under the thin sheet. *It will have to come off,* the doctors told her. Suddenly Terry was alert. *No. I will not sign the papers!* His voice was not much more than a whisper, but its strength was unmistakable. Reluctantly the surgeons reattached the ruined leg, tendons, bones, and muscle. It would be months before Terry could stand, never mind work or climb, and Julie knew that supporting the family was on her shoulders for the foreseeable future.

Reluctant to give up her role of housewife and mother, Julie nonetheless knew that luxury was a thing of the past for now, and she signed a new lease getting them restarted in the grocery, café, and climbing shop business. Soon Terry's Festerhaunt was offering everything from a tin of butter and a sack of flour to a climbing rope, carabiners, and sausage and onion pies personally prepared by Julie. A list of their customers and friends boasted some of climbing's most illustrious legends: Chris

Bonnington, Gaston Rebuffat, Paul Nunn, Doug Scott, and Dennis Kemp. Their life was full and exciting, and exhausting. When Kemp suggested to Julie that what she needed was a quick climbing vacation, she hesitated, the habit of duty stopping her. For years she had carried the work of the store, café, and home, reluctant even to climb with the children so young. Now she was enervated, Terry was all but healed, and the children were almost in their teens. She happily accepted the invitation to explore a series of limestone crags in Wales called World's End.

Days later Julie caressed the limestone rock almost lovingly. It felt so different from the sandstone of High Rocks, and she thrilled at its warm, silky texture. She found that she could massage it rather than cling to it, her fingers gliding easily from hold to hold rather than scraping painfully along the sandpaper surface. She looked down around her from her perch on the wall; she was many meters higher than the top of the Rocks in Tunbridge, and she still had many meters to go until she reached the top. She felt like she could climb forever. The air, the endless, gentle rock, the rolling green fields and hills of Wales stretching out in every direction—it was a perfect day, a perfect climb. After all the hardship, hard work, and struggle of the past year, she felt alive again.

As much as Julie loved climbing, it would be another, entirely different sport that prepared her for the physical and mental rigors of Himalayan climbing—aikido. Through its minute attention to the dance of breath, agility, strength, movement, and meditation, Julie learned an elegance she had never before felt. Inhibitions left over from her childhood fell away as she learned the grace, power, and patience of the art. After a few months of practice, she had rethought her entire approach to many things, including climbing. "Moving from the [body's] Centre makes everything easier, and understanding that tiredness and pain do not mean one has to give up, the body can go on, has saved my life on several occasions."

There are moments that, once lived, make life never quite the same again. And there are people who, once met, are instantly part of your life fabric, and you know without an ounce of doubt that they will be part of that weave for the rest of your life. For Julie Tullis, the legendary Kurt Diemberger was one of these people.

Born in 1932 in Austria, Diemberger was a successful mountain filmmaker and had climbed all over the world, including three 8,000-meter peaks, his first at age twenty-seven, when he and the great Hermann Buhl made a first ascent of Broad Peak. He met Julie and Terry Tullis on one of his lecture tours in England and called them in July 1976 when business again brought him to England. Terry insisted that Julie and Dennis Kemp take Diemberger on his first climb in the country. When Diemberger saw Julie climbing the sandstone cliffs off the Wales coast, something forever changed.

As Diemberger watched, Julie moved up the rock smoothly, "each movement expressing strength and a joy of living, just as an animal in its element expresses itself in movement," he wrote in his evocative journal. In one passage, while sailing off the coast of England with his brother-in-law, he muttered in almost a dreamlike state, trying to fathom another excuse to call her, to see her, to invite her to sail to France with him and his brother-in-law: "Will she say 'yes'? She hardly knows me, after all, and she doesn't know Herbert at all. Two Austrian mountain guides and filmmakers. Are these trustworthy professions in the eyes of an Englishwoman? Or will we seem more like buccaneers to her?"

Diemberger, although married to his second wife, picked up the phone to call her and like a breathless schoolboy put it back down before it could ring. His nerve failing him, he finally decided to wait to ask her until they next met.

"Why don't we sail across to France?" Diemberger asked when they were climbing on a sandstone outcrop in the Sussex woods. Julie looked at him thoughtfully. To Diemberger, the "air seemed to be vibrating, in small waves, dissolving into thousands of tiny dancing points, and I was sure that she wanted to come . . . I was held spellbound by her dark eyes. For several seconds I was incapable of thought, overcome by an emotion I could not recognize. Our gaze almost froze, and I felt sure that her voice could only say 'yes.'"

But she said no.

Taken aback by the invitation, Julie wondered why a man she hardly knew would invite her on a sailing trip across the channel to France. The only time she had been alone with him she had been rushing about hardly able to speak to him properly, and she thought their acquaintance was rather two-dimensional. To spend a weekend alone on a luxury yacht with two film directors, one she had never met and the other she hardly knew . . . well, she just wasn't sure. Not sure at all. Terry urged her to take advantage of the exotic adventure, but she demurred. *This is not the time to grow close to Kurt Diemberger,* she thought. *Not at all the right time.*

The next morning she and Terry dropped Diemberger at the Tunbridge Wells station for his train to London. Their good-byes were formal, even stilted. Diemberger, disappointed that she had turned him down, barely spoke as he boarded the train.

Three years later Terry and Julie were invited to represent the British Mountaineering Council at the Trento Mountain Film Festival in Italy, the oldest mountain film festival in the world. As they were fumbling with their hotel key Kurt and his wife appeared at the door of the room next to theirs. Suddenly Julie found herself engulfed in a bear hug while an exuberant Diemberger gibbered in unintelligible Italian. Julie did not know how he would treat her when they met again, but it seemed he did not harbor any ill will over her refusal of his invitation. During the festival she watched Diemberger being treated like a demigod, younger climbers and filmmakers hanging on his every word as he held court over heated discussions about the art and commerce of mountain filmmaking.

Almost a year later the phone rang, and again it was Diemberger asking Julie to come with him on an adventure. This time she wouldn't say no.

"Where are you?" Julie asked, expecting to hear that he was again at the Tunbridge Wells station needing a ride, or perhaps in London giving a lecture.

"Salzburg. I think you should come to the mountains. Will you come?"

Twenty-four hours later she was on the evening flight to Munich.

Julie thrilled at the adventure of it all, far from children's homework and dinner on the table. Suddenly she found herself in Viennese cafés drinking sweet coffee and talking through the night about climbing, filmmaking, and travel. She watched the heavily bearded man across the table with excitement. He was one of only two men to have a first ascent of two 8,000-meter peaks; Hermann Buhl was the other. He told her breathtaking stories of his adventures, his climbs, and of watching Buhl break through a high cornice and disappear over the edge of Chogolisa. She drank in the stories, eager to share in his world above 8,000 meters.

As their friendship grew, so did the adventures and assignments, and soon she was helping organize his lectures and slide shows all over England. She was an able assistant, cheerfully assuming the often thankless logistical nightmare of fees, venues, equipment, travel, and lodging while Diemberger continued with his busy climbing and filming schedule. After an unsuccessful expedition to Everest in November 1980, Diemberger called Julie to see how she had done in planning his lecture tour the following January.

She was pleased with herself. She had painstakingly scheduled a series of lectures, even during the British winter, a notoriously bad time to count on travel because a single snowflake could bring the roadways to a halt. She proudly reported that each was within forty miles of London, so he would be able to get to each venue on time, regardless of weather.

She held the phone to her ear, smiling, waiting for his excitement at her success. The phone line was silent.

"Oh," Diemberger said. He was disappointed. He had wanted to have another adventure with her. She rescheduled the entire month, allowing them a trip to Scotland, which he'd never seen.

The tour was a success, and the following November, as Julie looked around her cubbyhole of a house in the descending gloom of early British winter, the phone once again rang with an invitation. Did she want to be his sound technician and assistant while he filmed a French expedition to Nanga Parbat the following summer? Julie was surprised by the invitation, since she had little alpine experience—and none of it above 19,000 feet (5,790 meters)—and she knew little about audio technology. Nonetheless, she hardly believed her luck at being invited, and after Terry again gave his blessing to her adventure, she was soon packing for her first 8,000-meter peak.

Diemberger was busy on a shoot in China and planned to join the expedition after it had reached Base Camp, leaving all the logistics to Julie. He had rented filming and climbing equipment in Paris, and she took care of every detail of getting it packed up and shipped to Islamabad, then repacked and reweighed for the weeklong journey into the mountain. It was another thankless task with a lot of headaches and bureaucratic snafus, but Julie did the job without losing a single battery or carabiner.

The team was organized by Pierre Mazeaud, the same French politician and climber who had led Wanda Rutkiewicz's miserable trip to Everest in 1978 that had been so wrought with ego and aggression. It comprised six Frenchmen, two Germans, one Czech, one French-Italian, two Pakistanis, one Austrian—Diemberger—and Julie, the only Briton and only woman. Pierre had embraced her "as a friend" when she met with him and Diemberger in Paris, but once on the trail to Base Camp, with Diemberger far away in China, his treatment was anything but cordial. As soon as they started out of Islamabad, Mazeaud buried her with a "shot list," demanding a litany of scenes, settings, and people he said he needed for the film. Because she had signed a contract stating that she had to obey Mazeaud without question or risk being thrown off the team, she felt powerless to argue against his list, but each assignment was in her view a waste of energy, film, and morale.

As the team left the road and started the four-day walk into Base Camp, Julie knew almost immediately that she was in trouble with the men on the team. Feeling the urge to pee, she ducked off the trail at the first rock large enough to squat behind. Just as she was unbuckling her pack and lowering her pants, she heard giggling and looked around to see a sea of porters laughing at her vulnerable nakedness. Among them were many of her teammates, enjoying the joke. Mortified, she quickly pulled her pants back up and hurried down the trail, still unrelieved. It would be a persistent problem until a latrine was built at Base Camp and Julie could use it without fearing curious eyes.

A traditional rite of passage on the long trek into Base Camp in the Karakoram Mountains was the goat slaughter. A day of rest, celebration, and feast for the long-suffering Balti porters, the goat slaughter was also a bloody, nasty mess involving frightfully long, and sharp knives and a lot of caterwauling and shrieking, followed by singing and dancing late into the night as the goat was roasted over a fire. It was as close as the devout Muslim porters came to a bacchanal. Although it was a spectacle of fascinating local color, it was too brutal for most broadcasters, and Julie knew not to waste the precious film stock on a scene they'd never use.

Mazeaud ordered her to film the slaughter. Again feeling helpless fury, she did as she was told while he and the others watched, laughing at her obvious revulsion.

Even the team doctor, Jeff Mazeaud, Pierre's young nephew, seemed to be in on the harassment. On the last day of the trek Julie woke with a headache, likely suffering mild altitude sickness after the team's rapid four-day ascent to 13,000 feet; the near-90-degree heat didn't help. She asked Mazeaud for a common aspirin but was told she would have to wait until they got to Base Camp, where the bags would finally be un- packed and the medical kit located. Altitude sickness can be a serious ailment if not attended to, but the blood-thinning agents in aspirin make it relatively easy to treat. It would be the kind Pakistani cook who would dig his supply of aspirin out of his bags and give one to her.

When the team finally reached Base Camp, Julie was exhausted and still suffering a headache. All she wanted to do was crawl into a warm sleeping bag, but she worried that snow would fall in the night and immediately searched the area to find a stable and dry spot for their equipment and living tents. Working alone in the darkening night, fight- ing the urge to feel sorry for herself, she erected the tent, gathered the eight 25-kilogram (55-pound) loads from where the porters had left them scattered across the ground, and moved them awkwardly into the film tent. Suddenly Pierre rushed over.

"You must move these tents!" he demanded. "This is where I want the kitchen tent to go." Without asking why in hell he hadn't told her that before the hourlong effort to establish her tent, she silently obliged, biting the inside of her cheek in rage. It had begun to snow, as she had feared, but she took out all the boxes, drums, and bags, took down the tent, set it up a second time in a different spot, and moved the loads back into it. Again Pierre rushed over demanding that she move the offending tent.

She looked around her for help and support and saw only laughing faces. It was snowing heavily and was pitch-dark by the time she finally found a suitable spot for the tents, high above base and inconveniently far from the rest of the team. All the suitable lower spots had been taken by other climbers while she was moving her tent from spot to spot. Some, she noted ruefully, were placed exactly where she had earlier set hers up.

The next morning, exhausted from her long night and still suffering from a headache, she lay awake unable to sleep and unable to get warm. She dozed but couldn't summon the strength to rise for breakfast. She tried to rouse herself but found she didn't have the strength to stand. From the research she had done about high-altitude sickness, she knew she could be suffering from early hypothermia, maybe even pulmonary or cerebral edema. Hoping someone would notice her absence and come looking, she waited. No one came. Finally, by 10:30 she was having trouble breathing and called for help. One of the climbers came to her tent, and she asked that Jeff Mazeaud come see what was wrong.

Perhaps thinking that it would be easier to treat her with the medical supplies in his tent, Mazeaud said, "Tell her to come to me."

But Julie couldn't believe it. *How can a team doctor not come?*

Luckily two teammates helped carry her to Mazeaud's tent. Part of her problem was that her inability to relieve herself when she needed to had made her store urine, a dangerous condition that can lead to septic poisoning. Once Mazeaud gave her a diuretic and a blast of oxygen off one of the cylinders to clear her head, she felt much better and happier than she had in days.

When Kurt arrived two days later, she hoped team relations would ease, but they didn't. On an otherwise beautiful day, Jeff called her into the mess tent where a little group of men were waiting, barely stifled grins threatening to break across their faces.

"Come in, Julie," Jeff encouraged. "Gelaal [the team's Pakistani liaison officer] says he wants to fuck* you. Well, what do you say?" Julie stared in outrage as Jeff giggled in her face.

---

*Julie, too proper and probably embarrassed, wrote "f—" in her book rather than the offending word. Less proper and not at all embarrassed, I will fill in the missing letters for her.

Silently fuming, Julie walked away and left the men to their sneering and jeering. She never knew the source of the animosity, even cruelty, but she wondered if the Latin mentality of Frenchmen differed from that of British men, who "accept women more easily as equals and friends."

Diemberger later admitted to Julie that Pierre Mazeaud hadn't wanted any women on the trip, but when Diemberger insisted on Julie coming as his sound person, Mazeaud had relented, grudgingly. "Expedition leaders normally don't like to have women on expeditions because they think they cause trouble. Especially if they are not married [to someone on the trip]," Diemberger said, adding that he had to edit several passages in Julie's book for fear of her being sued by Mazeaud, even though he said she had written the truth.

The Christmas after Nanga Parbat the Bothy phone again rang with an invitation.

Not only did Diemberger have another film gig to one of the grandest and most challenging 8,000-meter peaks, but this one involved traveling for three to four months to and through one of the largely uncharted territories in the world: the North Ridge of K2 in China.

Terry, busy with the climbing school and unable to share such physically demanding adventures with his damaged leg, encouraged her passion for the mountains, even though it was becoming an all-encompassing force in her life, leaving little room for him or the children.

The North Ridge of K2 has been called Himalayan climbing's most beautiful line, and its unbroken rise from the glacier to the summit 12,000 feet above draws climbers like pilgrims to Mecca. But it remains relatively unclimbed because getting there involves a month of arduous travel by air, rutted and often washed-out jeep roads, mountain trails, the floodplain riverbeds of the Shaksgam River, and finally the great K2 Glacier. Only thirty-one men (and no women) have climbed the North Ridge compared to over 200 ascents via the southern routes. When Julie and Kurt joined an Italian team with its sights on the North Ridge, they were only the second team to attempt the route, and the first Europeans to set foot there since Eric Shipton's exploration of the area in 1937.

Julie couldn't believe she was getting her first crack at an 8,000-meter peak. She had strongly climbed to the 6,768-meter summit of Huascarán in Peru, all the while helping a man with prosthetic legs, but Mazeaud had told her they couldn't risk her collapsing and needing rescue on Nanga Parbat and forbade her to go above 5,000 meters. She was thrilled to be going to K2 with Kurt and with a team of true friends. She hoped to reach at least 8,000 meters, but she knew K2 was more mountain than she'd ever seen, let alone climbed. She would have to use every ounce of her experience, training, and knowledge learned over the years, from little Harrison's Rocks to Huascarán and everything in between.

After three flights and an endless payout in overweight charges to Aeroflot, Julie and the team arrived in Kashgar, China, proud home of the world's largest statue of Mao. But she was most enchanted with the colorful bazaars of this outlaw province of China, where the iron fist of Communist rule didn't quite reach. Julie took picture after picture of the people, a beautiful mixture of the various invading armies through the centuries. They left Kashgar and traveled south through the infamous Taklimakan Desert, a name she knew meant "If you go in, you don't come out," and they were stopped frequently at Red Army military checkpoints. Two weeks after she left Tunbridge Wells, Julie arrived at the end of the road and met her next form of travel: Xinjiang camels. As she had done a hundred times since the journey began, Julie fumbled to get out her camera. Although the animals would be with them for the next week, she had never seen anything so spectacularly ugly and yet majestic at the same time.

These original beasts of burden were an odd and unsettling mixture between a poodle with a bad case of scurvy and a furry ostrich that towered six to seven feet above the ground. The camels not only kicked, bit, and projectile-vomited as a matter of routine but screamed and roared like wild beasts, particularly when their Uygur (pronounced WEE-gur) drivers beat them with shovels. Julie was relieved to see that the beatings stopped as soon as the sure-footed animals assumed their 400–500-pound loads for the journey up and over the world's highest mountain passes and across torrential and frigid glacial rivers.

Every day Julie, Kurt, and the Italians trekked ten miles closer to K2 with the hairy, goony beasts, and the changing landscape reflected their increasing proximity to the mountain. After they left the greens and blues of the Surukwat River oasis and climbed over the 15,900-foot (4,846-meter) Aghil Pass, they reached the Shaksgam Valley, a serpentine, mile-wide riverbed in only varying shades of brown. Brown rocks, brown sand, brown water, brown cliffs, even the drizzle looked brown. While the camels stayed in the riverbed, Julie and Kurt climbed onto a high plateau to watch their progress: except for the plastic barrels and glacier glasses, the caravan could have been mistaken for Alexander's. Or Caesar's. Or Christ's, if Jesus had gone to Xinjiang. Nothing else had changed.

They had been on the move for three weeks, but because K2 was so remote and so deeply tucked into a valley, Julie had yet to see the mountain. Finally, as they rose from the Shaksgam Valley and reached the snout of the K2 Glacier, there it was, filling her field of vision, an impossibly perfect pyramid sitting twelve miles south, at the very edge of China. Its uppermost ridge was Pakistan. It was more beautiful than she could ever have imagined. The picturesque mountains of the Alps, the Andes, even Nanga Parbat couldn't compare to the majesty of the mountain in front of her. It rose out of the deep valley, its summit cone crowned by an enormous hanging glacier. If she looked long enough, she was sure she'd see the thing crack and fall off. With a stupid shock, she realized that if she was actually there, looking at K2, then she was as far from her home and family as she had ever been. Her body tensed with the exhilaration of exploration; she knew with every fiber of her being that having received this mountain into her soul, she would never again be the same.

As she reveled in the impossibly beautiful view, around her the camels were relieved of their loads; one by one they were untied and dropped in the dust at her feet. With a flip of their tails in the wind, the camels disappeared back down the rocky hill toward their homes in distant villages. Julie looked around her at the countless expedition bags, barrels, and bundles lying in the late-afternoon sun.

Now what? she wondered. She soon found out.

Perhaps there was no training that could have prepared her for the kind of labor she was in for, unless of course she had helped build the pyramids—that is, *if* the pyramids sat at 17,000 feet (5,100 meters) and at the end of a fifteen-mile glacier. Then maybe she'd have been ready. Julie hadn't helped build the pyramids, and she certainly had never experienced the ankle-wrenching hell of travel on a rock-strewn glacier, carrying her share of the team gear, load by load, through fifteen miles of boulder fields, with their sharp towers of ice looking like long lines of Ku Klux Klansmen on the rocky glacier and runnels of ice with murderously fast-rushing water beneath her. She carried every ounce that the men did, and she did so cheerfully. She'd wake up every morning with the same adrenaline coursing through her, unable to believe that she had actually been given this kind of gift. She embraced every aspect of the expedition, even the misery of load-carrying.

Once on the mountain, Julie fed off equal measures of thrill and terror, in one moment watching a full moon rise huge and luminescent over the east ridge of the mountain, and in the next seeing a rock fall from above and nearly decapitate Kurt as it sailed down the face of the mountain *rat-a-tat-tatting* like a Singer sewing machine traveling 100 miles per hour.

Her only truly awful moment came when she was safe and warm in her sleeping bag, snuggling next to Kurt in their tent at Camp II. Suddenly she felt her bowels roil, and she desperately grabbed for her sleeping bag and tent zippers to get out of the tent. As she fumbled she felt it go—*Ploof!* The "thin shits" had exploded out of her aching bowels and filled her two layers of pants all the way into her socks. Mortified and disgusted, she bounded out of the tent, hoping to spare Kurt the worst of the mess and smell. She stood on a perilous precipice, 6,000 feet above the floor of the valley, in her ruined socks, shivering in the cold, covered with her sickening slime. She burst into tears, as much from self-pity as sheer frustration.

Kurt, having heard her leave the tent, soon stood at her side admonishing her for not taking her gloves. *Julie! You are risking frostbite at this altitude!* As her tears turned to sobs she told him why her fingers were the least of her worries. With a tender calm, Kurt took charge, leading her to a safer place between the two tents at Camp II and clipping her onto a safety rope. Nearby, two Italian teammates peeked out of their tent to see what the midnight commotion was all about, then discreetly zipped the flap closed. Kurt pulled a thin foam mattress from the tent for her to stand on while she peeled off the fouled clothes. But without water and in the subzero temperature, she couldn't imagine how she could possibly clean up the foul ooze.

"Here, I found these." Julie would have laughed out loud if there had been an ounce of humor in her awful situation. Kurt handed her two towelettes, the kind and size restaurants pass out to customers after dinner. Still, she was grateful for his kindness and for something constructive to do. Using the towelettes and handfuls of the airy snow, she got as much of the sticky, smelly mess off of her skin as she could before gratefully putting on Kurt's spare pants and once again nuzzling into the warm security of her sleeping bag. As Kurt snored next to her, she smiled. It was all so amazing. A proper English housewife and mother, shitting all over herself in the middle of the night, being helped to scrape the mess off her skin by one of the world's best climbers and filmmakers, and all the while clipped into a rope at nearly 7,000 meters on the world's second-highest mountain in China! Her belly finally calm, Julie slept soundly for the rest of the night.

As the Italians climbed Julie and Kurt followed their progress on the mountain and on film. Through it all Julie was proud that she performed well, shouldering her share of the climbing and filming equipment, and she joined in the team's celebration when it put two of its climbers on the summit. Although she reached the magic point of 8,000 meters, she did not reach the summit. But she knew she would be back. K2 had gotten into her soul and under her skin. "On K2 I had learnt the real pleasures of high-altitude mountaineering and was totally captivated by the character of this beautiful 'mountain of mountains.' Even if I had reached the summit, I would have wanted to discover more about it, explore its other sides. As it was, I knew I would have to go back to K2. Of all the mountains, this one was the most special to me."

Just nine months later she was on her way back to her "mountain of mountains," this time filming a Swiss expedition for a British television station on the southern side of the mountain in Pakistan. Among the twelve climbers were four Polish women who had attached themselves to the permit, among them Wanda Rutkiewicz. Julie thought it slightly suspect that while they called themselves a "women's expedition," they were surrounded and supported by men. She meant them no ill will; she just thought it a bit disingenuous to go on about their strength and merit as women alpinists when clearly they used and even seemed to need the support of men. She knew she could never see herself on any kind of a "feminist" expedition.

After weeks of forbidding weather, the team gave up on its K2 bid and left the mountain, but Julie and Kurt decided to give nearby Broad Peak a try, since it was included on their K2 permit. On July 18, 1984, at the age of forty-five, Julie stood on the summit of her first 8,000-meter peak looking out over the peaks and glaciers of Pakistan and China, many of which she and Kurt had explored. One prominent peak stared back. K2, just across the Godwin-Austen Glacier, looked tantalizingly close, its infamous Shoulder at 8,000 meters nearly eye-level with Julie. She could clearly see the route through the Bottleneck, across the Traverse, over the last serac, and up its summit crown. She could almost spot the exact place where she and Kurt had established their Camp III at 25,000 feet (7,600 meters) only weeks earlier, before they were forced to descend. But again, K2 would have to wait. In the meantime she could relish her first 8,000-meter triumph and being the first British woman to climb Broad Peak. She and Kurt smiled for each other's cameras before turning down and beginning their descent as the last light faded across the western sky. Only a few hundred meters into the descent they realized that they would have to bivouac and spend the night tucked beneath the massive summit.

In the predawn gray of the next morning she felt Kurt struggle to free himself from his sleeping bag in the tiny one-man bivouac tent into which they were both crammed. Her eyelids felt like heavy compresses were holding them shut, and her body felt as if she lay under a lead blanket. She gave into the overwhelming urge to sleep.

Julie! Wake up! Get me my other boot! Kurt was yelling from outside the tent, the panic in his voice bringing her instantly awake. They had placed their high camp where the night's snow now funneled down in increasingly large sloughs. He had already diverted one moderate slide by standing in front of the tent and breaking its force to either side like the prow of a ship breaking the waves. The next could kill them, and she struggled against her high-altitude lethargy and the confines of the tent to find his boot, then her own, and get out of the tent before it was hit.

What takes an hour at Base Camp Julie was able to do in fifteen minutes at 8,000 meters: don her boots, put on layers of gear and gaitors, pack up the sleeping bags, tent, stove, gas, and food, and organize a length of rope to tie between them.

She followed in Kurt's footsteps across the unstable slope, waiting in dread for the force of their weight to be enough to send shock waves through the fragile snow and trigger a catastrophic release above them. They moved with awful deliberation; all she wanted to do was run. Kurt loomed ahead of her like a dark shadow in the increasing snowstorm around them. Like the Grim Reaper, he hunched over the rope, his ax poking at the snow in front of him, his expert eyes watching the slope for any telltale signs of weakness.

She didn't know if she felt it or heard it first. *Avaaaahhh,* she'd begun to whisper when her feet were knocked out from under her and she was instantly overwhelmed by a frozen wave, the force feeling like a waterfall dragging her body down the slope. She punched her right arm into the rushing snow, feeling the wonderful power of her aikido, and found air. After only a few moments she came to rest, grateful that it had only been a runoff slide. Suddenly, another jerk from the rope sent her spiraling. Her world went black and she crossed her arms over her chest, clutching her ice ax tight against her as she tumbled, rolled, crashed, drowned in the wet snow. She knew she was as close to death as she probably ever had been in her life, but her mind was calm. As she careened down the slope, moving as fast as a car on the roadway, she realized that she wouldn't mind dying in the mountains. *Better here than in some disabling accident in Tunbridge,* she thought. She couldn't stand the thought of being hooked up to machines and dependent on others for her care. No, if this was it, she knew she was at peace.

Himalayan avalanches travel at horrifying speeds, upward of 125 miles per hour as they careen miles down the steep slopes of the world's highest mountains. Even in a relatively small slide, the force and volume pack the snow and ice like cement. If climbers don't die instantly from blunt trauma, they usually suffocate within minutes, unable to dig out of their crushing tomb. Julie was lucky. She was hit high in the slide's progress down the slope, before it had murderous force. When she finally came to a rest, every aperture of her body was filled with the compacted snow, including her mouth and throat. She dug herself out, then leaned over and clawed the back of her throat, retching. Finally she opened her airway and fell back on the slope, gasping for air.

She was alive. Testing her body piece by piece, she found she could move. But where was Kurt? The rope between them was taut, but was he dead at the other end? As she prayed she heard him call out, "Julie, are you hurt?" She didn't think so, but when Kurt made his slow progress up to where she lay, he saw that she had wet herself, possibly indicating a broken pelvis. She struggled to free her rucksack from the hard pack beneath her and felt no pain, except for a badly bruised thigh. She had lost control of her bladder from the shock of the fall. Looking back up the slope, they saw that they had been hit at the foot of a rocky outcrop, over which the avalanche roared, carrying them first down a snow slope, then over a 120-foot ice serac, and finally crashing through tractor-trailer-sized ice blocks before Kurt became jammed between two and brought them both to a stop. She had probably first come to rest after her fall down the snow slope, but when Kurt was pulled over the 120-foot wall, she was plucked up and thrown after him through the boulder field of ice blocks, blocks that helped saved their lives by diverting and weakening the fall of the avalanche. They had fallen over 400 feet—higher than St. Paul's Cathedral Julie realized in awe—and they had survived!

But they still had to get off the mountain. Battered and exhausted, they cleaned their goggles and bodies of snow, digging at their ears and snorting through their noses and throats to clear them of the choking crystals, and continued down. Julie followed Kurt in a dreamlike state as the storm gathered real force around them. In the white-out blizzard that accompanied their retreat from the mountain, "it was only Kurt's expertly accurate route finding which saved us from getting lost," Julie wrote later.

When she returned to England, the media met her at Heathrow, blinding her with flashbulbs and pulling her toward "exclusive" interviews, her sleeves gripped in their rapacious fingers. She saw Terry in the sea of faces and felt the wonderful power of his arms around her. But before she knew it, she was plucked out of his embrace and pulled away by a reporter. Standing next to Terry, unseen and ignored in the crush, were Lindsay and Chris. Chris stood with the woman he was going to marry, patiently and proudly waiting to introduce her to his mother. His eager smiled faded as he watched Julie disappear into the crowds as quickly as she had emerged.

When she finally returned, Terry scolded her.

"They were standing right there and you just walked away, ignoring them!"

Julie, crestfallen, apologized. She simply hadn't seen them.

"But did you look?" Terry demanded. She didn't have an answer. She just hadn't seen them.

When asked how old he was when his mother died, Chris Tullis said eighteen. He was actually twenty-four. But it *was* when he was eighteen, in 1980, that Julie left on her first extended trip and her life began to be lived thousands of miles away from her home and family in England. And by 1986, when she left for what would be her third trip to her mountain of mountains, she thought mostly of those adventures, not of her life and loves at home. Perhaps there is just so much room in a life, and hers was increasingly filled with mountains and Kurt Diemberger.

"She didn't have time for us as a family really," Chris remembered. "It was all publicizing the next expedition or a book or just working toward where she was going to go next."

Julie had made a meteoric rise from climbing the crags of Tunbridge and Wales to navigating 8,000-meter peaks, mostly through her friend-ship and collaboration with Diemberger. It was not a leap lost on her children.

"She wasn't really a mountaineer, as such," Chris thought. "She went from not very much to a lot in a short space of time. At least that's the way it seemed."

But you never would have known that judging from the mountains she chose, or those that were chosen for her. On Diemberger's wings, the humble "middle English housewife" was suddenly thrust into the world's most thrilling and dangerous landscapes.

The attention from her first British female ascent of Broad Peak got her a first-ever invitation for a woman to join a British expedition to the North Ridge of Everest in 1985. But again, terrible weather conditions on the mountain kept the team low and frustrated, and after the death of a member, the team finally departed without a viable summit bid. She returned to England feeling a frustration she had never felt before, but it was soon forgotten. Ten days after leaving Peking she was on another flight to Pakistan, this time to revisit Nanga Parbat.

Her second expedition to the mountain proved much happier than the first, although she felt troubled, almost haunted, by her surroundings. Many climbers speak of the spirits, both dead and alive, benign and threatening, that surround the mystical peaks above 8,000 meters, but Julie had never been one of them. On this trip, however, they seemed to be everywhere, swirling the winds with vicious strength, swallowing them in avalanches, peppering them with rockfall, even allowing them to lose a precious rucksack of exposed film and gear. She felt she had met the evil spirits of Nanga Parbat and survived—"we had a future."

But perhaps those spirits weren't evil. Maybe they were actually benign, and instead of trying to do harm, they were trying to warn Julie of far greater ill will beckoning her from a nearby Karakoram peak.

CHAPTER 6

THE BLACK SUMMER'S
FINAL, TERRIBLE TOLL

Alpinism is the art of suffering.

—WOJTEK KURTYKA

Somewhere in between her now back-to-back expeditions, Julie found time to sell her autobiography, and she stole precious moments in early 1986 to write down her life story. In her short Himalayan climbing life, she had been on five expeditions, some lasting as long as four months, between 1982 and mid-1985, but as she wrote the final chapters of the book she lamented that the whole of 1986 was, at that point, "a horrible blank" on her calendar.

Again with a phone call, that blank became a dream. Could she leave for five months? Diemberger had booked a doubleheader filming job that would take them first to Nepal in the early spring and directly from there to their beloved K2 through the summer.

Julie left the Bothy in March 1986 for a trip that would first take her to Tashigan to film life in a remote mountain village and then immediately from Kathmandu to Pakistan for the third attempt she and Kurt would make at what they called "their" mountain. With her ride to the airport waiting, she and Terry had an emotional good-bye in the low doorway, both crying and holding their embrace longer than usual.

The expedition began well. When Julie and Kurt once again joined up with the "Quota 8000" Italian team, they found there were several members from their 1983 trip to the North Ridge of K2. Agostino Da Polenza, their leader from 1983, saw Julie across the Karachi airport, ran over, and swooped her up in an enormous hug, her feet dancing inches above the cement. Julie laughed and hugged him back, happy to be on a team that felt more like a family. When they reached Skardu several days later, they found the K2 Motel filled to overcrowding with climbers and spent their first night on the floor of the lobby with a collection of other unlucky climbers as the haunting prayers of the imam floated through the hotel from a nearby mosque. Julie and Kurt knew it was going to be a record year for climbers attempting K2, among them Wanda Rutkiewicz, the French couple Maurice and Liliane Barrard, and an assortment of British climbers whom Julie had met over the years as they came through her climbing shops. With so many teams heading into the Karakoram, finding an adequate supply of porters was sure to be a problem, so the Italians rose at 3:00 A.M. to get a jump on the competition. But Kurt woke with a nasty flu, and he and Julie decided to hang back and make the trek at their own speed, letting the teams battle it out ahead of them.

Julie loved the slower pace, traveling just a few miles a day, taking time to stop and marvel at the changing scenery they passed; the towering rock faces of the Cathedrals and Mustagh and Trango Towers, Masherbrum, the majestic Gasherbrum IV, a close runner-up to World's Most Beautiful Mountain, until finally K2 itself appeared around the last corner. "I love this place," she wrote Terry and said that it was her most enjoyable approach to the mountain yet.

As the teams settled themselves for their two- to three-month stay on the glacier, Julie noted where each would be climbing. Three other teams would join them on or near the South Southwest Ridge: a large Polish team that included three of the women they had met on K2 in 1984; a small American team; and Renato Casarotto, who, despite learning of his unexpected company on the route, would attempt to climb solo, something that had never before been done on K2. But if any man could do it, Casarotto had the experience, strength, and determination to pull it off.

Casarotto had been to the mountain once before in 1979 with Reinhold Messner, who had made it his very public goal to climb K2 via a so-called Magic Line, a route that closely followed the SSW Ridge. But once at the mountain, Messner abandoned his Magic Line and turned his energy toward the Abruzzi, as so many teams have since done once faced with the reality of alternative routes: unrelenting slopes, avalanche dangers, and 12,000 feet (3,660 meters) of unroped mountain. Perhaps feeling cheated out of the original goal, Casarotto was back to climb what was now *his* Magic Line. Joining him was his wife Goretta, a climber in her own right whose blond hair, blue eyes, full lips, and ivory skin reminded many of the models on the fashion runways of Paris and Milan. They were a popular and respected couple at Base Camp, although when their summer of expected solitude was shattered by the increasingly noisy rabble of other expeditions, they kept quietly to themselves in their large bluish-green tent.

The beauty and grace of Julie's trek in and the early days at Base Camp quickly turned to disaster and anguish. Two weeks after Julie and Kurt arrived, Base Camp was awoken on June 21 by the thunderous roar of an avalanche. As climbers jumped from tents littered along the glacier, all eyes went to the mountain, where a fine dust of snow still hung in the air below the SSW Ridge. *Was anyone climbing this morning? Did anyone get caught?* Word soon spread: four Italians were higher on the route, safely at Camp III, but two Americans had been climbing low, below Camp I, when the avalanche broke off.

Al Pennington's body was quickly found in the debris and buried the next day at the Gilkey Memorial. John Smolich was never found. Julie wrote Terry that their "glacier village is a mixture of emotions—extreme sadness, and worry for those still up."

The avalanche began a chain of events whose actual toll will never be known. Deeming the SSW Ridge too dangerous, the large Italian team switched its route to the more popular Abruzzi, and Julie and Kurt switched with them. Launching their first summit attempt only days later, the Italians reached 7,850 meters before being turned back by storms. As they descended to Camp I they told Julie and Kurt of further bad news: the Barrards, who had made the summit on the 23rd, were missing. In an eerie foreshadowing, Julie had worried about the Barrards' determination to have Liliane be the first woman to climb K2 and hoped they wouldn't "kill themselves in the attempt." It seemed they had. Liliane's body was found at the base of the mountain nearly a month later, 10,000 feet (3,050 meters) below where she was last seen in the Bottleneck.

Julie and Kurt did not attend her service at the Gilkey, instead choosing to remain quietly in their camp. "It was like shying away," Kurt wrote, "as if we tried to keep news of further disaster at bay. After these harrowing experiences of the Black Summer '86, we could certainly have done one thing: forfeit our mountains of dreams. But nobody who has been up there takes this as a serious option. To fulfill their dreams, men frequently dare death and destiny."

The mountain had claimed its third and fourth climbers of the Black Summer of 1986. But it had only gotten started.

Teams struggled physically and emotionally to get back on the mountain. The weather continued to roll in storm after storm, causing a pattern of climb, retreat, wait, climb, retreat, wait, which further sapped the energies and morale in the "village."

Climbers dealt with the deaths and ever-escalating danger differently. Some simply abandoned their climbs, packing their expeditions back into bins and duffels and retreating down the glacier to home and safety. Others attacked their routes with new ferocity, setting out on their summit bids before their bodies were fully acclimatized, only to find themselves sucker-punched by the mountain and its weather; they returned to Base Camp exhausted and chagrined at their hubris. For Julie, the emotional warring was perhaps easier. Without a word, she would disappear through the ice towers that bordered both sides of Base Camp, taking only her samurai sword with her, and follow the silent meditations of aikido until she found her equilibrium. "I have two passions," she said. "Mountains and the martial arts." Then, when she was again able, she would share stories with the Casarottos, drink tea with the Brits, or play guitar and sing with the otherwise antisocial Austrians.

In many ways, Julie Tullis was the last person you'd expect to find on a Himalayan mountain, and some at Base Camp worried about her lack of high-altitude experience. Jim Curran, a jovial member of Al Rouse's

British expedition, was on board as a cameraman-climber hoping to film the first British ascent of K2. A friendly and well-liked climber from the Sheffield climbing scene, Curran carried extra weight from many a night in the local pubs that caused one of his blokes to comment: "Curran'll never get a tan because the Save the Whalers'll keep rolling him back in the water." It was the kind of joke that in the hypoxic world of Himalayan climbing can cause a ripple of laughter to erupt for months. At Base Camp, Curran watched Julie with a sense of alarm: "I always felt that she'd slightly skipped quite a big chunk of mountaineering training in that she'd gone from being very much a rock climber to a Himalayan mountaineer without doing too much in between. So there was always a slight sort of question mark; where did she come from?" There was also the question of her drive on K2. "I think everyone on K2 in '86 was quite aware that there was quite a gap between the grand old man, Kurt, and his protégée. It was a bit like a guide and a client. There was no question that Julie would never have in a month of Sundays been on K2 without Kurt being there. I suppose the idea was that Kurt's experience would see her through. But every time she got away from the fixed ropes, like on Broad Peak, they seemed to be pushing it pretty near the margins."

Climbers tend to be a superstitious lot, wearing the same lucky clothing climb after climb and never using words like "conquer" or "vanquish" in talking about climbing a mountain. Ed Viesturs, an American well on his way to achieving his goal of climbing all fourteen of the world's 8,000-meter peaks without supplemental oxygen, said that you don't linger on an 8,000-meter summit relishing your victory—you "tag the summit and run like hell" back down. Curran, watching Julie and Kurt in 1986, became increasingly wary of their lofty claims. "They both kept using this 'K2 is our mountain of mountains' as if they owned the thing, which I felt was a bit worrying that she'd got some sort of destiny to climb it. I tend to be fairly pragmatic, and I think if you start confusing climbing mountains with destiny you are playing with fire."

July 16 dawned clear and calm, a perfect summit day in a place that rarely provided perfection. But for Renato Casarotto high on his route up the SSW Ridge, his climbing season was over. He was exhausted, and after a heroic effort of climbing alone and belaying himself to 8,300 meters (27,230 feet), he was calling it quits. He radioed Goretta at Base Camp; he was admitting defeat, retreating in the face of his own exhaustion and frustration with the route and the weather. As night fell he had almost reached Base Camp, a tiny speck in the vast expanse of the Filippi Glacier behind Base Camp, when he disappeared.

Diemberger, who had been watching Casarotto's progress down through the crack-filled glacier, ran over to Goretta's tent and urged her to raise Renato on the radio. Insisting that he couldn't be that low on the mountain so soon, Goretta hesitated, but seeing the urgency in Diemberger's face, she reached for the radio.

"Goretta, send help. I've fallen, *tutto rotto*, I'm dying. Come quickly," Casarotto's weak voice cracked over the radio. *All broken, I'm dying.* Alone and unroped, he had fallen 120 feet (37 meters) into the bowels of the glacier. Renato had been descending on his normal route, a route he had traversed countless times as he climbed and descended all summer. But this time, perhaps with his mind filled with frustration and defeat and all but jogging down through the Filippi Glacier, instead of jumping over a telltale snow bridge with its perilously thin ice, he had crashed through it and fallen into the narrow and deep crevasse.

Base Camp became a buzz of activity as people scrambled to find a rope for his rescue. Ironically, as more and more climbers aimed to ascend in the "fast and light" alpine fashion, finding a spare climbing rope in a Himalayan Base Camp was a difficult task. Finally, Diemberger and Julie grabbed their own rope and some ice screws and ran toward the glacier. Da Polenza, younger and faster, soon caught up with them, took their rope, and while keeping the injured Renato talking from his icy prison, sped through the maze of crevasses up to where his friend lay.

Gianni Calcagno, another member of the Italian team who had run up behind Da Polenza, descended into the crevasse and found Renato sitting against its wall. They embraced, and one can barely comprehend what Renato's relief must have been when he saw Gianni's smiling face join him in the deadly underworld. Water was all around him, and Renato complained that he was numb and that his head was cold.

Although initially able to help pull himself out, he soon slumped on the rope, a deadweight that those above struggled to wrest out of the hole. When they finally got him to the surface, he was semiconscious, but he immediately collapsed onto the glacier, dead.

When Curran and his group reached where Renato lay, he remembered something "sinister" about the scene. "Beneath a sleeping bag, a plastic boot protruded. Bev [Dr. Bev Holt] carefully carried out his examination before replacing the bag, and in a choked voice confirmed what we already knew." Curran looked at what only days before had been a robust man, his now pale arm emerging from his rolled-up sleeve, hanging limp and lifeless on the ice.

Wanda Rutkiewicz wept quietly. She had rushed up with the other climbers, sure that they could save him, determined that there wouldn't be yet another death. Her summer of triumph had become one of darkest memories. She later wrote, "I can feel no pleasure at having reached the summit of K2. . . . I lost too many friends in 1986."

Stunned climbers stood by the body, a dark shadow against the white snow, headlamps occasionally glancing off its rounded contours. As the first light of morning began to lighten the sky above Broad Peak, Agostino, sobbing, called Base Camp to tell Goretta.

Back in the Casarottos' tent, Julie sat holding Goretta's hand, watching her give calm instructions: her husband would be buried in the crevasse from which he had just been released. But before they lowered him, she wanted to come up to say her final good-byes. Hearing that she was on her way up, the climbers slowly made their way back to camp to give Goretta a measure of privacy in the midst of such sorrow. But weeping in Julie's arms, Goretta realized that she wasn't capable of watching her husband be lowered into his icy tomb, of seeing his body, once so strong and able, now broken and lifeless.

Curran started back down the glacier for Base Camp, turning back one last time in the waxing light. He saw two dark figures flanking a horizontal third. Suddenly there were just two. Renato had been returned to the crevasse, where it was hoped the body would remain in relative peace, not subjected to the constant grinding motion of the glacier's surface. But like so many others over time, Renato's body was disgorged and found by climbers in 2004, when it was once again quietly returned to its cold depths. For years after Renato's death, Goretta returned to K2, a widow visiting her love's gravesite. But by the mid-1990s she had stopped, having said all the good-byes and "I love yous" she could say. When his remains were found in 2004, Goretta again went back to the mountain, finally and thankfully to say good-bye to the body and the man she had been unable to say good-bye to eighteen years before.

Curran hoped the Black Summer had had its fill of death. Casarotto's had been the worst he'd seen, and he'd seen a lot of death in his years of climbing. He just couldn't imagine it getting worse. He prayed it wouldn't.

It was July 17, and after gently rocking Goretta's sobbing, inconsolable body for hours, Julie decided she had had enough climbing for one season. When Goretta finally fell into an exhausted slumber, Julie put pen to paper to tell Terry and the children that she was coming home. No more summit bids. No more death. While she had to remain on the mountain to film, she would not be climbing into harm's way again. "I have buried so many good friends," she wrote, "and so many good climbers have died, that I have little heart left to climb my mountains of mountains."

But days later, when she sat outside her tent at Base Camp, the sun warming her back as she stared up at the mountain, she wasn't so sure. She felt safe, the mountain looked beautiful, she and Kurt had already gotten to within 300 meters of the summit, and they were ready. Should she once again leave K2 in defeat or give it one last try? She was there, after all, and it seemed so ridiculous not to try. Perhaps the mountain had had its fill of death. Perhaps the weather would clear, finally, and give them that week of good weather they needed for a credible summit bid. What if they turned away, as they had in 1984, only to be greeted by a week of perfect weather in which they summited Broad Peak instead? Would she get a *fourth* chance at K2? Would she even want it? She could sense that Diemberger was still eager to try for the summit, but he didn't say anything, just watched her out of the corner of his eye. She didn't want to disappoint him. She didn't want to be the one to call it quits. But she was emotionally spent, empty. There had been so much death. She didn't want to see any more. She didn't want to bury any more bodies. She didn't want to risk that the next one could be her own. But how could she let Diemberger down? He wanted it so badly.

Rather than commit to a full summit bid, they decided to climb at least to Camp II with their filming equipment. Although their Italian team had since summited and left the mountain, Diemberger and Julie remained because Diemberger felt they had more filming to do before they could leave the mountain. Once at Camp II, he thought, they would then decide whether to go for the summit. They never discussed this compromise, but Julie must have felt his burning determination to continue because when she began packing it was not for merely a climb to Camp II but included all the gear necessary for a full summit bid. Diemberger watched her with growing hope that she had indeed changed her mind and would accompany him to the summit.

She was stuffing a large pile of gear into her increasingly heavy pack when Jim Curran approached her. He asked whether she and Kurt were going for the summit.

"No," she said, but knew already she was lying, "we're just going up to Camp II to get the rest of our film equipment." She was glad she was wearing dark sunglasses. Lies were easier when you knew your eyes were invisible.

"Besides," she continued, looking into his kind and concerned face, "I'm terribly homesick and am eager to get started back for home."

Curran was unconvinced. He walked away, worried, and she watched him go before turning back to her packing.

By early August the Abruzzi was a crowded place. The string of deaths caused team after team to abandon earlier, more isolated routes. Along with a trail of fully stocked camps, the Koreans had roped the entire Abruzzi to and through the Traverse above the Bottleneck and stocked many of the camps with oxygen. While K2 remains the deadliest mountain on descent, not one of those deaths happened to a climber who used oxygen on the way up. Most climbers choose to ascend the mountain without the extra weight and cost of bottled "gas," but knowing it's there if disaster strikes provides a small measure of assurance.

Climbers often espouse a purer style of ascent while readily depending on the supplies, lines, and oxygen of larger teams. This is particularly true on K2, where climbers often denounce those who join "assault"-style expeditions for not being true mountaineers, but "austere" alpine climbers often utilize, even demand, the supplies and strength of those larger, well-equipped teams when trouble hits high on the mountain. Julie and Kurt were climbing in just such a self-sustained style, but like many others on the mountain that year, they were depending on the supplies and gear of other teams on the mountain.

An original count of nine teams on the mountain that year had been shaken down to four disparate groups: four Koreans and their three high-altitude porters, three of the Austrians, Julie and Kurt, and Al Rouse and Mrowka Wolf, the woman who had climbed with Wanda Rutkiewicz. Wolf had come to the mountain with a strong Polish team that included Wojciech Wroz, Anna Czerwinska, and Krystyna Palmowska. But after weeks on the as-yet-unclimbed South Southwest Ridge, Wolf opted to jump to the less challenging Abruzzi and climb with Al Rouse, who had abandoned his Northwest Ridge route and agreed to team up with her.

Rouse worried about Julie's reaction to the move. "Julie Tullis will go ape-shit if she thinks we'll try the Abruzzi," he told teammate Adrian Burgess. Both men thought she was driven to climb K2 as well as to become the first Briton to do so, and if the stronger Al Rouse climbed it first, then "a shadow would be drawn across her life." They also worried because she and Diemberger were "insanely" slow climbers. More than once Aid Burgess had stood in Base Camp, holding out his thumb in front of him, and placing it on the distant specks of Kurt and Julie climbing on the mountain, waiting for them to move. Sometimes it would take five minutes, sometimes ten, before they emerged from behind his thumb.

On July 29, Julie and Kurt turned from the death pall at Base Camp and once again faced *their* mountain, determined it would be their last attempt. The next morning they rearranged their gear at Advance Base Camp. Kurt, his mind in constant silent conversation about the decision ahead of them, turned to stare at Julie. Without looking up from her pack, she quietly said, "I know I didn't want to go up anymore, but I've changed my mind."

Just like that, the decision was made. They were going for the summit. Diemberger could barely contain his joy and relief, a joy he was sure Julie shared.

They made slow but steady progress, having already left caches of equipment high on the mountain and obtained permission to use the abandoned gear of departed teams: the Swiss at Camp I and the Spanish at Camp II, as well as a small, light tent lent to them by Michel Parmentier that they planned to use at Camps III and IV.

Between their 1984 attempt and this year, they were making their ninth ascent up the Abruzzi. They knew it well. As they neared 7,000 meters they were met with devastating news: an avalanche had destroyed Camps III and IV, and nothing was left. Julie turned to Kurt, fear licking at her eyes. "Do you think the avalanche danger is still high? I don't want to die, you know," she said quietly. He assured her they would turn back at the first sign of avalanche; it was an illusory promise high on a mountain as dangerous as K2. She bowed her head and continued climbing.

They climbed well, and except for Diemberger's loud tantrums when other climbers disrupted his sleep, there was no further trouble. Meanwhile, a tempest was brewing ahead of them.

The Austrians had refused to believe that their high camps had been destroyed in the massive avalanche days before and left Base Camp climbing light and without replacement tents, sleeping bags, stoves, or gas. But their worst fears were confirmed when they reached Camp III and saw that the only remaining tent belonged to the Koreans. Hannes Wieser radioed down to the Koreans lower on the mountain and asked to use their Camp III tent; in exchange, he and his teammates would then move it up to Camp IV for them. Being a day ahead, Wieser said he and his team would use the tent the night of August 1, go for the summit on the 2nd, and then continue descending in time for the Koreans to arrive, saving the Koreans the effort of carrying another tent to Camp IV. All parties reportedly agreed, although because they communicated in English, a language foreign to both the teams, whether the terms were clearly understood will never be known.

When Julie and Kurt reached Camp IV, they set up their *petit* tent in the lee of the large, three-man Korean tent, hoping it would create a windbreak. Once up, Julie jumped inside and immediately began brewing water, a crucial factor in maintaining strength and cognition above 8,000 meters. In a steady stream, she handed Diemberger cup after cup of tea, mushroom soup, and finally bottles of hot water that would provide the almost erotic pleasure of a warm sleeping bag in an otherwise frigid night. Diemberger, who had been watching the slow progress of the ascending Austrians above them on the summit cone, suddenly yelled in to Julie, "I am very worried—the Austrians are retreating in a bit of a hurry." Inside, Julie was shocked as well. Between the Koreans' tent, Al Rouse and Mrowka Wolf's tent, and their small French bivy, there were three tents and seven people on the Shoulder. There simply wasn't room for three more.

The Austrians descended from their failed bid and announced that they would give the summit another try in the morning. Insisting that the Koreans had told him they would bring a second tent to Camp IV, allowing the Austrians a two-night stay in the large Korean tent, Wieser and his teammates refused to descend. There was a noisy and nasty argument. At 8,000 meters it couldn't have helped the physical and mental state of the climbers. Tempers flared until the three Koreans finally allowed two of the Austrians to cram into their already full tent. The climbers then turned to Kurt, who steadfastly refused to take in Alfred Imitzer, the extra man, insisting that the Austrians should bivouac or descend. *Why should we sacrifice our chance at the summit by having a bad night beforehand?* Diemberger yelled at the miserable group. *Besides,* he said, *we have only a tiny French bivouac tent, barely enough room for Julie and me, let alone three.* Imitzer was left standing on the Shoulder, his sleeping bag trailing in the wind. Finally he turned and climbed down to where Al Rouse's tent was set up several meters below the other two. Rouse opened his door, and the third Austrian crowded in with him and Mrowka in their small two-man tent. The seven climbers in three crowded tents tried to rest before their summit bids in a few hours.

August 3 promised perfect summit weather: clear, cold, and calm. The Koreans rose first at 4:00 A.M., but preparations that should have taken an hour took three in their cramped tent as the men struggled to dress, eat, and pack with two additional bodies in the way. Why the Austrians didn't vacate the tent to give the Koreans moving room is not known. Diemberger and Julie, counting on the Koreans, the Austrians, and Al Rouse to break trail ahead of them, waited in their tent sipping tea and staring darkly into the misty halo rising from their mugs. Occasionally Diemberger would yell impatiently across the narrow divide between the nylon tents, "Are you ready yet?" Julie sat silent, waiting.

After a sleepless night jammed into a corner of his tent, Al Rouse announced that he couldn't make a summit bid and would wait until the next day. Likewise, the Austrians, exhausted from their bid the day before, opted to rest a day before their second attempt at the summit. By the time the Koreans finally got themselves organized and fed and left camp at 7:00 A M, Diemberger also decided it was too late and announced that he and Julie as well would wait until the next day.

Nowhere is hindsight more 20–20 than in mountaineering. The concept of a rest day at 8,000 meters is absurd. At that altitude the body is dying so fast that every minute is measured like precious gold against the loss of brain cells and body fluids. The thought that they would be more motivated and feel *better* after another day in its death rattle is unfathomable. And yet a handful of the world's strongest climbers reasoned that a day of leisure in the thin air was better than trying for the summit sleep-deprived.

Back in Base Camp word filtered down that the Koreans had made the summit and that they were followed by three of the Poles who had made a heroic ascent of the South Southwest Pillar—the route for which Casarotto had fought so hard—with little more than the clothes on their backs.

Curran felt nothing but dread. He knew that August 3 was Rouse's planned summit day. *Where are Al and Mrowka? What has happened?* His mind raced with worry and anguish. *Why have only the Koreans left Camp IV for the summit?*

On descent, one of the Koreans decided to bivouac rather than continue down in his exhausted state. Therefore, Imitzer was able to tuck into the available sliver of room in the Korean tent with his two teammates and the two descending Koreans, leaving Al and Mrowka able to stretch out and get comfortable in their tent. Nearby, Julie and Kurt continued to brew and nibble on breads and soup. It was a calm afternoon; the skies were clear and hopes high. *Tomorrow is our day, Julie,* Diemberger told her, but Julie just sipped at her tea, quiet and staring off into the thin air between them.

Suddenly his calm assurance turned to panic when three figures were spotted descending the ridge headed right for Camp IV. It was the Poles, obviously. For whatever reason, they had opted to descend the Abruzzi rather than the SSW Pillar they had climbed. Diemberger and Julie were outraged. *How dare they come down here without having made any plans for their food and shelter?*

Plans or no plans, Przemyslaw Piasecki and Peter Bozik stumbled into camp around 2:00 A.M., clearly shattered from their ascent. The epic achievement of climbing the mountain with little more than a bivy sack between them had cost them dearly. Knowing the Abruzzi was an easier route and strung with safety ropes and stocked camps, they chose to descend via it rather than back down the barren SSW Pillar. As they began their descent their teammate Wojciech Wroz disappeared. Korean climber Kim Chang Sun, trying to make sense of the jumble of fixed lines through the Traverse, had cut and retied a section, leaving the short end dangling. Wroz apparently had clipped onto the short rope and simply slid off its untethered end. It was dark, and his teammates felt rather than saw his body whir past them into the abyss. He didn't scream as he fell to his death.

Having witnessed Wroz's death, the two surviving Poles arrived in Camp IV physically and emotionally devastated. Diemberger had little sympathy. Julie stood at his side while he railed against the climbers for their poor planning and for being at the mercy of others' beneficence. Again Diemberger refused to help, and again it was Al Rouse who took in the stranded climbers, allowing the two exhausted Poles to collapse in his tent's relative warmth and comfort while he dug a snow cave outside it and hunkered down for the long, bitter night.

Back in Base Camp word again spread that another climber, the seventh of the summer, had been lost. When Krystyna Palmowska received the news in Base Camp, in an instant her heart froze, and she realized that her love of climbing had frozen with it. She would never climb again. "There have been too many deaths," she said.

Finally, at 5:30 A.M. on August 4, under a clear, blue-black sky that was littered with stars so bright they vibrated, the seven climbers began their summit bid. Miraculously, Rouse had the energy to lead the way, breaking trail and releasing ropes that had been frozen into the slope during the night. Behind him, Wolf followed closely, then came Alfred Imitzer, Kurt, and finally Julie. Willi Bauer and Hannes Wieser waited for nearly ninety minutes before they started out, but Wieser turned back, saying that his gloves were wet; his summit bid was over. By 7:00, six people formed a human trail up the steep summit pyramid. They had already been above 8,000 meters for two days, some of them for three. The clock was ticking.

By midmorning the sky was streaked with the first signs of a storm, "mare's tails," light, wispy lenticular clouds that streaked across the sky as benign indicators of the malice to come. If noticed, the warning went unheeded by the ragged group, tiny ants inching inexorably up the final slopes toward the summit. At this altitude every step was measured against a lead weight across the shoulders and filling the boots. Each step required ten, twelve, fifteen ragged breaths of the desperately thin air. Titanium ice axes that weighed less than a pound felt like a caveman's club. The ice slope was as steep as a wall and as hard as steel; kicking their points of their crampons into it for purchase took every measure of concentration and energy.

After Rouse broke the trail to within 100 meters of the summit, Bauer and Imitzer caught up and passed him while he paused to rest. If Rouse resented the Austrians' exploitation of his work only to pass him within meters of the summit, he didn't say so. But he did mutter his relief, perhaps tinged with sarcasm, at finally having help with the backbreaking work of establishing the trail. Bauer was first to the summit, followed closely by Imitzer and finally the steady plow horse, Al Rouse.

Below them, Julie and Kurt inched across the frightening Traverse, every step measured against their terror of their crampons losing their grip on the brittle ice, or of the entire slope sliding out from under them. "Julie! Be careful!"

"I know, don't worry," she assured Kurt, her voice low, barely audible in the airless world, her words coming out in puffs of exhalation. "Just. Keep. Moving! No. Time. To. Lose!"

Kurt kept his eyes constantly flitting between the ice at his feet and the progress of the four above him. They were moving slowly, but they were all still moving.

With every ounce a deadweight across their backs, Diemberger asked Julie if he should leave his rucksack clipped to the last piton anchored into the slope; they were 300 meters below the summit. Julie pushed her dark goggles above her eyes so she could see him better. *Yes,* she gasped between labored breaths, *let's leave it,* Diemberger saw that her eyes were shining before she replaced her goggles. Diemberger left his ruck-sack of emergency bivy gear while Julie continued to carry a load of essentials in a smaller hip sack. No matter how far they got, they would now have to return at least to this piton, their only survival gear above Camp IV.

As they reached 8,400 meters (27,550 feet) they found Mrowka. Unbelievably, she was asleep, her head resting comfortably on her right arm, her ash-brown hair framing her calm face, her hands holding fast to her tools. Earlier in the day Bauer had found her, head on her hands, asleep above the last fixed rope. Incredulous, he snapped a picture, the icy slope yawning behind her under the hot sun. Julie and Kurt were frustrated and afraid that her slow progress ahead of them would impede their ability to reach the summit within a safe time frame to descend in daylight. As Kurt shook her awake he held tightly to her yellow anorak, fearing she would pitch off the slope if she woke up suddenly. "You should go down," he urged. "No!" she insisted. "I am fine. My naps are perfectly normal." The Ant was not ready to give up.

Mrowka jumped up and continued climbing. Julie, terrified that Mrowka might fall and hit them on descent, yelled to Diemberger to overtake the newly energized woman. But he could not. She raced out ahead of him, and after a few desperate attempts he sagged back and decided to let her climb out of their fall line. Taking the opportunity to rest, Julie and Kurt leaned into the slope and looked at the world miles below them. Along with the flotilla of mountain masts sailing in the serpentine Baltoro and Godwin-Austen Glaciers, they also saw that the weather was worsening, and the sky darkening.

"Look!" Julie suddenly shouted, pointing above them. Yes! Two stick figures, their arms raised in triumph. The summit. It was that close. It was 3:15 P.M.—they should have plenty of time.

Willi Bauer was the first to descend, and when he reached them 150 meters from the summit, what he said puzzled Julie.

"Are you sure you still want to go up?" he asked, obviously concerned at how late in the day it was. Julie didn't understand. Kurt had said it would take only an hour from where they were. "No," Willi said, "it took us four hours to get from there to the summit," but he pointed to a distant point down the mountain.

"Ahh, that's a different story," Kurt assured Julie. "We are fine. We have plenty of time." But he wasn't so sure, asking Bauer if he had seen any good spots for a bivouac if they ended up making the summit late. It was already four o'clock, the time they had determined would be their summit or turnaround time. But they were so close. Julie looked at Kurt, her eyes excited, smiling.

"I feel very fit!" she assured him. They lowered their heads and continued up the unrelenting wall toward the summit.

Suddenly they came upon Mrowka, now resting her head on her arm with every step. They took the opportunity to pass her, and when Rouse appeared over an ice bulge on his descent from the summit, Julie implored him, "Please take care of your partner. We cannot. She won't listen to us."

Al leaned close, putting his arm around her bent shoulders. *It's too late, Mrowka. Come down with me. Please.* Crying tears of frustration and exhaustion, she nodded against his chest, straightened herself, adjusted her gear, and followed Rouse down. She knew she would jeopardize the summit bids, even lives, of those around her if she were to continue up. As much as she loved the mountains, she was not willing to risk others' lives or her own to climb them.

. . .

Finally, after three years and as many attempts, Kurt made the final steps and reached the summit of K2 sometime in the early evening, with Julie joining him moments later.

"Our very special mountain," she whispered as they embraced on the curved expanse of the summit crest. The sky above them was clear with the first stars of the evening, but the clouds now obscured everything below them but the nearest ridgelines of the mountain. She looked about her in dull awe, her brain struggling with a growing numbness to register that here she was, the third woman and nearly the first Briton to reach this point. She looked over at Broad Peak, its three distinct peaks in a swirl of clouds. Just a year ago she had stood there, looking here! It looked so close that she felt she could touch it, but she knew, she had learned, that it was farther and more difficult to reach than the moon.

After about forty-five minutes on the summit, with the clouds darkening to a sinister gray and the wind bringing a new chill, Julie was increasingly anxious, knowing all too well the pitfalls on descent.

"It's high time we left," she said, and they turned to begin their long journey home.

Diemberger decided to descend first, reasoning that they would be quicker with his greater skill at finding the route. But it was a risky choice. Usually the stronger climber stays above the weaker on descent so that if the lower climber falters or falls, the higher climber can stop the lower climber before momentum is built up that could peel them off the slope.

As they made their painstaking way, the light fading with every step, Kurt suddenly heard a scream.

"Oh! Kuuuuuuurt!" Julie yelled as she fell.

With the instincts of four decades behind him, he swung around and, gathering all the force he could muster, rammed his ice ax into the slope. Throwing his body on top of it, he prayed beyond reason to hold them against the awesome power of the fall about to hit him. Her body flew past him down the slope, already at an incredible speed, and with a vicious shock the rope between them became taut, and he was catapulted into the air and followed her down the icy wall toward the glacier 12,000 feet below. *This is it,* he thought. *This is finally it. After all of our efforts, and success, this is it. I can't believe we are going to die on K2, of all mountains. Our mountain.*

Suddenly they stopped. It was deathly quiet, the wind whistling around them the only sound. Julie was above him on the slope, unable to free her ice ax from under her body, and Kurt lay in a natural self-belay position, hands and feet firmly gripping the ice.

"Are you all right, Julie? Julie!" Kurt's voice emerged from the void beneath her.

"Yes!" She tried to sound convincing, but her head hurt and she was twisted all around. She tried to maneuver herself off the ax but found herself again slipping down the slope, this time thankfully coming to rest gently against Kurt.

"We must stop for the night," he said. She barely nodded in agreement. *Whatever you think.* But when they tried to dig a snow hole, the ice was so hard that their axes bounced off it like staples trying to penetrate a steel tank. Their emergency stash was hundreds of feet below them, hanging uselessly on the piton. With only a couple of hard candies to share, wearing just their down jackets and shell pants, they spent a wretched night, hugging and rubbing each other's limbs, trying to stay warm and awake. Sleep could be fatal. But all Julie wanted to do was sleep. *It wouldn't be so awful,* the thought moved through her muddy brain slowly. *I could just close my eyes and that would be it. Just to fall asleep and not wake up.* She knew she wanted to die in the mountains eventually. Hell, maybe "eventually" had come. Her face hurt, particularly her nose, which was throbbing in the cold, and her fingers had begun tingling. Somewhere she had lost a glove. Deep in her brain she knew that a lost glove at 8,000 meters was disastrous. She rested her head against Kurt's chest, her eyelids feeling like magnets held them shut. In the end it was the pain that kept her awake as one by one the cells of her face and fingers froze, the ice crystals tearing through the tissues, destroying them.

When the black night finally gave way to shades of gray, Julie looked around her and felt an awful terror rise in her chest. She could barely see. The world was fuzzy, unreal. *Maybe it's just the snow. But no, even*

Kurt, right here, is blurry. She didn't tell him, didn't want him to worry. Besides, what could he do? She held her bare hand close to her eyes and saw that it was white and felt like a block of wood. *At least the pain has stopped,* she thought dully.

She and Kurt barely spoke as they stretched their frozen, cramped, painful legs and arms and started down toward Camp IV. She tried to focus on her aikido Centre. *Breathe from it,* she told herself. *Breathe from your Centre and from your Centre will you find power.* It had been her mantra in many tough spots, and she intoned it now, hoping it would provide some help as she struggled against the pull of the mountain. It seemed to want to pluck her right off its frozen slope.

During their pitiful bivy the threatening storm had held off. But as they started down the winds picked up and the first flakes of snow became a gray fog that rapidly enveloped them, obscuring their way. Soon they were zigzagging across the steep ice below the Bottleneck, desperately looking for the flat plateau that would lead them to the tents, terrified that they might wander off one of the Shoulder's sheer faces. *Perhaps this is where Maurice lost Liliane,* Kurt thought, increasingly anxious at being adrift in this 8,000-meter pea soup with mind-numbing drops on either side. Finally, the slope leveled off, and Julie sank to the snow to rest. Kurt yelled into the gray-white void, "Hello! Is anybody there?" He wondered, *Has everyone left Camp IV? Are Julie and I alone in the featureless hell?*

"Yes! This way!" Willi Bauer's voice answered from the mist. Kurt urged Julie to get up. Hurry! But she stayed low, hugging the ground.

"I can't see well," she finally admitted. "I'd rather crawl into camp."

Bauer, horrified, watched as Julie emerged from the white cloud and approached the tents on all fours, her nose blackened from frostbite and skin hanging from her bare fingers on one hand.

"Willi, please take Julie in with you and get her some tea," Kurt begged.

"Of course," Bauer said, guiding the semiconscious woman to the Koreans' tent. Diemberger then collapsed in the small French tent alone, glad to have someone else take care of Julie, to drift off into grateful sleep.

Julie half-sat, half-lay in the Austrian/Korean tent, glad to be alive. Surely the worst was over. She knew her hand was in bad shape, but she'd live. Whatever was wrong with her eyes would be fine as soon as she could breathe the thick air of Base Camp, even of Camp I or II. The plain black tea was delicious, as good as her fine mulled cider that she had steeped over her Bothy stove for hours. But she had trouble bringing it to her mouth. She kept missing her lips, instead hitting her cheek or chin. The Austrians pretended not to notice. When she was finished, she put down the empty cup and mumbled her thanks. Snuggling into her sleeping bag, she was able to give in to her heavy exhaustion and sleep, finally safe.

By the time she awoke hours later, the storm was upon them with a fury. The sleep had done her well and her head felt a little better, although her vision remained blurred, off balance somehow. But she wanted to be with Kurt. It seemed odd that she was not with him after what they'd been through, and were still going through. She thanked the Austrians for their generosity and help and squeezed out of the tent, bracing against the blast of brittle air that hit her as she steadied herself outside. She didn't need 20–20 vision to know the only thing to see was white. She could feel its oppressive strength, its complete wall, preventing even an attempt at descent. *Well, maybe tomorrow will be better. Maybe tomorrow we can start down.* She needed to feel her lungs fill with thick air, something that was simply impossible at this altitude. No matter how hard she breathed, the suffocating desire to breathe ever deeper continued. She just couldn't satisfy the craving for air. *There isn't enough to support a tick up here. Why should my lungs be any different?*

Kurt heard her struggling outside to open the tent door. "You could have come back earlier," he grumbled into his beard, feeling grouchy and out of sorts. She barely heard the accusation in his voice, the annoyance. She was exhausted from the effort of moving between tents. She fell into the tent, and he pulled her into an embrace.

In the morning he felt remorse for snapping at her, for not expressing the joy he felt at seeing her again. But she was expressionless, unable to share in his celebration over having conquered their K2.

"I don't know . . ." was all she'd say.

Kurt watched her with a growing panic: the poor vision was a sure sign of a concussion or cerebral edema, a fatal leakage of fluid on the brain that if not treated with immediate descent was almost always fatal. Its exact cause still a medical mystery, cerebral or pulmonary edema results when the oxygen-thin air upsets the natural flow of liquid between the membranes of the brain or lungs, causing fluids to leak where they shouldn't go. In the case of the brain, it causes the already wet sponge of the cerebral cortex to become water-logged, pushing against the rigid skull. Victims suffer a range of symptoms, among them headaches, nausea, dizziness, impaired vision, lack of motor skills, apathy, and an enervating exhaustion. Staving off death, the brain shuts down all but the necessary functions and pulls the last of the blood supply into the body's core.

Watching Julie struggle to focus and hold a teacup, he reached over and felt that her lips were cold. Her body was shutting down, giving less and less blood to the superfluous lips, feet, hands, nose. She showed him her blackened fingers, and he silently realized that she would probably lose at least two of them. "Don't worry, Julie," he lied, "they'll be okay." She looked at him with such sadness and panic, he felt like his heart would break. *But what if I can't hold my sword*, she wondered, her eyes wide with fear and sadness. *My sword, my power, my peace.* He felt a helpless dread; there was nothing he could do. The storm had trapped them all at 8,000 meters and until it broke, descent would be suicide. But still, he had never seen her so weak, so vulnerable. He pulled her close, snuggling her into the warmth of their down sleeping bags.

The snow continued as the temperature plunged to –20 degrees Fahrenheit and the wind gusted to 100 miles per hour. Julie felt rather than watched the sides of the small tent push further and further in. She tried to find the motivation to get up, get out of the sleeping bag, find her boots, find her remaining glove, get out of the tent, dig it free of the crushing snow. But she just couldn't seem to move. The effort to leave her warm sleeping bag was just too much. Kurt also knew he should mobilize, but he didn't. Soon their entire entrance was under snow, trapping them inside. Kurt yelled for help. Al Rouse came immediately to their rescue and began digging at the entrance like a dog in a snowbank. After many minutes of heavy huffing and puffing, Rouse announced that he hadn't yet found the entrance but couldn't dig anymore. Diemberger shouted for Willi Bauer to come help them. Bauer soon stood outside, swinging his ax to clear the snow away from the door. Finally, he found the door, now reduced to a small porthole.

"You'll have to do the rest," he called in to Kurt, and he'd have to do it fast, before the door closed over again in the swirling snow. Kurt, desperate to get out of the tent fast and fearing his boots would get him stuck in the narrow opening, wiggled out of the tent without them. While his climbing brethren had long since switched to the lighter, more water-resistant plastic double-layer boots, Diemberger held fast to his age-old trusted leather ones, which, while more comfortable and durable, were prone to becoming soaked and then frozen solid in the arctic conditions. Now standing in his stocking feet, he looked at the ruined tent, its support poles bent and worthless against the endless snow.

"Julie," Kurt called into the tent, "we have to separate. The tent is finished."

"Let me go with the Austrians, you go with Alan," she called back, handing him his sleeping bag through the collapsed entrance.

Kurt called over to Bauer, "Willi, please, take Julie in with you. Can you help? Now, immediately!"

"Yes, of course," Bauer, replied, reemerging from his tent.

Julie struggled through the compressed snow to get out of the tent, its pressing walls suddenly filling her with a claustrophobic panic, but she couldn't move. There was just too much pressure, and she didn't have the strength. She stuck her hand through the entrance, feeling the biting cold drill into her skin. "Help!" she yelled, waving it in the air. Relief flooding her, she felt a strong hand grip hers. *Kurt, yes, help me out*. But it wasn't Kurt.

"Willi will help you. I'm cold, I have to run. See you later!" Kurt's voice faded off as he stumbled down to Al's tent. "Please let me in!"

Kurt's voice was thin with panic. Without hesitation, Al Rouse opened his tent and Diemberger crawled inside.

Willi pulled Julie through the small entrance of the wrecked tent, and she reached back in for her sleeping bag, then followed Willi back to the Austrian tent. It was August 6.

For several indistinguishable days the seven climbers sat in various states of hibernation in their lofty prison, the wind blowing the snow horizontally over the wide Shoulder, rattling their tents. It sounded like a freight train traveling over the ridge doing about 175 miles per hour. Without his boots and having taken off his wet clothes, Diemberger lay naked in his sleeping bag while Al Rouse and Mrowka Wolf did the necessary work of shoveling the tent free of snow and gathering new snow for the endless supply of water and tea needed to keep them all hydrated. At 8,000 meters the climbers breathed fast but deep as their lungs desperately tried to get enough oxygenated red blood cells to their brains. The increased respiration burned even more of the body's precious fluids, and climbers knew they had to drink as fast as the gas could melt the snow. But with the snow less than 10 percent water content, a four-cup pan would yield less than a quarter-cup. Even with the gas burning constantly, they simply couldn't keep up.

At some point that first or second day, Julie forced herself to get up and put on her boots. She had to see Kurt. She had to make sure he was all right. She had to hear his reassuring voice. Surely he would tell her that the storm had to end soon, that they would be able to start down. She made her way to Al's tent, bent nearly double in the storm, the snow hitting her face like pebbles.

"Kurt, are you all right?" Her voice sounded odd to her, as if coming from someone else.

"Ah! Julie! Yes, yes. Please, lean down so I can see you." Kurt struggled from the far side of the crowded tent to see her face.

But she didn't seem to hear him. Maybe she was expecting him to emerge from the tent, to give her a hug, to encourage her, but he didn't.

"I'm feeling rather strange," she finally admitted, her voice carried away in the wind. Kurt struggled to get a glimpse of her face, but all he could see was her long brown and gray hair swinging in the wind.

"As soon as I have my boots, I will come visit you," he told her. "You must drink and tomorrow we will go down." He tried to sound reassuring as she moved off into the white mist, still a faceless form.

"Bye-bye," she said and retreated back to the Austrians' tent.

Two miles below them, Jim Curran, one of the few denizens left in the deserted Base Camp, was watching the mountain with increasing dread. He knew the climbers' planned schedules; if all had gone accordingly, his friend and teammate Al Rouse should have been back in Base Camp that day. Now. But there was no sign of him as Curran scoured the route with high-powered binoculars. A few days before, on the afternoon of the 5th, the Koreans had made it back to Base Camp, and the morning of the 6th the two surviving Poles had returned. They had been the last to come off the mountain.

The blizzard had blown through Base Camp for the past two days, but the morning of the 7th looked hopeful. "I've woken to a wintry landscape, but the wind has dropped," Curran wrote in his journal. "K2 is clear up to the Shoulder, and the pinnacle behind which Camp IV lies is also visible, so the whole of the Abruzzi and the whole of the descent is out of the clouds. . . . Anyone up there will, I imagine, be hotfooting it down."

But they weren't hotfooting it anywhere, and by noon the winds had picked up and the snow was again blowing across the Shoulder, obscuring the route above Camp III. The small porthole in the storm had opened briefly and slammed shut again, and no one had left Camp IV.

Julie lay in her sleeping bag awake, but she could feel sleep pulling her back down into its comforting womb. Willi, Alfred, and Hannes were so close that she could barely distinguish where her breath ended and theirs began. Their long leg bones pushed against hers, their arms occasionally knocking her head or chest. Their beards were coated in the same frost as the hair that framed her face. She stared up at the tent bucking and fluttering in the constant roar of wind. She had been in storms before, both here on K2 and on Everest, but this was different. She had gone from panic to anger to dread, and now, to what? She hardly felt a thing. Her blurred vision helped her stay cocooned away from the worst of the reality they faced. The men were taking good care of her. The Koreans had left them with a well-stocked tent, and she drank as much tea as her shrinking stomach could handle. Eating was more difficult, but she managed to choke down some dry breads and odd fishy soup. As the wind screamed over the tent fabric and pushed anew at its poles, she thought of Terry and Chris and Lindsay. Of their funny Bothy and its cozy, narrow living room, a room crowded with only four people in it. She thought of how the sun would flood in the southern window and warm the entire room on a chilly November day. She thought of the first time she had seen Terry and his remarkably blue eyes, and how she had marveled the first time she saw Christopher suckling at her breast. What an odd, indescribably joyful sensation that had been. She thought of her wonderful Vespa and tried to remember what had finally happened to it. Had she toppled it one too many times? It was a wonder that thing never killed her. Her lips cracked in a faint smile remembering how many bushes she christened until she figured out the damn brakes and clutch. And finally she thought of the way the rocks at World's End felt under her fingers, and how the warmth caressed her skin and allowed her to feel like she was floating up the wall, effortless, tireless, weightless. It was freedom, and she breathed deep remembering the release of her body.

Then she closed her eyes.

Diemberger's and Bauer's accounts differ as to the exact day, but the morning of either the 7th or the 8th Kurt was awakened by a voice calling to him.

"Kurt! Kurt!" Willi Bauer called across between the tents. "Julie has died in the night."

As simple as that. She was gone. K2 had claimed its third woman in as many ascents. The Black Summer's lethal count stood at nine.

Kurt heard the words, but they seemed barely to register. Al and

Mrowka tried to comfort the inconsolable legend they housed, but he recoiled from their touch and curled deeper in his sleeping bag. He scarcely moved for the next three days.

When Diemberger didn't appear to see Julie for the last time or help with removing the body, Willi and his teammates pulled her out of their tent and over to the ruined French bivy. Once again taking his ax, Willi cut through its roof with one swift arcing swipe. Carefully tucking her hands over her chest, they slowly lowered her in. With a last look, touch, perhaps a lingering hand on her arm, they pulled the flapping fabric of the shredded tent around her and walked away.

While the men put Julie to rest, Kurt remained in his sleeping bag. With Julie's death, his hibernation became almost a coma, his thoughts focusing on one fact: he needed to get his boots back. He couldn't leave without them. Thinking about Julie, about bad choices, if-onlys, could-have-beens, only caused him more pain, more grief. They were the unchangeable past. His boots at least were the future.

Sometime on the 8th the camp ran out of high-altitude cooking gas, and the climbers were left trying to melt the snow in their mouths or in plastic bags between their legs. But most of their blood had moved away from their extremities in order to keep their vital organs alive. There was no warmth between their legs, under their arms, or in their mouths. The bags of snow remained cold and dry, their mouths filled with airy powder. They all began to show signs of severe dehydration, starvation, and a slow hypoxic descent into hypothermic death, particularly Al Rouse. The man who had night after night relinquished his tent to climbers in need and who had broken trail most of the ascent, particularly on the last grueling summit day, declined quickly into semiconscious ranting, waving his arms about and talking wildly about Jesus Christ and how desperately thirsty he was.

Diemberger dimly registered Rouse's increased agitation and incoherence, wondering why Rouse was wasting so much energy, while he dozed, curled up naked in his sleeping bag, waiting for someone to bring him his boots.

Finally, on August 10 he awoke to find that the tireless Mrowka had retrieved his boots and put them under his head. After nearly a week in the subzero temperatures, the soaked leather was frozen solid. It would be a long, wretched climb down in them, if he could even get his feet into them in the first place. He saw what looked like shadows of sunlight on the outside of the tent. It was now or never. Diemberger looked at Rouse, who begged for water. Mrowka looked away. There was none. Unable to get out of the tent, Rouse would have to be left where he lay. After sacrificing so much for others, there was no one left who could in turn help him. Nearby Willi Bauer tried to rouse Imitzer and Wieser, who had fallen into dazed stupors.

Diemberger went over to where Julie lay in the crushed tent and, almost shyly, reached in to touch her for the last time. Seeing that she was lying under a sleeping bag that he hoped would give Rouse a measure of comfort in his sure death, he took it off Julie, said a final goodbye, and walked it over to Rouse's tent, where he stuffed it inside near Rouse.

"Please, water," Rouse's pitiful rasp begged Diemberger as he stood to leave.

"Yes, Al, I'll go find you some water," Diemberger promised the dead man, and walked away.

Finally, the ragtag group of five stumbled away from the wretched Camp IV, but Imitzer and Wieser made it less than 300 feet (100 meters) before collapsing onto the snow. Finished. They would stay where they fell. "Try to get back to the tents," Diemberger urged, but he knew it was useless. They didn't have the energy to crawl.

Slowly, painfully, Diemberger, Bauer, and Wolf began their descent. After a week above 26,000 feet (8,000 meters), six days of it stuck in a tent without food or water, they were truly the walking dead, but they were walking. Willi was in the lead, burrowing through the waist-deep snow like a plow, the tiny Mrowka right behind him, Diemberger following at a distance. They reached the Koreans' tent at Camp III at 7,300 meters only to find it destroyed by avalanche and wind, so they continued down, praying that Camp II hadn't met a similar fate. Every inch they descended was one inch closer to safety, one ounce more of air pressure filling their oxygen-deprived lungs and brains. Inch by inch. Mrowka was moving with particular care, slowly switching from

rope to rope with an awkward abseiling device, while Willi and Kurt
had switched to just sliding down the rope on a carabiner; now that
they were on a less severe slope they didn't need the extra safety of a
descending device, but Mrowka wasn't taking any chances. Kurt, frustrated and anxious to get down, clipped around and ahead of Mrowka,
leaving her as he quickly descended the last meters to Camp II at 6,700
meters. There, like a mirage, he found Willi brewing soup. Willi silently
handed him a steaming cup.

"Where's Mrowka?" Willi asked, and Kurt said she was a short distance behind him, on her way.

By midnight Mrowka had not arrived. They waited all night and in the
morning were unable to ascend to look for her. If they had, they would
have found her, as climbers did the following year, on the ropes, her head
calmly resting on the slope, her anchors holding her fast to the mountain.
She had once again simply fallen asleep and needed, as she had many
times before, a nudge to wake her up and get her going. But no one had
been there to give her that gentle shove. The Little Ant, who had been
strongest of the miserable cluster at Camp IV, digging out others' tents,
bringing tea while there was still gas, getting Diemberger his boots, had
finally worn herself out. The Black Summer, which began with the death
of Smolich and Pennington six weeks before, had claimed its last victim.

Willi was the first to make it to Base Camp, an awful apparition,
stumbling like a drunken ghost through the rocks and ice toward the
tents. He mumbled that Kurt and Mrowka were somewhere behind
him, and teams were quickly organized to try to rescue the survivors.

Jim Curran, desperate for news of Al, rushed up to the base of the
mountain and at midnight nearly bumped into Kurt as he inched backward down the last steps of the mountain, face into the slope, crampons
and ice ax tapping rhythmically into the slope.

"I've lost Julie" was all he said.

Weeks later Terry Tullis made his way to Kurt's hospital bed in Innsbruck, where he was recovering from surgery to remove three frostbitten fingers on his right hand. When Kurt turned and saw who was there,
he cried, "Oh, Terry, you've come," Tullis remembered, tears filling his

eyes telling the story. "I think it was a relief to him that I'd come to see him. Without a shotgun." But he'd come to offer solace, not shame, which Diemberger gratefully accepted.

Terry believes that K2 would have been Julie's last Himalayan adventure. "I think she would have settled back in here and become as she was before, just a straightforward mother, loving the garden, getting out in the sun, teaching handicapped children, walking the dog. In fact, she was a very normal lady. It was just this sort of aberration that she had," he said, laughing at the understatement of her fascination and passion for high-altitude mountains.

When asked years later why he and Willi Bauer survived and the others did not, Diemberger said that his experience taught him to conserve his energy. "They were also very fat and very slow," Jim Curran said less kindly but nonetheless accurately. Curran's loss of his dear friend Al Rouse remains a raw wound, and the jovial, gentle man bows his head in grief when he relives that awful summer. "Al was built like a Greyhound. Kurt and Willi were big, big men, and I think they just carried enough reserves to stick it out for that time. I think Kurt has the perfect survivor's physique and also fantastic willpower. Stubborn, stubborn old bastard just stuck it out and refused to give in."

While Wanda Rutkiewicz did not condemn Diemberger for leaving Mrowka behind, she did question whether he treated the Polish woman differently because they were not climbing partners: "Julie was important to Kurt, but Mrowka had been an intruder endangering their lives." Wanda wished, at the very least, that he had been able to admit to his own human frailty, even perhaps a clouded judgment. "After K2, Kurt could not say, 'Maybe I did not behave as I should have, but I couldn't think about the others; I had to save my own life.' But he never did, and I have this irrational bad feeling about him; it's irrational because I cannot judge him. I survived. I'm alive."

As she speaks of her sister, Zita Palau Latham's British-controlled emotions spill over when she thinks, not about how Julie died, but of what her sister is missing.

"She would have loved to be a grandmother," Zita says, pausing to let a horribly loose cough rumble through her tiny body, one gnarled hand holding onto her chest, the other keeping her cigarette aloft so that the ash doesn't fall on the velvet settee. It sounds like a freight train moving through a rickety covered bridge with a thousand loose boards. When she can again speak, with her eyes red from the effort and the emotion, she says, "She would have been so proud of Chris and Lindsay."

With his salt-and-pepper hair cut into short bristle, wearing a T-shirt and jeans, Chris Tullis belies his forty-one years. It's hard for him to realize that Julie has been gone from his life almost as long as she was in it. In fact, until recently his wife, also named Julie, never once heard him mention his mother's name. And now he's sitting on a memorial stone built for her near the climbing wall, talking about his "fun-loving, unpredictable, crazy" mother and how her death didn't come as a huge shock. Growing up in the climbing community exposed young Chris to the vagaries and violence of sudden death.

"I'd lived with it all my life, people going away and then you hear how all of a sudden somebody's been killed, and yes, one day I suspected that maybe it would be my mother that didn't come back from an expedition. There was a certain inevitability about it."

But what really upset him was her postcard, received only days before the family got word that she had died.

"She said she was coming home and 'there's been too many deaths' that year and that was it." For several days he tried to believe the postcard, not the reality. But like Julie herself, Chris Tullis finds a certain measure of peace in her dying.

"I'm actually really pleased she died somewhere doing what she wanted to do, rather than in a plane crash or car accident or something like that." Even so, it is not a life he would choose for himself, particularly now that he has children of his own. "I just wouldn't want them to go through that uncertainty." Although Chris himself lived with that uncertainty, he insists that he doesn't resent her choosing a life quite apart from being a mother and grandmother.

"People have to do what they want to do, and I think my mum probably had the urge to go and do stuff a lot earlier on. The opportunity came along for her to do it, and I think she grabbed it and good for her.

My mother went out and did what she wanted to do. She had a desire to go and climb big mountains. She loved it." But surely he must wish she were here now, part of his life, his children's lives?

"I think she would have enjoyed it, yes," he says, jiggling his leg, as if to offset his quivering chin, "and I think she would have loved that we are all climbing. Me and the kids."

And indeed they are. From Julie and Terry's humble beginnings with their small climbing crag, Soft Rock Climbing and the recently opened Evolution Indoor Climbing have grown into a bustling outdoor climbing area and indoor gym, tucked into the bucolic English countryside.

"I think she would have loved this," Terry acknowledges, looking at their grandson lead a climb up the 90-degree wall. "She would have loved this a lot."

"What?" Thor Kieser said out loud, sitting up in his tent. "What the fuck was that?"

He and his 1992 American-Russian team had arrived at K2 Base Camp only a few days before for their attempt on the mountain. It was a dark, still night, and the air at Base Camp was unusually quiet, so still he could hear the stream dribbling over the rocks at the edge of camp. But he had heard something else, something entirely different. It was a voice. A voice on a radio call.

"Camp IV to Base Camp, do you copy, over?" Shit, there it was again.

Adrenaline pumping, he jumped out of his tent, the rocks cold under his stocking feet. He looked over; his teammate Scott Fischer stood outside his tent looking around. The two men looked at each other—both knew what they heard.

"What the fuck was that? There's no one on the mountain, is there?"

"No way, man, no one," Fischer said, almost in a whisper.

That was it, they never heard it again. But the sound of that voice will be in Kieser's head for the rest of his life.

"Camp IV to Base Camp, do you read, over?"

It was a female voice. A British voice. He can still hear it.

CHAPTER 7

THE PIONEER
PERISHES

Don't stand at my grave and cry; I am not here anymore.
I am thousands of breezes in the wind.

—INSCRIPTION ON WANDA RUTKIEWICZ'S TOMB

By 1990 Wanda Rutkiewicz was approaching fifty years of age, her major mountaineering achievements were behind her, and much to her dislike she was being called the Matriarch of the High Mountains. She had been the first Pole to reach the summits of both Everest in 1978 and K2 in 1986, but that was ancient history, and raising money and climbing the big mountains were becoming ever more difficult challenges. Once a hero of Polish climbing, she was finding herself ignored and overlooked by a new, young, brash group of climbers entering the mountaineering world. Not all of the disregard was the fault of changing times; much of it was rooted in her own iron will, which compelled her to fight even the most innocuous confrontations as if they were life-and-death battles.

One day she and Ewa Matuszewska were on a beach in Ustron Morski working on a particularly daunting chapter in Wanda's biography. Suddenly a volleyball from a nearby game flew toward them and hit Wanda on the head. With the speed of a tigress, she jumped up and returned the ball with a clean, powerful throw. Soon a handsome gentleman from the game appeared and invited her to join their game. With obvious pleasure, Wanda threw herself into the match. She was the only woman playing and did so without a hint of femininity. She had played professionally for the Polish national team, giving it up only when she realized she could go no further in the sport. But facing able competitors, she was diving for every ball, sending murderous serves, spiking at the net, and exploiting every weakness in the opponents' moves. The game, which until her entry had been for fun, suddenly became a true battle, a fascinating combat with each player playing to his maximum. Not surprisingly, the makeshift tournament gathered a crowd that cheered her every-victorious point.

It was not an isolated event. Wanda was absolutely determined to never be or play the victim. She was walking home one evening after training in a local gym when a mugger grabbed her bag and ran. After a few shocked moments, she chased after the thief, rapidly gaining on him. When the hapless crook turned and saw the fierce resolve and rage on her face, he wisely threw the bag back at Wanda and kept running.

The grit, pride, and sheer will that had kept her alive for so many years had also cut her off from many of her former friends and colleagues. For years Rutkiewicz had been able to gather Europe's best female climbers for first-ever attempts on the world's highest peaks. Now she was operating as an independent agent, choosing to buy onto already established expeditions in order to save time and money. By the end of the 1980s her expeditions were with relative strangers who often seemed to resent having "the great Wanda Rutkiewicz" suddenly part of their team. On one of her expeditions into the Karakoram a male teammate told the local Pakistani children that the word for candy was "pussy," and if they said this to Wanda she would give them candy. Unaware of the "joke," Rutkiewicz was followed through the dusty, narrow streets of Rawalpindi and Skardu by flocks of children screaming, "Wanda! Pussy!" in her bewildered face.

Although she had accomplished more than any woman ever had, she was often shunned and ignored by the climbing community, particularly the Poles. In the days of its struggling Cold War communism and then burgeoning Solidarity, Wanda had been a convenient posterwoman for the fraught country. But as a new Poland maneuvered itself into position for the twenty-first century, its legacy of women climbers was increasingly replaced by male climbers, and she was all but forgotten. In the Polish newspaper *Warsaw Voice*, a 2003 listing of the great

Polish mountaineering feats of the last twenty-five years totally omits Rutkiewicz.

In 1988 Wanda took a rare break from high-altitude climbing and traveled to the United States, where she gave lectures in Seattle and Berkeley and spent a weekend climbing in Yosemite. Wanda loved the feel of the warm, dry rock under her hands, as well as the carefree climbing world gathered at Camp IV, the hippie-like epicenter of scruffy climbers who gathered in Yosemite's main camping area every summer. Dressed in a flowing India print skirt and white blouse, her hair neatly styled, she was a feminine icon in their shabby midst.

Back at home, Matuszewska feared that Wanda's loneliness had become entrenched. As the two women conducted their years-long interview, Wanda told her that she had never met a man who supported any of her achievements. "They're always threatened by my passion," she said, "and jealous of the time I give to climbing. So I choose to be lonely. I have learned there is no other choice." Ewa looked at her friend, sadly realizing she was right. Once the mountains had been Wanda's refuge from the pain of her isolation, but now they were becoming another venue for that isolation.

When she climbed Gasherbrum II as part of the British Women's Expedition in 1989, she stood at the summit but felt a deep sadness looking at the sea of peaks where she had lost so many friends. K2 stood in brilliant relief against the cornflower-blue sky. She looked across the skyline of mountains at its stunning summit pyramid only a few kilometers away and thought of 1986. It had given her the greatest satisfaction, but now, three years later, she felt nothing but sadness. If she had had it to do over again, she would not have climbed the mountain. It had cost her too dearly.

While Wanda was in the Karakoram, she fulfilled a promise she had made to Barbara Kozlowska in 1985. That autumn Wanda had made another attempt on Broad Peak, but the trip had ended in disaster when Kozlowska, exhausted and descending the mountain alone, slipped as she crossed a thigh-deep glacial stream. She had not put on crampons and was thus unable to gain purchase in the icy, roaring water even though she was attached to fixed ropes that breached the stream. When Wanda descended the mountain later that day, she came upon Kozlowska's body hanging from the ropes, her face in the frigid water. Wanda cut her free and buried her in the rock scree at the base of Broad Peak. Wanda had vowed to return with more support and give her friend a proper burial at the Gilkey, as she had Halina.

It had taken her four years, but she kept her promise. She asked her friend Carlos Buhler, an American climber she had met a few years before, if he would help carry her friend's body from the makeshift grave to the Gilkey Memorial several hours' walk away. As they approached the spot where Wanda had put her friend four years before, they could see that the rocks had shifted and that areas of Barbara's body now lay exposed. The sun, wind, and shifting glacier had also torn at the clothing and flesh, rotting it where the sun was able to bake away at the skin, and flash-freezing it where it lay submerged in the ice. They choked back the bile that rose in their throats at the stench of decay. Clenching their jaws, they lifted the body and struggled to fit it into a rucksack. Unlike the newly dead, this body held no stiffness from rigor mortis; instead, the limbs hung heavy with muscle and bone, loose like Raggedy Ann arms and legs, the head looked like it might snap off as it fell back almost at a 90-degree angle from the neck. Silently, they folded her in half, her head down between her knees, and put her bottom first into the sack, allowing the legs and arms to poke out of the top. Before starting out for the Gilkey Memorial, Wanda wrapped Barbara's ruined face in a scarf, like a mummy before entombing.

They trudged up the glacier, heads bowed, taking turns at carrying the grisly load, its arms and legs bouncing along with each step. Slowly, painfully, they made their wretched progress to the Memorial. Finally, with the sun disappearing behind the ridge to the west, Wanda and Carlos bowed their heads and prayed, as much for those who had been lost as for themselves and each other as they turned from the grave once again to face their fates in the mountains.

In October 1989, Wanda drove to Ewa Matuszewska's house and pounded on the door. Ewa opened it, and Wanda walked in without a word and slammed a liter of vodka on the table in the small but cozy kitchen.

"He's dead," Wanda told her.

Jerzy Kukuczka, Poland's pride, a powerhouse of a climber and a sweetheart of a man who had carried her on his back the last kilometers into K2 Base Camp like a queen, was dead. Jurek was lost, perished on Lhotse, a mountain he had already climbed.

"Damn it, why did he have to try again? But he was so proud," Wanda said. "He needed to have a first ascent of an unclimbed route, he couldn't leave it alone. If he can die, none of us is safe." Wanda opened the bottle with a single twist of the cap. Ewa went to the cupboard and pulled out two glasses, almost expecting to see Wanda put the bottle to her lips before she had a chance to put the glasses on the table. Ewa brought one for herself: she wasn't much of a drinker, but she wanted at least to reduce the amount Wanda could drink by herself.

Wanda poured the clear 100-proof liquor quickly, and both glasses overflowed onto the table. Wanda picked up her glass, put it to her lips, jerked her head back, and downed the entire contents in one gulp. She put the glass down on the wet tabletop and refilled it. Ewa stared at her friend. She urged Wanda to slow down, but she didn't and soon the bottle was empty. When Wanda had swallowed the last drop, she stood up, surprisingly steady, and walked to the door.

Ewa knew she should stop her from leaving, from driving, but she didn't. She couldn't. You just didn't tell Wanda no.

Ewa gave Wanda a quick hug and told her again how sorry she was about Jurek's death. She knew what the man had meant to her. She knew that Wanda didn't have many friends, or many men that she loved more than Jurek, and she knew his loss would be carried heavily for the rest of Wanda's life.

Wanda looked at Ewa with sad, tired eyes but said nothing. The door closed behind her, and soon Ewa heard her sports car rev up and then screech out of its parking space. Ewa sat at the table and listened until it drove out of earshot.

The friends never mentioned the night again.

· · ·

In 1990, as her body slowed and her prospects dwindled, Wanda nonetheless went about planning her climbing life with a new frenzy. Perhaps hoping to quell speculation that she was past her prime, she announced to the world late that year that she would become the first woman to climb all fourteen of the world's 8,000-meter peaks. But she set the bar impossibly high. Having achieved six of those fourteen by 1990, she devised a media scheme called her "Caravan of Dreams" in which she would climb the last eight peaks in *just over a single year*, something never before planned, let alone achieved. Sponsors were less than eager about pouring a lot of money into the scheme, Wanda Rutkiewicz or no Wanda Rutkiewicz.

Ewa Matuszewska tried to help her out, suggesting that she trade on the value of her name and status by opening a mountain gear store. She told Wanda, "You won't have to do a thing; the store would use your name and give you a percentage of the profits." Wanda sat quietly, listening to her idea. When Ewa was done, Wanda looked at her coldly and snapped, "If you think it's such a good investment, why don't you quit your job and do it?" Hurt and insulted, Ewa never mentioned it again.

Wanda's life outside of the mountains was entirely focused on how fast she could return to the mountains, with every minute she spent measured against its worth in getting her back on an expedition. Refusing to waste a single moment waiting in line, but unwilling to give up her car, she would set her alarm for 3:00 A.M., dress quickly in her small two-room apartment, and drive to the nearest gas station, just to avoid the gas rationing queues. She also stopped buying ham and meat; both items required hours-long waits in markets.

Wanda continued scrambling for expedition monies and equipment and trying to plan a workable climbing schedule. She had climbed an 8,000-meter peak every two years since her first, Everest, twelve years before, and now she wanted to climb the remaining eight in less than two years. Even she admitted that it was an "insane" plan, but nonetheless she rationalized in her press release that "reducing the interval between climbs can maintain the climber's body systems in a permanent state of altitude acclimatization." What she didn't mention was that even the fittest body typically needs four to six months to recuperate after climbing above 8,000 meters and that most Himalayan climbs require a minimum of six weeks, given the trek in and out, weather delays, and conditions on the mountains. But she was undaunted, lightly brushing off her critics as she rushed headlong into a flurry of activity organizing her impossible Dream. "I am not going to wait until I'm sixty to realize my dreams."

By the end of 1991, with only a few months left in her schedule, she had climbed only two of the eight, Cho Oyu (8,201 meters, 26,906 feet) and Annapurna (8,091 meters, 26,545 feet), and the latter came at great physical and emotional cost.

First climbed by the French in 1950 during Maurice Herzog's harrowing expedition, Annapurna has an astounding ascent to death rate of 42 percent, the deadliest of the Himalayas. It claimed some of mountaineering's greatest climbers, among them Anatoli Boukreev and Wanda's own friend, Alison Chadwick-Onyszkiewicz, in 1978. In the fifty-plus years since it was first climbed, Annapurna has had only 130 ascents, while suffering 54 deaths, mostly due to avalanches and rockfall. Even the most climbable side of the mountain is an avalanche trap, and like many mountains, it has suffered the ravaging effects of global warming, raining down on climbers an unpredictable flurry of rocks, ice seracs, and cornices that are melting out of the mountain at alarming rates.

When Rutkiewicz arrived at Base Camp in October 1991, she found herself on a fractious and angry team. The irrationally quick schedule of climbing her eight Dream mountains required that she come in to a Base Camp at the last minute, relying on her teammates to do the work of establishing the high camps and fixing the ropes on the dangerous sections of the mountain. Her lack of involvement and work on the mountain angered her teammates and prevented her from really bonding with them.

Determined that late was better than never, Wanda threw herself into helping establish the last remaining high camp. Less than two weeks after her arrival, she left Base Camp for her first summit bid but was turned back by heavy winds. After a few days' rest, she and teammate

Bogdan Stefko tried again. This time the weather was in their favor, and the pair climbed strongly. But only hours out of Base Camp Wanda heard the *pluck-pluck-pluck* of rocks bouncing down from the slope above. She knew not to look up; if one of the rocks were to hit her face rather than her helmet, more than just her climb would be finished. With nowhere to go, she plastered her body against the slope and prayed that the worst of the rocks would miss her. Suddenly a blinding pain exploded in her thigh. With a sickening fear, she knew it was her bad leg. When the last of the rocks skittered off below her, she looked down to assess the damage. Luckily, the rock hadn't torn through her climbing pants, and as she gingerly ran her fingers along her femur bone, she breathed a sigh of relief: even if it had rebroken, it wasn't a compound fracture like before. No bone protruded from the hard line of her thigh. *But damn, it hurts!* she thought. *Maybe the rock has severed some muscle tissue and tendons.* A wave of nausea made her swallow hard as an excruciating pain traveled up her body. She waited for it to pass and for the black in front of her eyes to clear. Then she turned to Bogdan. "Let's go," she said. She may have been hurt, but she could still move.

Krzysztof Wielicki watched from Camp II as she made her agonizingly slow progress up the mountain. As team leader, he decided her climb was over. She was never a fast climber, even on a good day, and now she was dangerously slow. When she reached camp, he told her that Bogdan would continue up the mountain, with him, and that she should descend immediately and attend to her damaged leg.

"No! I won't give up. Don't take my climbing partner," she cried. "I don't want to climb alone." But Wielicki would hear none of it. Without another word, he and Stefko continued their ascent, leaving her to climb the mountain alone.

Fighting back tears, she grabbed the fixed line and jammed her ascending device onto it. She slid the jumar up the rope but found she was unable to lift the damaged leg. She had taken painkillers to dull the ache, but she couldn't lift the leg with the injured muscle. So with one hand on the jumar and the other hooked under her left thigh, she pulled with the ascending device and hoisted her leg with the other, step by step, camp by camp, thousands of feet up the mountain. Thankfully, the team had established miles of fixed line on the mountain, enabling her to inch her way up the hazardous South Face of the mountain, one of the most difficult routes in the Himalayas. As she climbed she talked aloud to herself, as she had so many times before. *How much better it would be to have a companion, even a friend, to travel through these infinite spaces,* she thought, *but it was my choice to join this team as a free agent rather than a partner. My choice. Now I have to deal with it. No one caused my injury, no one promised me anything.* It was painful and terrifying, but she wasn't about to quit. Suddenly she remembered her failed attempt on Broad Peak, when she had looked down into a crevasse high on the mountain and seen the body of a climber lying at the bottom. Transfixed and terrified, she had stared at the broken man and wondered at her fear. Why should the dead frighten her? But the image haunted her still. *Stop it, Wanda!* she said, giving the jumar a rough push upward. *Just stop it. You're going to climb this mountain, alone, hurt or otherwise!* Her words were carried away in the winds swirling around Annapurna, and she pushed and lifted, pushed and lifted.

When she stopped for the night, she peeled off her climbing clothes to assess the damage to her leg. Just as she had thought: there was no break, but the bruise was purple and black and swelling to a large, angry mound on her upper thigh. She elevated it as best she could and reached for the radio to call to Krzysztof and Bogdan. She told them how far she had made it and asked again that one of them wait so that she would not have to climb the last 800 meters of largely unknown terrain by herself. Again they refused. "You are a liability," they radioed down to her. "If something happens to you, what about us? It's not a risk we are willing to take. I will come and help you down," Bogdan offered, "but it is not safe for me to climb with you. You should go down."

Going down was not an option. Not only was her leg not going to get any better, but one of Wielicki's teammates, Ingrid Baeyens, a beautiful climber from Belgium, was breathing down Wanda's heels on her way to the summit. Wanda knew she had only a day's lead on the woman, and she was not about to let the pretty, blond Belgian have the first female ascent of the South Face. *If I have to crawl, I will.*

"Okay, then, don't bother about me. I'll sort myself out," Wanda said before throwing the radio across the tent and watching it bounce against the nylon wall. *Chams! Kurwa bastards! Fuck them!*

In the morning the pain was duller, but she had not gained any mobility. She also wasn't feeling very well and thought the residual shock and painkillers probably hadn't helped her system at all. She brewed some tea and forced herself to eat. She would need every calorie and drop of liquid for the day ahead. She dressed slowly, painfully working her injured leg into her outer pants. Even bending her knee to adjust her boots and crampons made her lightheaded with pain. At first light, she left the last camp and began the long ascent to the summit. Shortly out of camp she met another climber on descent and asked him about the route in front of her. He looked at her skeptically and hesitated. She couldn't believe it. *Does he think I'm going to use the information to lie about making it all the way to the top? Incredible!*

"Listen," she said, "we both know there are cheats who lie about reaching the summit, but I'm not one of them, okay?"

Finally he told her to look out for bad ropes before he turned and continued down the mountain.

That's it? she thought, *bad ropes?* She felt like screaming at him. *What about the terrain, the seracs, crevasses? I know to look out for bad ropes!*

But the man was gone, and Wanda was again alone.

Almost twelve hours later, as the sun was blinking over the western horizon, Wanda made her final steps to the summit. She stood in the beautiful twilight, the setting sun baking nearby summits in a wash of rosy alpenglow, as if the Dome of the Rock had made its way from Jerusalem to here, tens of thousands of feet high in Nepal. She had reached her eighth 8,000-meter peak. No woman had come even close to her record, and those who were trying had only two or three 8,000-meter peaks to their credit. Her hurt and isolation were forgotten. Apart from reaching her eighth mountain, she had set another benchmark in the history of female alpinism by becoming the first woman to climb the perilous South Face of Annapurna, and doing so alone. The route had been her most challenging, even more so than K2.

Standing unsteadily on her bad leg, she shot some photos of the darkening valleys and fading mountains around her before the camera froze up. She gave it a shake, trying to release the shutter, but was unable to get the camera properly working. *Piece of junk,* she screamed, and threw it into the snow. The action helped release her rage. She reached down to retrieve the camera, carefully brushing the snow off it with her bare fingers. With her hands increasingly cold in the frigid air, she gave up on the camera, shoving it back into her pack, and put her hands back into her mittens. She stood quietly in the still air, absorbing the beauty around her in the waning light. Then a full harvest moon rose over the opposing ridge, and she thought she'd never seen anything quite so spectacularly, simply magnificent. Finally she turned and started the long, lonely descent.

Entirely, utterly alone, she prayed that she would find the right route off the summit. Unlike Everest or K2, Annapurna's summit ridge fell away in every direction down ice and rock walls. There were no deep footsteps in the snow to follow. She reached up to click on her head-lamp, but nothing happened. She took it off her head and moved the switch back and forth. Nothing. The batteries were dead. Now, with the moon her only light, she struggled to discern the path and found herself once again talking out loud against the fear. *Wanda, step by step, careful, careful. You can do it. You've done it so many times. The weather is good, you are not too cold or thirsty, just be careful.* One hundred meters down her chosen route, she found herself teetering on the front tips of her crampons, four narrow steel teeth the only things that held her to the ice cliff. The wind swirled around her, pushing her, pulling her, shoving her with its gusts. With a yawning void at her feet, she knew she had taken the wrong way. She looked back up the sheer ice, trying to shield her face as crystals broke loose from above and cut at her cheeks and eyes as they fell. Even though she was exhausted, climbing back up was better than down. At least she knew where "up" went; down was a terrifying black emptiness. She adjusted her weight on her front points to make sure they were secure before she released her ax from the ice. Swinging her arm as far back as she dared reach, she thrust it into the ice higher, felt that it was firmly embedded, and foot by foot pulled her crampons out of the ice and rekicked them in a few inches above.

As she climbed she continued to talk to herself. *There is only peace, Wanda, no fear. No death. Only peace.* It took her several hours to reclimb the 100 meters and regain the ridge. As she sat resting at the top, watching the moonlight play in the shadows of the mountain, she realized that her fear was gone. Down on the wall, she had feared she was going to die, but the very action of finding a plan and executing it had replaced her doubt. *Well, so much for my ability to find a route in the dark, full moon or not,* she thought, and instead got on all fours, dug a small snow cave out of the slope with her ice ax, and curled up inside it for the night. Her adventuring was done for one day.

In the morning Wanda descended to Camp II, where she radioed Base Camp about her success in reaching the summit.

Wielicki asked her why she hadn't radioed when she made the summit, as climbers do when they reach the top. He told her he had been watching her from Base Camp on binoculars, and it looked to him like she had turned around shy of the summit.

Wanda couldn't believe her ears. He actually doubted she had made it. He was calling her a liar, a fraud.

"Krysiek," she shouted, using the more familiar version of his given name, "you've known me for twenty years! I gave you your first climbing lesson! I am not a liar!"

But Wielicki refused to believe her. She wondered at his ill will. Perhaps he was more interested in having the pretty Belgian get the credit for the first female ascent of the South Face.

Wanda started down from Camp II tired and defeated. Her own teammates, countrymen, were down there calling her a fraud, a cheat. *What is this nasty business I'm in?* She tried to get into a down-climbing rhythm, a steady dance between feet, arms, and rope, but her troubled mind and the pain in her leg prevented her from finding that hypnotic pattern. Instead, her focus was on reducing the weight her left leg absorbed with every step. Descending from the summit to her high camp hadn't been that bad, but as she collected her gear from Camp II, the weight and painful downward momentum became almost intolerable. Her plan was to leave immediately for Dhaulagiri (8,167 meters, 26,794 feet) in her ongoing *Caravan*, so she didn't have the luxury of leaving equipment behind.

She radioed to Base Camp several times asking for help, but no one came. When she finally reached camp two days later, in tears of loneliness and pain, she realized why no one had responded to her radio call: most of the team had left without her.

When she returned to Poland, no reporters and no group of friends greeted her, only a scandal. She was devastated. Jozef Nyka and Hanna Wiktorowska went to the airport to warn her that Wielicki was publicly doubting whether she actually reached the summit, and the Polish Alpine Club had launched an investigation. In the midst of a growing national scandal, Wielicki and other teammates were called before the Polish Alpine Club. After testifying, Wanda met him on the stairs of the club.

"Krysiek, what the hell are you doing calling me a liar?" she screamed. "What's in it for you, you bastard?" They stood staring at each other in the stairway.

"We said you made the summit, but fuck you, we don't believe it," he said, impassive. She stared at him in disbelief. *How could our friendship, our comradeship, have gone so bad? I taught this kurwa how to climb twenty years ago! What have I done to piss him off so much?*

Several days later she received her expedition film back from the processor. As she flipped through the pictures she stopped and yelled out loud. The camera had worked. When she had flung it to the ground, the shutter had released. The picture was blurry and dark, but there it was—the view from the summit of Annapurna! She had her proof. She showed the film to the Alpine Club, and her summit was deemed authentic. She hoped the messy topic would be closed, but the damage was done: Wanda Rutkiewicz, the Polish heroine, an icon of Himalayan climbing, had been publicly doubted, called a liar, rebuked by her fellow climbers and countrymen. She wore the shame heavily and wondered whether her success as a woman climber was at the root of all the ugliness.

Having made the summit of Annapurna, it brought her 8,000-meter total to eight, the same number as Wielicki. Wanda speculated that he was resentful of her matching his achievement, and doing so on the South Face, a route he thought beyond her abilities. But the animosity was short-lived; though Wanda probably never forgave him his censure, they needed each other in the highly controlled and competitive Polish Alpine Association. Within months they were planning an expedition together for the fall of 1992.

If her reputation suffered in Poland, elsewhere in the climbing world it remained solid. Reinhold Messner never doubted her claim.

"When I wrote my book on Annapurna, I had Wanda in it, without question, as one of the summiteers. No doubt in my mind she made it."

Back in Poland, her former climbing partner Krystyna Palmowska was shocked that Rutkiewicz's word would be doubted. "When I heard the news, I just couldn't believe this. She was not the sort of person who could lie. I believe it was really a tragedy for her and all who participated. One should look at her whole career, not the last part, because I think it was a kind of tragedy that she couldn't find anything else to fill her life. This was the time for her to withdraw [from the 8,000-meter mountains]." Instead, she was delving deeper and deeper into their icy void.

By early 1992, Wanda had been to only three of her eight 8,000-meter peaks, climbed two of them, and failed on the third, Dhaulagiri. She was far behind schedule. Her Caravan of Dreams had become something of a nightmare. She was also increasingly lonely. Over the years she had struggled to find a balance between her love of the mountains and her love of men. After two failed marriages and some painful affairs, when she found and fell in love with yet another doctor, German cardiologist Kurt Lyncke, in 1988, she thought she had finally found the balance she so craved.

"It's hard to find someone in total harmony with yourself. I was ready for a third marriage, and this time I really believed it could be for life. I'd known him for two years, and I was sure I'd found a man like me—free and independent," she confided to a friend later.

Unfortunately, it didn't last. While Lyncke was descending from Camp II on Broad Peak in 1990, he fell 400 meters and died instantly. A climbing partner saw the fall. He said that while it appeared that Lyncke could easily have arrested his slide by jamming his ice ax into the slope, he didn't and instead fell like a rag doll to his death, most likely the victim of a cerebral hemorrhage, stroke, or aneurysm. Wanda

ran up from Base Camp when she heard what had happened and was
devastated by the sight of her lover, crumpled on the slope, blood running out of his mouth and nose, his backpack and ice ax scattered down
the slope. Wanda knelt by his broken body, staring at his handsome
face. She put a hand on his neck; it was already cold. She sat back on
her heels, stunned. Her teammates, Jószef Gozdzik and Christian Kunt-
ner, stood by, increasingly nervous.

"Come on, Wanda, there's nothing we can do. Let's go down before it
gets dark," they urged. They didn't like to look on her face. It looked
wiped clean. Nothing. No emotion, no tears, no grief.

She didn't seem to hear them. After what seemed like hours, she
slowly got up. She looked like she had aged a decade in that afternoon.
Without a word, she turned down the slope. Jószef and Christian scrambled to stay with her. When they got back to Base Camp, Wanda went to
her tent and stayed there until the porters arrived days later to take
them back out to Skardu. Finally, as the team started walking down the
glacier, Wanda allowed the tears to come, tears she had held in tight
rein while in the close confines of Base Camp. Now, with the team scattered along the long glacier, with only the rocks and ice to hear, she let
the sobs course through her body. She stopped occasionally when the
pain became too much and bent over her ski poles as she wept, her
moans echoing between the mountains to her left and right. She
noticed nothing of the trek through the towering peaks except the crevasses. As she passed their gaping mouths she would linger, staring
down and imagining Kurt's face looking up from their icy depths. *It
would be so easy, so simple, so fast*, she thought. And then she would
walk on.

After nearly twenty years spent in the mountains she loved, Wanda just
seemed to be counting peaks, as if eager to have them behind her. With
so many of her potential climbing partners either dead or retired, she
found it easier to pay her way onto already established teams with
climbers she barely knew and rarely climbed with. And with her Caravan
schedule, she came into a mountain directly from the one before; with
no time to get to know the team, she ended up climbing virtually alone.

Once, when watching the American Western *Magnificent Seven* with Ewa Matuszewska, Wanda was irritated with her friend's fascination with the movie. Then she heard Robert Vaughn's character utter words that spoke to her heart; "Home? I don't have a home. Family? I don't have a family. Friends? I don't have any friends. Enemies? I don't have any enemies, at least none who are still alive." Something about the clean finality and stubborn pride of those words deeply resonated with Wanda's own definition of her life.

"Wanda had nothing but the mountains toward the end," said Henry Todd, an irascible British expedition leader infamous for decking a journalist at Everest Base Camp. "She had a flat in Warsaw and a dog, but she was lost."

When Jim Curran watched Wanda give a slide show presentation at the Katowice Film Festival in early 1992, he felt a nagging sadness. "She seemed very isolated and very lonely. And I felt terribly sorry for her. I remember saying good-bye to her and thinking, 'I'm not going to see her again.'"

He didn't.

In March, Wanda turned her eyes to Kangchenjunga (8,586 meters, 28,169 feet), the world's third-highest mountain and the only 8,000-meter peak at that time still unclimbed by a woman. Kangchenjunga remains the hardest for women to conquer; only one has climbed it, and four have died in the process, and even that one ascent, by Briton Ginette Harrison in 1998, was disputed by some eyewitnesses watching from Base Camp. They claimed she could not have made the summit and returned to Camp III in the time she said she did. Harrison died on Dhaulagiri in 1999.

Kangchenjunga translates as "five treasure houses in the snow." Tibetan mythology deems the mountain the sacred seat of the Gods and says it contains their five treasures: gold, silver, copper, corn, and divine books. Although climbers have traditionally gotten to within feet of the true top but out of respect stopped short of that holy ground, it has become increasingly trampled by climbers with little or no spiritual connection to the sacred surroundings who want to tag the true summit.

For women climbers, simply avoiding the hallowed ground evidently isn't good enough to mollify the Mountain Gods; local legend has it that the spirits don't want women anywhere near the sanctified summit for fear they will "pollute" its purity. Many devout believe this is why women have had so little success on Kangchenjunga.

Even though Wanda had no patience with such mystical thinking, she and her teammates all had dreams about a young girl telling them that the Gods of Kangchenjunga didn't want a woman to climb it. And though she didn't speak of it, something *was* different about this trip. Before she left for the mountain, she drove to her mother's house to say good-bye. As she had many times before, Maria Blaszkiewicz led Wanda toward a small shrine she had set up in the corner of her living room. But this time Wanda found she couldn't pray with her mother. She didn't know why. It had always been a comforting, loving ritual for both women, but this time she couldn't light the candles, say the words, bow her head. Her mother looked at her with sadness and concern. Wanda bent to pull the small woman against her. *Don't worry, Mama, I'll be fine. I'll come home. I always do.*

After she left her mother's house, she drove to see Janusz Onyszkiewicz, the widower of her friend Alison Chadwick-Onyszkiewicz. Onyszkiewicz had lost two wives and scores of friends to the mountains, he didn't want to lose another. He feared that she had become bewitched by the 8,000-meter game. "Please, Wanda, reconsider this trip," he urged. For four hours he tried to change her mind. He wasn't successful.

Carlos and Elsa Carsolio, a young Mexican couple who had already been on several expeditions, invited her to join their young expedition to the North Face of Kangchenjunga, and she readily signed on, happy to be once again with friends in the mountains. In Elsa, Wanda found a peer and a friend, and in Carlos one of the world's strongest climbing partners. In 1996 Carsolio became the fourth of only eleven[*] men, and at thirty-three years old the youngest, to climb all fourteen 8,000-meter peaks. A darkly handsome, compactly built man, Carlos said he asked

*As of June 2005 that number now stands at thirteen.

Wanda to join the team feeling a bit like a teenager approaching a rock star for an autograph. In Carsolio's eyes Wanda was not only a legend but a friend. With six strong climbers, all of them good friends, it was a capable team, and although Wanda was old enough to be their mother, there was deep respect for her and her accomplishments.

Arriving at the mountain in mid-March, the expedition had begun well, but by early May four of the six climbers had been so weakened by illness and frostbite that only Carlos and Wanda were capable of a final summit bid. As they sat in the murky cold of the team's mess tent, they talked about the climb ahead. Wanda seemed particularly gloomy.

"I have lost so many friends in the mountains, Carlos," she said, staring off into the deepening dark of night, absently stirring her tea.

Carlos was taken aback. He knew that she had been sad on this trip, perhaps feeling her age. Early on he and Andres Delgado, his buddy from Mexico City, had started calling her "Grandmother," and Wanda had laughed along with the joke, but then she came to Carlos furious and hurt. "I'm sorry, Wanda, we didn't mean any disrespect," he had said, but still she stomped back to her tent and didn't speak to them for the rest of the day. But she *was* old enough to be their mother, plus she was fighting an intestinal bug and still suffering pain in her leg. She had been climbing slowly but strongly, and he had no doubt she could make it to the top. But he didn't like the sound of her thoughts.

"But you have many good friends, yes?" he asked, struggling with his English and with understanding her heavy accent.

"*Ja*, but all of my best friends are gone." She looked at him with eyes so sad that he felt like he might start crying. She reached into her pocket and pulled out a photograph and handed it to him.

Carlos looked down at a silver-haired man with carefully sculpted facial bones and long, muscular legs that were bare under the hot sun at some Base Camp. But Carlos stared, not at the handsome man, but at the beautiful woman sitting next to him in the picture. This was a different Wanda than the one who sat before him. The Wanda in the picture was dressed in a little tank top, her arms were bare and tan, and she wore a pair of shorts so small they revealed her long, muscular thighs.

She rested her chin in the palm of her hand and smiled at the man splayed out in front of her. Carlos had never seen that look of coquettish pride and simple happiness in the Wanda he knew, the one who now sat with the evening shadows playing across her lined, tired face, her eyes enormous dark orbs. Carlos knew the death of Kurt had been particularly shattering for Wanda because she was still in the early days of love. Unlike the other times she had fallen in love, this love never had the chance to succumb to the demands of her enormous and stubborn personality, the way all of her other affairs had done. This, he knew, was a loss of the heart.

"He's waiting for me out there," she said, her voice empty. "And soon I shall find him."

Wanda's leg was still bothering her from the accident on Annapurna, so she decided to leave Base Camp two days ahead of Carlos and meet up with him at Camp IV so that they could go for the summit together. Even with that much lead, Carlos soon caught up to and passed Wanda, and he was the one waiting for her at Camp IV. As they packed their gear for the morning Carlos was relieved that all of Wanda's gloomy ramblings were past; she didn't talk about lost friends and about how slowly she was moving. She talked only of the mountain. As she did on K2, Wanda had made two previous attempts on Kangchenjunga, and she was determined this would be her last.

They brewed tea and soup and tried to get a few hours' rest before they started out into the predawn cold for the summit. At 3:00 A.M., they began the arduous process of putting on their boots, crampons, and climbing harnesses over their down one-piece climbing suits. Even though it weighed heavy against her waist and the fixed lines stopped a few meters above them out of Camp IV, the harness was habit for Wanda if there was a chance she'd need it.

Soon after they left their high camp, it was apparent to both of them that Wanda was moving too slowly for Carlos. He would have to go ahead or risk hypothermia moving at such a slow pace.

"You go," Wanda urged. "I'll be fine." Carlos nodded and went for the summit alone. He occasionally looked down to gauge her progress, but she became a smaller and smaller black dot in the ocean of white below him. Then, when he reached the Pinnacles, where the route traversed over to the south face of the mountain before the last few meters to the summit, he lost sight of her completely. He reached the summit at 5:00 P.M., took a few pictures, and began his long descent.

It was getting dark and bitterly cold, and his progress down the icy slope was as fast as he dared. His water had run out hours before, and the meager bits of food he'd nibbled on during the day had only whetted his hunger. Nearly three hours and 1,000 feet into his descent, he came upon a rope across the trail. He picked it up, looking toward its source. And there was Wanda. She had dug a tiny cave out of the ice slab slope and half-sat, half-lay in its meager shelter from the wind. In their efforts to climb fast and light, they had left all of their emergency bivouac gear in their high camp. Wanda had no stove, no food or water, no sleeping bag or bivy sack. They had both planned on making it to the summit and back to camp in one long day of climbing. To make matters worse, at the very last minute she had decided to take her lighter-weight one-piece suit given to her by the French climbing gear company, Valandré. She had laughed when she first saw it because it was yellow and electric pink, her least favorite color. She always thought pink a frilly, silly color for a woman. Plus it made her skin look a terrible yellowish-green. But she had gratefully accepted the three "Combi" suits; they were expensive and very well made. Pink or no pink, it was a great suit, and she was glad to have it. But now, as she sat hunched over in the cold, she cursed her choice. Her big bulky yellow one was heavier and warmer, but it sat thousands of feet below her. She looked at Carsolio with huge eyes.

"Can I have your jacket? I am so cold," she asked him.

Carlos felt a terrible wrench of guilt. As much as he wanted to give her something to help her warm up, he didn't have an extra, and he needed his to survive. "Wanda, I'm sorry, but I have nothing else to wear. It's so cold, maybe you should come down with me?"

"No, no, I will be okay. I'm just cold. Once the sun comes up, I will be warm and go for the summit."

Carlos couldn't believe his ears. Go for the summit? She could barely move; she had no food and no stove or gas to melt snow for even a sip of water. How was she going to have the strength to climb in the morning? He looked at his Himalayan hero shuddering and huddled against herself in the miserable ice hole. His instinct was to scream at her: *Come down with me, now. It's too cold, you must come down and rest at camp, then maybe try again with proper gear.* But he said nothing. He didn't dare. *She is the great Wanda Rutkiewicz. Who am I to tell her anything? Just some kid from Mexico who's only been on a handful of expeditions. She is the best female climber the world has ever seen.* As he watched her struggle against the frigid cold, he marveled at her stubborn pride. Maybe all she needed was to be told what to do, forced to get up and go down before it was too late. But he said nothing.

"Are you sure you won't come with me?"

"No, I want to try for the summit in the morning."

It was her decision.

He sat with her in the snow cave as long as he dared, but he remembered his failed 1986 bid on Manaslu. He had been slow, too slow, and took drugs to boost his circulation. Instead, they had robbed his already thick blood of vital fluids. Only his health and youth had kept him from losing fingers and toes, but still he had endured months of skin grafts from his legs to replace the dead tissue, tissue that would forever be susceptible to extreme temperatures.

After fifteen minutes that seemed like hours, he looked at Wanda. "I have to go down, Wanda, it's too cold." She looked at him, barely registering his words. Finally, with his own descent ahead of him, he reached over and touched her arm. "Good-bye, Wanda. Be careful."

"Don't worry, I'll be all right," she said.

He turned from where she sat and continued down the dark slope, looking back only once, but by then she was indistinguishable against the night shadows playing across the snow.

He reached their high camp at 7,900 meters (25,900 feet) and waited the night, then the next day. She never came. Physically spent and unable to reclimb the mountain, he left Wanda a thermos of water and descended farther, reaching Camp II at 6,900 meters (22,600 feet), where he was trapped by a ferocious blizzard. He couldn't imagine what was happening higher on the mountain as he hunkered down in a tent, relatively safe and warm, waiting for the storm to abate for his final descent. Finally, when the storm broke, he knew he couldn't wait any longer. He left Wanda a fully stocked tent with food and water. But he knew it was for her spirit; she wasn't coming down.

As he rappelled down Kangchenjunga's North Face, a wall of ice and rock, Carsolio himself was close to his limit, that dangerous edge where climbing is more a flirtation with death than a celebration of life. He was hallucinating, his brain numb after a week on the mountain, his hands barely able to hold the rope, when he made a mistake that has killed many exhausted climbers. In moving from one rope to another, he failed to clip onto it with his descending device. When he leaned back to continue his rappel, he was anchored to nothing but air and found himself in a freefall down the sheer wall of ice. Luckily, his arm became tangled in the rope, and he was able to self-arrest, his feet dangling thousands of feet above the glacier beneath. As he gathered his wits, set his crampons firmly into the ice, and finally clipped into the rope, he heard a voice.

"Don't worry, I will take care of you."

"Wanda? Is that you?" Carlos swung wildly on the rope, looking around him. The voice was so clear, so near, it sounded like she was anchored right next to him on the ice. "I will take care of you, Carlos." Her voice was calm, like his mother's used to be when she would comfort him after he'd skinned his knee. Carlos leaned his head into the wall and cried. He knew Wanda was gone. Finally, completely gone, and there was nothing he could do to save her. He didn't know what happened when people died, but perhaps they became voices in the minds of those who loved them. Maybe Wanda would live forever in him, in his thoughts. A small sob escaped his lips when he remembered how she had always treated him like a mother, with such gentle care, and yet when she needed him he hadn't been able to return that kindness, that concern. The tears froze to his cheeks as he continued his lonely, bitter retreat from the mountain.

When Carlos reached the base of the mountain three days later, the which had been waiting out the storm with growing concern that something had gone terribly wrong, rushed to meet him. Even though the chance of survival after so many days, in those kinds of conditions that high on the mountain, was worse than none, the team stayed several more days, waiting and hoping Wanda would return, but she didn't. Finally, the team left Base Camp and the mountain. As they walked away many turned back for a final glimpse of the mountain, hoping for a miraculous glimpse of Wanda making her way down the icy slopes, but the storm and reality kept that hope nothing more than fantasy.

It was May 21, 1992, and somewhere on the holiest peak in the Himalayas the great Wanda Rutkiewicz, the first woman to climb K2, had finally perished.

News of her death did not reach Poland for nearly two weeks. After many nights of grief-stricken insomnia, Ewa Matuszewska was finally able to fall into an exhausted, empty sleep. She was awakened in the middle of the night by the phone. She scrambled to answer it.

"Hello?"

"Ewunia?" There were very few people who used that derivation of her name.

"Oh my God, Wanda!" Ewa exclaimed, instantly awake as her heart raced in her chest. She clutched the receiver so hard her fingers hurt. "We are all in despair. Where are you?"

"I am cold, I am very cold, but don't cry. Everything will be fine."

"But why aren't you coming back?"

"I cannot now," she said, and the phone went dead.

When Ewa woke up in the morning, she thought she'd had an incredible dream. Then she heard the buzzing of the phone—it lay off the hook on her bedside.

Reaction to Wanda's death was immediate and passionate from climbers all over the world. Today Reinhold Messner misses Wanda terribly, the friend as well as the climber, and says she left a void in mountaineering history. "She doesn't know, but I am missing her. How happy it would make me to be able to call her up and talk about the mountains."

"She was one of my heroes," said Peter Hillary, son of Sir Edmund, "one of my Himalayan heroes."

"She was the best female Himalayan climber there ever was," said Jim Curran, who also found her a formidable lady. "She wasn't a lion in a cage; she was just a lion standing around, and I thought, 'Oh no, she'll definitely bite me arm off.' She was very, very attractive, but she was just such a strong woman, you just knew you'd come out mauled."

"She was a great lady," Charlie Houston said, getting up from his living room chair overlooking Vermont's Lake Champlain to get a mounted rock off of his bookshelf. "She brought me this rock from the summit of K2 and had it mounted. A sweet gesture. A good woman."

When Janusz Onyszkiewicz heard that she had died, he wanted to scream at her, "Why didn't you back down? Why didn't you obey me?" Onyszkiewicz's reaction to the loss of yet another climber to the mountains was anger. "I'm an egoist. I want them near me."

Sadly, many who might have added to her eulogy were already gone, from Jerzy Kukuczka to Alison Chadwick to Halina Krüger. Perhaps her own words are her best epitaph:

> I never seek death, but I don't mind the idea of dying in the mountains. It would be an easy death for me. After all I've experienced, I'm familiar with it. And most of my friends are there in the mountains, waiting for me.

Courtesy of the Library of Congress

In 1899 American vanguard adventurer Fanny Bullock Workman became the first woman to get a glimpse of K2 during her exploration of the vast Karakoram Range and its glaciers.

Dianne Roberts and husband and team leader Jim Whittaker on the trek to K2, May 1978. Forty years after Charlie Houston's 1938 team reconnoitered the mountain, Americans would finally reach the summit on September 6 and 7.

Jim Wickwire

After she broke her femur climbing in the Caucasus, Wanda refused to cancel her 1982 Women's K2 Expedition, even though it meant making the grueling 100-mile trek from Dassu to Base Camp on crutches.

Wanda Rutkiewicz collection

Friends and fellow Poles Wanda Rutkiewicz and Jerzy Kukuczka at the base of K2 after their historic ascents.

Wanda Rutkiewicz collection

Wanda posing in a Valandré "Combi" climbing suit in 1990. Five years later her body would be found on Kangchenjunga and identified by the trademark pink and yellow Valandré suit it still wore.

Niels-Henrik Fritsbøl

September 19, 1987: Just as she had on Everest and K2, Wanda Rutkiewicz became the first Pole to climb 8,013-meter (26,291-foot) Shishapangma. Hours later Jerzy Kukuczka reached the summit, realizing his dream of climbing all fourteen 8,000-meter peaks, the second man to do so.

Wanda Rutkiewicz collection

Alain Bontemps

Liliane and Maurice Barrard in their Base Camp tent at Nanga Parbat, 1984.

Alain Bontemps

Liliane and Maurice in their garden at La Beauce, France, after her first-female ascent of Nanga Parbat, 1984.

Wanda Rutkiewicz collection

Wanda Rutkiewicz, Liliane Barrard, and Barbara Kozlowski at the base of Broad Peak in 1985. Days later, Kozlowski tragically drowned in a glacial stream and in 1989 Wanda returned and carried her friend to the Gilkey memorial for burial.

Opposite: Found in Maurice Barrard's camera at K2 Base Camp, this is the last known picture of Liliane, taken as she climbed through House's Chimney on her ascent of K2, 1986.

Courtesy of Alain Bontemps

Julie Tullis, circa 1970.

Terry Tullis

Julie in the backyard of the Bothy.

Julie with Kurt
Diemberger at the
Trento (Italy)
International Film
Festival in 1979.

Terry Tullis

Terry Tullis

Courtesy of François Mauduit

Chantal Mauduit (age two) with her sister Anne and brother François on a family trek through the French Alps, circa 1966.

Chantal climbing the Shield on El Capitan in Yosemite, California, May 1997.

René Robert

Chantal at K2 Base Camp, 1992.

Charles Mace

After her ascent of K2 in 1992, snowblind and exhausted, Chantal collapsed on descent, and to get her down alive it took the efforts of several climbers, including Americans Thor Kieser and Ed Viesturs, who here administers analgesic drops in her swollen eyes above Camp III.

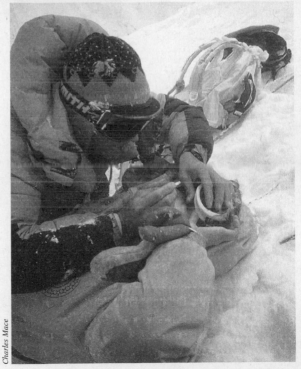

Charles Mace

Guy Cotter

In 1995 team leader Rob Hall urges an exhausted
Chantal to turn back from her seventh and last
attempt to climb Everest without oxygen. They are
standing on the South Summit at 28,700 feet, less
than 350 vertical feet from the true summit.

Chantal crossing Pakistan's
Gondogoro pass after
her 1997 ascent of GII,
pointing back at K2.

René Robert

John E. Hargreaves

Three-year-old Alison Hargreaves on Bunster Hill in Derbyshire, after climbing her first mountain, 1965.

John E. Hargreaves

Alison with Tom on her back, hiking near Chamonix, France, 1989.

Courtesy of Kim Logan

Taken at Base Camp the day before their final summit bid, this is the last known photo of Alison, Rob Slater, Jeff Lakes, and Bruce Grant, August 9, 1995. *(Left to right, standing)*: Peter Hillary, Fida Hussein (cook), Slater, Lakes, Grant, Mohammed (cook), *(seated)* Alison and Kim Logan.

Jennifer Jordan / Fox Television Studios

Alison's children Tom, 14, and Kate Ballard, 12, stand with their father, Jim Ballard, in front of their home, Stone Cottage, in Scotland, May 2003.

CHAPTER 8

FINALLY, ANOTHER SURVIVOR

Over all the mountaintops is peace.
— JOHANN WOLFGANG VON GOETHE

For six years K2 stood silent and waiting, and unclimbed; not one man or woman had been able to reach the summit from its southern side in Pakistan since the Black Summer. The tragedies of 1986 had cast a deathly pall on the mountain, particularly for women, three of whom remained on the mountain, forever entombed in its frozen rocks and tragic legacy. Now the only one who had made it down alive, Wanda Rutkiewicz, had died on Kangchenjunga. Athletes tend to be superstitious—some tennis players wear the same shirt in every tournament, and baseball players often perform a litany of ritualistic pats, taps, and adjustments before they swing at each pitch. Climbers are no different. After the killing season of 1986, many began to fear that for women, K2 carried a curse.

Then in 1992 a beautiful Frenchwoman with no fear of ghosts or lingering evil spirits approached the Savage Mountain.

When they climb, many mountaineers fill their minds with nothing more than the rocks and ice at their feet. Others mentally and methodically envision the crux of the route ahead of them, placing their spiked toes and axes strategically with each move. But some recite poetry. Chantal Mauduit was one of them. Her favorite to recite softly as she climbed was written by a Tibetan Tantric monk:

Quand j'étais petit poisson,
je n'ai pas été pris comme grand poisson
Malgré les nasses, personne ne m'a dompte
Et maintenant je vagabonde dans l'océan immense.

When I was a little fish,
I wasn't caught like the big fish.
Despite the nets, no one tamed me,
And now I wander in the immense ocean.

—DRUPKA KUNLEGS (1459–1529)

Chantal Marie Agnes Mauduit was easily recognized among the scores of children playing in the schoolyard as she ran from game to game; she was the one who was always laughing. She moved as if her body had no limits and her mind held no fear. She moved with joy. But it was a costly joie de vivre, and she suffered numerous broken bones and torn ligaments before she was even out of her teens, including a damaged knee tendon in her first skiing accident when she was five.

Born in Paris in 1964, the youngest of three children, Chantal and her family soon moved to Chambery, where her playground became the foothills of the French Alps. Like the Bontempses and many other European families, the Mauduits spent their summer holidays not on lengthy car trips but on two-month treks through the mountains near their home, often including ten- and twelve-hour days of hiking. At four years old, Chantal had to run to keep up with nine-year-old François and seven-year-old Anne, but no matter how long the day's journey, she would never tire. Hour after hour Chantal skipped along while the family hiked from peak to peak, from hut to hut, in their alpine adventures, her laughter sparkling through the trees.

A pretty child with enormous green eyes, wild brown curls, and a wide, smiling mouth, Chantal's energy was infectious. When she did sit still, it was usually to write in her journal, something she did from the age of six. As she matured she wrote compulsively and emotionally, pouring her heart onto the pages in often opaque ramblings. By the

time she was a teenager, her ebullient mood had darkened some, and
she appeared more contemplative, her smiles less habitual. But one day,
sitting with her diaries, she became dissatisfied with every word she had
written, and she threw the stack of small books she'd been painstakingly filling for years onto her bedroom floor. She sat down in front of
the pile, pushing her wild mane of dark curls away from her face, and
methodically ripped every page out of each book, then tore the pages
into tiny shreds. She sat looking at mounds of words, paintings, and
poems, then gathered them up and threw them into the trash. Finally
satisfied, she sat down and started a new journal.

"Despite the dangers," she wrote, "I want to become an alpinist."

Like many children who grow up in the Alps, Chantal climbed as a matter of course, the way American children grow up tossing a baseball or
football around the front yard. From her first touch of the rock under
her fingers, she felt a connection to the stone, loving its sensual power
and her ability to scale up it as well as, if not better than, the boys
around her. But she also knew the sport had lethal risk. By her early
teens, she had already witnessed her share of climbers losing their lives
in the pristine world above Albertville, Chamonix, and Les Houches.
When Chantal was fifteen, death would make a very private visit. Without warning, her mother began to tire easily and her usually robust
complexion became sallow and gray. Chantal never asked why, and the
family never discussed it. One day Renée Mauduit suddenly collapsed
and was rushed to the hospital. Thinking it would be less traumatic,
Renée and Bernard had decided not to tell the children that she had terminal cancer. Not until her mother lay dying did Chantal learn that she
would lose her. Only weeks later, she did.

Chantal left the gravesite with her dark head bowed and her jaw set.
She refused to talk about her grief with the family and instead carried it
very deeply and very privately. She sat alone for hours in the family's
Catholic church, lighting candle after candle for her mother, until one
day the parish priest appeared next to her in the pew and invited her to
come join a youth group. Reluctant at first to join any group, let alone

one in which she would have to share her private pain, she finally said yes—she would come to the next meeting. She did, and the resulting discussions helped Chantal finally share her pain.

While many climbers tend to avoid the reality of their dangerous sport, after her mother's death Chantal seemed to embrace the peril, as if hoping it would help her better understand life. At fifteen, she realized what many people never do: everyone is going to die, so she might as well live a passionate life while she was here.

Her first hell-bent passion was skiing. In the winter of 1980, she and François climbed high above Chamonix to a 45-degree, 500-meter couloir in the shadow of Mont Blanc. They reached the top of the narrow couloir and carefully balanced on the slick, steep surface, putting on their skis. Pausing only to flash François a devilish smile, Chantal deftly hopped off the corniced ridge and sailed down the icy channel, veering perilously close to other skiers who were climbing the gully. As she sped past snow from her sharply angled skis sprayed them in a wide arc.

"Who is *that*?" several asked as her tucked body flew by them, a mass of curly hair floating out behind her in a dark cloud. François tried to stay with her, but she was too fast for her older brother. She was fifteen.

As she progressed and began downhill racing, the combination of speed, strength, and sheer nerve narrowed her focus to the steel edges under her feet and the course flags flashing by her. There was nothing else in the world as she weaved down the inches-wide track, traveling sixty, seventy, close to eighty miles per hour, leaning so far into turns that she was almost at eye level with the tips of her skis, the trail of flags becoming a solid ribbon of color.

She earned a college degree in physical therapy but lacked the discipline of a scholar. What she did possess was the raw physical talent of an athlete. After a short stint in a local hospital, she turned to the mountains for her living and signed up as a sponsored athlete with the French Skiing Association. She was on tap to join the professional ski racing circuit but found she hated the controlling bureaucracy of the FSA. She couldn't help but bristle when time after time the association would dictate her skiing style as well as her life on and off the slopes. Finally a

series of nasty accidents made her rethink her calling, and she decided
to get her certification as a mountain guide.

Having climbed many of the rock walls near her home as a girl, she
returned to their smooth warmth in summer and to the ice falls in winter, rediscovering the thrill of physical exercise coupled with the daring
and independence of climbing hundreds of feet off the ground. After
only a few years she found herself leading routes for some of France's
best male climbers. When Chantal was twenty-two, she saw an announce-
ment in a magazine for an ice climbing competition. Reading that top
climbers from around Europe would be competing and that there
would be cash prizes for the top finisher, she thought, *Why not?* and
signed herself and her boyfriend up. When they showed up at the meet,
she recognized many of the famous faces from magazine articles and
the posters hanging in Chamonix cafés and bars. What she didn't see
was another woman. Taken aback by the beautiful woman adding her
name to the list of competitors, the event organizers watched slack-
jawed as Chantal floated up the demanding course time and again; she
finished third out of twenty-five male competitors. The French National
Mountaineering Association had a new star.

Chantal signed on to climb with the association's team, and as
France's newest poster child for ice climbing, she traveled to some of
the biggest ice walls in Europe, the Canadian Rockies, and the Tetons.
Everywhere she went she gathered a crowd. In a sport dominated by
men, the presence of a woman created an excitement in the air; one as
beautiful as Chantal positively electrified it. Soon she was fielding offers
from her admirers, ranging from dinner around the corner to expeditions around the world. One such invite was to the Andes. With very little deliberation, she accepted.

Her trip to the Andes was her first venture above 5,000 meters. She
not only climbed one 6,000-meter mountain, she climbed three of them
and paraglided off two, including Huascarán, Peru's highest mountain.

Paragliding, a sport slower to catch on in the States, has been a
perennial fixture above the town of Chamonix for decades. Consisting
of a large rectangular sail fastened to a small sling-seat for the driver,
the paraglider is Chamonix's form of "air pollution": around the peaks

of Mont Blanc, Brévent, the Grand Jorasses, and the Bonatti Pillar floats a cloud of brightly colored sails. On any given day in the 1980s and 1990s, one of them was inevitably Chantal's.

As she floated down from Huascarán through the cathedral of Peruvian peaks, a group formed below watching this tiny, agile, beautiful woman glide toward them. When she landed, one of the climbers approached her and said they were planning a trip to Everest. Might she want to join them? Again without hesitation, she said yes. After phone calls to her grandmother and François to borrow the necessary money, she was on her way to Nepal.

A few months later Chantal stepped out of the airport into the cacophony that was Kathmandu and felt immediately blessed to be there. She felt like she had finally come home. She loved Chamonix, but somehow this was different. This felt not only like her heart's foundation but like her soul's. Looking around her at the hot, crowded maze of dark faces, the sharp smell and deafening din of too many cars, mules, and people sharing the same streets assaulting her senses, she raised her hands to her chest, pressed her palms together, bowed her head slightly, and whispered into her fingertips, "Namaste."

The mountains, the culture, the children, and the people of the tiny Himalayan country that contains most of the world's largest mountains reached out and grabbed Chantal and never let her go. The warm smiles that lit the faces around her were more beautiful than masterpieces in the Louvre, the exchanged *namastes* were lullabies in her ears. She walked through the streets alone, marveling at the sharp colors, bitter smells, and cloying heat, laughing as the strange language tickled over her tongue. She embraced all of Nepal's exotic extremes without hesitation.

Chantal was traveling with the minimal amount of gear and expense; having learned to climb from the icons of French mountaineering, she adhered to their austere style of "fast and light." Christophe Profit, Benoit Chamoux, Maurice Barrard, Pierre Behgin, Michel Parmentier, Eric Escoffier, Thierry Renault—they had all espoused an ethic that demanded climbers be strong and talented enough to carry their own gear and their own asses up the mountains. Not only did they steer clear of supplemental oxygen, but they rarely used high-altitude porters. Chantal decided to adopt their stringent and immensely more difficult style and vowed she would never use supplemental oxygen. Reinhold Messner had said, "When you climb an 8,000-meter with bottled oxygen, you have reduced it to a 6,000-meter mountain." She too wanted to meet the mountain on its terms. If she wasn't up to the task, so be it; she would try again.

"To climb Everest, Roof of the World, is the dream of a child, the dream of a climber, my dream," she wrote. "Without oxygen, without aid, to discover the ultimate dimension, like a cyclist climbing a pass without a motor, digging deep, physically, mentally. . . . To be at 8,000 meters without oxygen offers the opportunity to open up to the rebirth of senses in these high magical Himalayan places. The harmony with the Earth transcends. The internal horizon blooms."

She climbed well and strongly, acclimatizing quickly to the thin air. Upon reaching a camp high on the mountain, she saw that her tentmate was ill, unable to keep any food down and complaining of a migraine. Hoping to spare him more nausea at watching her eat, she discreetly devoured her dinner, then, as politely as she dared, asked him for his. He weakly motioned to where it was. As she ate, the man lay miserably in the tent, unable to quell his upset stomach or still his pounding headache. Later he looked over at Chantal. She was peacefully and soundly asleep.

Although the team was turned back from its summit bid, Chantal was thrilled at having climbed well on her first 8,000-meter peak. Her first trip to Everest ended as each of her many subsequent expeditions would: without the summit but with a deeper and abiding love for the people and culture at its base.

As Chantal matured and developed as an alpinist, she gathered about her a coterie of friends as well as enemies. In a sport lacking high-profile women, Chantal more than stood out, and like many beautiful women living in a male milieu, she polarized people around her. Because she attracted a literal bevy of men in any Base Camp, many charged that she used her sex and sex appeal to manipulate those minions. The fact that they were by and large willing suspects did not quell the criticism, nor did the fact that much of that criticism came from men whom she didn't favor with attention. And though she was obviously well suited to harsh environs, her critics labeled her presence on an expedition as "trouble." It was a label that stuck.

On her second trip to Everest in 1991, Chantal's very presence created an internecine battle so outrageous that men actually challenged each other to a stone-throwing competition for her attentions. Thor Kieser, an American who was attempting the West Ridge that year, watched the shenanigans from afar, amused until he himself was stung by the "black widow," as he called her. Kieser had been happy to devote his energies to the mountain until one night when he heard a scratching outside his tent.

"Thor? Thor? Are you awake?"

The red-blooded American man was instantly awake and hastily made room for Chantal, who was already crawling into his tent with a bottle of champagne and an offer he couldn't refuse. Their sex was so frequent and incendiary that he found himself climbing the mountain just to get some rest away from her and her insatiable appetite. By the time the expedition folded its tents, he was infatuated, obsessed, blinded by his love and lust. Later, as they relaxed in Kathmandu, lazily walking through the busy markets and enjoying a sort of honeymoon romance after the mountain, they planned a trip to climb Mount Fitzroy, an 11,000-foot pinnacle of snow, ice, and loose, unstable rock in Argentina.

In Chantal, Thor thought he had found everything he had ever dreamed of: a hard-core climber; a beautiful, desirable, phenomenal athlete; and an insatiable sexual partner. He felt like a teenager in love for the first time, following her around doggedly, heart racing until they met again. When they parted at the airport, he bound for Colorado, she for France, he immediately began counting the days before their trip to Fitzroy the following January.

Back in Chamonix, Chantal worked occasional guiding jobs, ferrying tourists through the alpen attractions, but as the Fitzroy trip approached she told Thor she didn't have the money for a ticket to Argentina. Thor, desperate to see her again, took an extra job delivering Domino's pizzas around Golden and Denver to pay for Chantal's ticket. Within a few months they were on their way.

After meeting up at the Santiago airport, they organized their gear and were soon bumping along dusty high mountain roads through hairpin turns as their bus climbed toward El Chalten, a tiny village nestled at the base of Fitzroy. The Patagonia Mountains were breathtaking, but Thor couldn't stop staring at Chantal. He had pretty much dreamed nonstop of her since leaving Nepal months before, and here she was, sitting right next to him, their legs touching on the hot vinyl seat. As they traveled along the rutted road Thor told Chantal of some trouble he was having with his business: one of his competitors in the guiding world had begun spreading a rumor that he had abused Sherpas on his recent expedition. Suddenly Chantal yanked her hand out of his, her eyes turning to ice. "I don't want to hear of your problems," she said and turned her face to the window.

Thor felt like he had been slapped. He reached over for her hand, but she held it firmly out of his grasp. He tried to stroke her shoulder, but she shirked away from his touch. He tried to ask what was wrong, but she wouldn't talk to him. Stunned, he barely noticed the looming peak out the front window of the bus.

That night in their tent at Base Camp, she turned on her side facing the tent wall with her back to him. She had simply turned off her love, and he lay there wrestling with how to get it back. They continued to climb as a team, but the friendship, to say nothing of the intimacy, was gone. Weeks into the climb they approached a pitch unknown to both of them.

"Thor? Will you take one or two ice axes with you?" Chantal asked.

Thor, looking up the route, knew that he didn't want to get caught unprepared. "Two. I don't know what's up there, and the weight of an ax isn't worth the risk of needing it."

She looked at him as if he had said he was taking the elevator up and he half-expected her to mutter "wimp" under her breath. Instead, she said, "I think I know better than you. I have more experience, you see. It looks easy enough. I will take only one."

"Suit yourself," Thor said, ignoring the insult, and started up the wall.

After only a few pitches into the climb, he encountered an 85-degree runnel of ice about twenty feet high. Smiling to himself, he grabbed his second ice ax and clicked right up it, thinking, *Now* this *is going to be interesting*. He sat at the top of the chute, and within minutes he heard a whimpering voice below him on the route.

"Thor? Thor? Can you lower me an ice tool, please?"

Resisting the urge to say, "Told you so, bitch!" he lowered the tool to Chantal, who quickly climbed up with it. When she reached the top of the runnel, she handed his ax back to him without a word. No "thanks," no "I'm sorry," no "I was wrong." Nothing. She had rewritten the rules of their relationship, but Thor was still desperate to change them back.

Toward the end of January they had made several failed attempts at the summit. Time was running out. As they packed their backpacks for a final assault, Chantal said to Thor, "If we make it to the top, I think everything will be all right between us." Thor didn't know what that meant or why the summit would change her feelings toward him, and he didn't ask. He didn't care. All he wanted was to get her back, to feel her love, to hold her body again. As they started up the route Thor realized that he was going to get this woman on the summit and didn't care if it killed him. It almost did.

He had been leading most of the route, compensating for small mistakes Chantal made, like down-climbing to retrieve the jumar she left on the rope. At around 11:00 P.M. he found himself leading a 5.9 section, about eight pitches from the summit. They had been climbing nearly eighteen hours, and rain had soaked them to their skin. He was as exhausted as he'd ever been, the fatigue feeling like lead on his shoulders and in his arms and legs. Still, Thor refused to turn back. He was almost there. Just a few pitches more, and he would get her to the summit. Everything would be okay. She had promised.

As he reached up in the dark, miserable night he grasped a good-sized rock for his next handhold and began to transfer his weight from one hand to the other when he felt the stone move. He tried to freeze, to stop the momentum of his weight moving toward the rock, but it was too late. The rock came loose in his hand and fell into the dark void. As he yelled a warning his brain went into immediate overdrive, praying the rock would ricochet away from the wall, avoiding Chantal and the ropes. But it landed squarely on their 9-millimeter rope, cutting it cleanly in two. Thor, on lead, was immediately pulled off the wall. As he bounced from rock to rock, he thought, *Well, at least I'm not dead yet.* Sixty feet later, he finally came to rest, alive but severely injured. His eyelid had been ripped nearly off his face and his right hand was broken. But he was alive. Other teams above them on the climb came to their assistance and were able to get him safely back to Base Camp. Climbers hustled about boiling water to clean his wound and finding a splint for his hand. His climb was over, but Chantal announced that hers was not. She had been invited by another team to stay and go for the summit at first light.

"I just don't love you anymore" was all she would say.

Thor returned home devastated and broken. He sought psychiatric help to ferret through the jumble of pain and emotions. His doctor told him that she was bad news and that because of his feelings for her, she was dangerous, like poison when it mixes with water. He told Thor never to climb with Chantal again, and he thought he never would, but when he heard that she had signed up with a Swiss team going to K2 later that spring, he scrambled to find an expedition that still had room for one more climber.

Soon he was packing to join a large American-Russian team, boasting such power horses as Ed Viesturs, Scott Fischer, and Vladimir Balyberdin. Once he arrived in Skardu, rather than wait for the rest of the team to join them from Russia, Kieser ran up to K2 Base Camp as quickly as he could to see her. "I was hoping. I still loved her, was still obsessed with her."

When Chantal had entered Pakistan a few weeks earlier, she found its patriarchal restraints frustrating and its men boorish and insulting, particularly in comparison to her beatific Nepal and its gentle Sherpa people. She felt that Pakistani men were sexually repressed and that in her case that repression manifested in overt sexual harassment. Like many Western women climbers, Chantal was asked by a local Pakistani reporter for an interview about her upcoming attempt on K2. As she sat down in the hotel lobby, the first interview question was, "Do you want to give me and my friend a nice kiss?" She looked at the man in disgust, but he merely laughed, not understanding why she would take offense. She had walked through the streets revealing her bare head and arms and wearing tight pants. Why should she mind sharing a little attention?

For Pakistanis, there were two types of women, virgins and nonvirgins, and within the latter group there were wives and whores. In their minds, Chantal was clearly a whore and passing through Pakistan, in part, to spread her particular charm.

Not wanting to make a bad situation worse, Chantal suffered through the man's inane and sometimes insulting questions as best she could, giving pert, quick answers before she stood, muttered a quick "Shukria, merci," and left the men chuckling and snickering about her bottom as they watched it leave the hotel.

Chantal had come into Pakistan separate from her Swiss teammates, and she immediately found it impossible to travel as a single woman through the maze of bazaars and markets that litter Rawalpindi outside of Islamabad. She had wanted to wander through the world-famous rugs and silks, alabaster and gold, but everywhere she went a crowd of dark, angry faces greeted her, some even stopping and questioning her. *Why are you here? Where is your father? Your husband?* She ignored them at first, then tried to charm them with her laughter and bright smile, but finally she just fled their cloying fascination and repressive maneuvering, almost jogging back to the relative safety of her hotel.

Later she met up with a female friend, and the two women headed for a local restaurant rumored to have clean food. But they had barely ordered when three Pakistani men at a nearby table insisted they join them. Repeatedly Chantal and her friend politely said, "No thank you, we are old friends and would like to talk privately." Snickering that perhaps they enjoyed women more than men, the men's harassment and beer consumption escalated until finally the beer won. The three tripped drunkenly out of the restaurant, giving Chantal a final leering guffaw as they went.

Her distaste for Pakistan and its patriarchal chauvinism wasn't helped when the owner of her hotel in Skardu showed up at her door late in the night. She answered it wearing only the T-shirt she slept in, trying as best she could to cover herself. She thought there might be a problem; otherwise, she would have ignored the insistent knocking. The man looked at her with the look of a starving man at the buffet. As his eyes roamed her body with a wolf's leer, he suggested that perhaps, since she was alone, she might want to sleep with him?

Again mindful that she was alone and that he had a passkey to her room, she resisted the urge to spit in his face, kick his enlarged crotch, and slam and lock the door in his face. *No,* she told him, *no thank you, I am fine,* and tried to push the door shut. But the man put his weight and foot against it.

"But I am young, I am strong, I will not disappoint, yes?"

"No!" she said, and with a mighty push finally shut the door. She spent the remainder of the night listening for his passkey in the lock.

Part of her problem with Pakistani men may have been her dress. In the strictly Muslim, see-no-skin society, many Western women opt for total anonymity, hiding themselves, their bodies, their hair, and their faces behind the traditional *shalwar kameez,* a billowing three-piece outfit of caftan, pants, and head shawl that obscures everything female about the woman beneath. Eschewing the local garb, Chantal upset the locals as well as other climbers when she insisted on wearing her Lycra tights in public. Even Western men have admitted to feeling uncomfortable wearing shorts in a place where the only visible legs are on mules and cows.

Once she met up with her Swiss teammates and started out of Skardu, Chantal thought only of the towering peaks of the Karakoram and K2 as she made the ten-day trek into Base Camp. There, she and the Swiss climbers told other teams that they would ascend the mountain alpine-style and did little to help fix rope on the Abruzzi or establish high camps. However, climbers saw them clip onto old ropes to descend, ropes that more than once broke under their weight as they made their way on the route. For her part, Chantal hated carrying the heavy loads necessary for true alpine climbing and usually relied on her partners to supply the necessary gear of tent, stove, gas, and food high on the mountain. Her backpacks were notoriously tiny; one even sported a stuffed duck on its frame but lacked anything heavier inside. When American Marty Schmidt, a boisterous climber who couldn't help but wonder how much team gear she could carry in such a ridiculously small rucksack, called out, "Hey, Chantal, that's some tiny pack," she shot him an angry glare but did nothing to add any weight to her load.

To many it didn't appear as if the Swiss were making a serious stab at climbing the mountain. After a few weeks even Chantal seemed to distance herself from the team, setting her tent away from the Swiss and closer to Americans Ed Viesturs and Scott Fischer, as if placing her bets on a different horse. After a month the Swiss decided to go for the summit even though their highest camp was barely at 6,300 meters (20,670 feet). To climb the remaining 2,300 meters (nearly 8,000 feet) without any ropes, tents, or caches of gear on the mountain was foolhardy at best, suicidal at worst. Fortunately, they were stopped by a storm at 7,000 meters (23,000 feet). They descended the mountain and packed their bags for home, saying the mountain was now too crowded for them.

"They got their asses kicked," Thor said as he watched the team walk down the glacier toward Concordia and home. He looked over at Chantal and waved. She had been unwilling to leave the mountain without a serious bid at its summit, and Thor, ever eager to please, urged her to stay and climb with him, even though the Pakistani mountaineering rules strictly forbade a climber from jumping from team to team. Never one for following rules, Chantal decided to stay on the mountain, waiting at Base Camp writing poetry while Thor and his team continued to work the route.

Her intrusion on the American-Russian team was like the release of tear gas through their ranks. As Thor struggled with his warring emotions, Chantal began sleeping with Ed Viesturs. Meanwhile, teammate Charley Mace, also on his first Himalayan expedition, watched from a distance, his distaste for her antics growing with every day. Although she was pretty and charming, Mace didn't trust her motivations and decided to keep as far from her web as possible, fearing its silken threads. While his team, joined by Kiwis Rob Hall and Gary Ball, toiled on the route, Chantal held court at Base Camp, walking from mess tent to mess tent, commanding center stage from audience after audience of rapt men. Those not so rapt were awestruck at her hubris, but said nothing.

Chantal had no such turmoil. In her mind she was an independent player, climbing when and where she wanted to; having carried some of her equipment to a high camp, she figured she was done. She didn't consider the fact that a lot of hard work had to go into her ability eventually to clip onto ropes and climb the mountain. *Why should I? I only want to climb the mountain. There are plenty of men here to see to the drudgery of preparing the route.*

And so they did, with almost no complaint. While many men have slacked off from the hard work of climbing an 8,000-meter peak, few seemed to take the work of others for granted the way Chantal did.

On July 28, Kieser, Viesturs, and Neal Beidleman, another climber with the American-Russian team, left Base Camp for their summit bid, reaching Camp III on July 30. Two Russians, Vladimir Balyberdin and Gennady Korieka, were 300 meters above them at "Camp III.2." While Viesturs and Beidleman slept in a nearby tent, Thor was alone when he heard a little voice outside the tent.

"Thor?" It was Chantal. He had had no idea that she was on the mountain behind them. She had waited in Base Camp for the men to make their bid, and then she quietly put on her crampons, filled a water bottle, and started up the mountain. She carried no gear, picking up her stowed sleeping bag lower on the mountain. She climbed in with Thor, who was surprised, and thrilled, to see her. Nearby, Viesturs and Beidleman said they didn't like the look of the weather and decided to descend.

July 31 dawned cold and clear, but burdened with a tent, sleeping bag, stove, rope, and food, Thor was carrying a load too heavy to make much progress up the slope. After he and Chantal ditched their sleeping bags, most of the rope, and a lot of the food, they continued up but were stopped for the night by a 300-foot ice wall. After a miserable night bivouacking without sleeping bags, Thor's feet were totally numb. Chantal, even though she was wearing only a one-piece suit, was fine, apparently impervious to the cold. Maybe she just didn't need all the extra gear; her own body armor did better than most. With the weather holding, Thor told Chantal that he was going to go down and get his bag; he couldn't risk another night without it. "While you're there, please bring mine too," Chantal asked. He did.

As he descended he encountered Alexei Nikiforov, who said that he also hadn't brought his bag high on the mountain because he knew his teammates were ahead of him. Could he fold into Kieser and Chantal's tent for warmth if he didn't make it to their Camp IV tent? Kieser agreed, glad for the help in the trail-breaking to come. The three then continued up and reached the Shoulder at 4:30 P.M., but seeing that they were still hours away from Balyberdin and Korieka's Camp IV tent higher up on the Shoulder, they decided to camp there for the night. They pitched Kieser's tent and crawled in, Nikiforov nestled between the two sleeping bags for warmth.

August 2 was yet another beautiful day, and the troika made it to the Russians' Camp IV by noon. There they encountered Balyberdin and Korieka on their descent; they were the first men to make it to the summit via the Abruzzi since the disaster of 1986. But having bivouacked at 8,400 meters on descent, they were in no mood to celebrate or linger, and they hurried down the ridge, leaving their tent and a sleeping bag for Nikiforov.

"Tomorrow is our day," Thor said. And it nearly was.

Before the sun had peaked over Broad Peak, Thor rose and left Camp IV first, breaking trail for hours through two feet of new snow recently dumped by a storm. Hours later Alexei Nikiforov followed. Using the slow and methodical pace of a Russian-trained climber, Nikiforov made careful progress up the slope. When Kieser reached 8,450 meters (27,700 feet), only 550 feet below the summit, he nevertheless knew his chances of reaching it were gone. He was depleted from his rapid pace as well as the exhausting work of plowing through the deep and ice-crusted snow alone, particularly through the most dangerous section of the entire climb up the mountain, the notorious Traverse.

A 50-degree wall of unstable snow on a frozen waterfall of ice, the Traverse stretches 150 feet across an open abyss where, if climbers cared to—most don't—they could look between their feet and see 10,000 feet down the face of K2. It is here that many climbers have turned around, and it is here that many of those who have continued on have died. Jim Wickwire, who climbed the mountain in 1978 and barely survived a harrowing bivouac at 28,000 feet, called it "the nastiest spot on the entire climb," and Carlos Buhler, who climbed the mountain in 1991, said that "climbers' crampons, as well as their brains, are pretty dull by the time they reach that ice field," leaving little room for mistakes.

Thor found the route had a wind-crust that he continually fell through. Turning around, he hoped to see Chantal or Alexei near him so that they could take over the exhausting work of breaking trail. They were still tiny figures far below him. He sat against the slope, trying to cry from the sheer frustration and exhaustion, but his body refused to respond to even the most basic of commands. His mind a gauzy haze, he sat studying the curvature of the earth and the endless mountains at his feet. Suddenly a clear, powerful voice pierced his dull brain: "If you want to live, go down." Thor looked around him, almost expecting to see somebody talking to him; the voice was that clear. He was alone on the barren slope; Chantal and Alexei were still tiny black dots far below him on the route. Unwilling to risk his life any more than he had, he turned and began to descend. "I always want to live, so I err on the conservative side."

Chantal had left camp last, worried because her toes were cold. She waited over two hours after Thor and Alexei had left Camp IV for the sun to rise before finally starting out for the summit. Following in the now-established trail, she quickly caught up with Nikiforov in the Bottleneck and met Thor as he descended back through the Traverse. "Thor," she urged, "climb with me! We'll make the summit together."

Tempted but not swayed, he told her no, he didn't have anything left for the summit. He'd spent his last dime.

"No matter what happens," she said to him, "I think you are a really nice guy." Thor, physically and emotionally numb, barely registered the peculiar comment. He told her he'd wait for her at Camp IV.

Good thing. His retreat saved not only his own life but most likely Chantal's and Alexei's as well. When he reached the top of the Bottleneck, he saw that Alexei had left their 50-foot coil of relatively thin but strong Kevlar™ rope hanging from ice screws, obviously betting he wouldn't need to carry the extra weight for the remainder of the climb. Thor stopped to set anchors in the ice and loop the rope through them, thereby providing a safety rope through the worst section of the Bottleneck for Chantal and Alexei. It was the section of the climb where Liliane and Maurice Barrard were last seen before falling to their deaths. Above him, Chantal was making her final steps to the summit.

Chantal concentrated on her breathing, listening to it rasp through her throat. She watched her boots, counting her steps against her breaths as she climbed, five, six breaths, step, six, seven breaths, step. *So long as my feet are on the ground, I'm safe. But am I dreaming? It all feels so unreal.* She sat back on her heels to rest. Far below her she saw the ribbon of glacier where Base Camp sat, realizing how far she was from its safety. Above her hung the summit of K2. Images flooded her brain; among them she saw her mother, smiling, loving, proud. She felt a peace she had never known. *Is it the altitude? Is it God? Is it Death?* She felt totally mystical, one with the spirits around her, one with herself. She rose from the snow and took her final steps to the summit of K2.

It was 5:00 P.M. on August 3, 1992, and K2 had a fourth female summiteer. She looked over at Broad Peak where she knew a group of her Basque friends were climbing. She dug her radio out of her pocket and called them. Great whoops of joy and congratulations filled the quiet air around her. It sounded like a symphony to her.

"Hola! I am right here!" She laughed and waved across the great expanse to K2's neighbor, thinking they must be able to see her. She said good-bye and sat back once again on her heels to take it all in. Quietly she thanked God, told her mother she loved her, and wept joyous tears.

When avowed nonbelievers in a Supreme Being sit on the rim of the Grand Canyon in Arizona for the first time, most are awed into a stunned silence by the sheer power and beauty at their feet. When they are able to speak, many admit that maybe, just maybe, there is a God after all; it's that sublimely gorgeous a place. Maybe this is what Chantal experienced—a lot of cathartic tears and an emotional embrace of what she now saw as God's unknowable plan for her mother and for her. Then she rose and turned to begin her long descent.

When Alexei passed her moments later, she gave him a strong hug, assuring him that he was almost there. She continued down, but her blissful reverie lasted only as long as the waning light. Having broken her clear-glass night goggles, she was forced to descend without their protection from the cold, wind, and tiny particles of airborne ice. Cold, exhausted, and not trusting herself to cross the Traverse alone in the dark, she curled up to wait out the night in a snow hole dug at 8,400 meters two days earlier by the Russians. Alexei found her crouched miserably on the icy slope and urged her to get up and follow him down. She did, although her eyes were already burned by the cold and ice in the darkness. As she made her painstakingly slow progress through the Traverse and the Bottleneck, she began to lose feeling in her feet and hands, even momentarily falling asleep on the line, as Mrowka Wolf had done six years before.

In front of her, Alexei clipped into the rope that Thor had set just hours before. As he transferred his weight from one foot to the other, he felt his crampon come loose from his weighted foot and hang useless from the strap that held it to his boot. He fell several frightening meters before the rope allowed him to gain purchase. Without that rope, K2 would have claimed its twenty-eighth victim. It didn't because Thor had found the mind and the mettle to make the descent safer for those above him. For Chantal. He knew she might need the anchor, but it was Alexei whose life he saved.

By the time he finally made it into camp, Alexei was nearly comatose with exhaustion, fear, and hypoxia and fell into Thor's tent near collapse. "Where is Chantal?" Thor asked. Alexei pointed into the air. "Behind me," he whispered.

Forty-five minutes later he heard her stumbling toward the tent. He jumped out and found her staggering, arms out in front of her like a child playing Pin the Tail on the Donkey, trying to find her way. She was snow-blind and barely conscious. When he got her in the tent and peeled her boots off her feet, he saw that they were dangerously cold, but not yet frostbitten. He quickly brewed tea and soup and fed them chocolates, hoping to get them rehydrated and energized for the long descent.

Having spent three days at Camp IV, the last twenty-four hours waiting for Chantal and Alexei, Thor knew his own clock was pretty close to winding down, and now he needed to get not only himself but two barely ambulatory people off the mountain and out of its Death Zone.

The stricken trio started out of Camp IV around 1:00 P.M. on the 4th, Thor and Alexei supporting Chantal between their shoulders. Barely moving and unable to see the snow at her feet, they had to carry her a few meters at a time, then sit her down to let her rest, then drag her back up, move another few meters, and again set her down to let her rest. It took them three hours to go less than 200 feet to the edge of the Shoulder and the beginning of the technical descent. Thor feared that trying to guide Chantal down the steep slope beneath them at night would be suicidal, so he set up the tent while she sat in the snow, incapacitated. Alexei, scared for his own life, continued down, leaving Chantal and her rescue to Thor. Thor couldn't blame him. That's all he wanted to do too, to get down and fast. Instead, Thor turned back to the tent to begin melting water for more soup and tea. He and Chantal had been near or above 8,000 meters for six days. Their luck with good weather was miraculous. Even more so, it continued as their descent dragged on.

The next day they were rewarded with the most beautiful morning Thor had ever seen in the Karakoram. They woke to brilliant sunshine sitting just above a thick blanket of clouds at their feet. The only things poking through the blanket were peaks above 7,800 meters (25,500 feet). The white summits of Broad Peak, the four majestic Gasherbrums, and far-off Nanga Parbat were like ships sailing in a milky sea. He described it to Chantal, who still could not see farther than her feet, but he was glad to see she was stronger; the constant supply of brewed drinks, soup, and food were reviving her energy.

Thor radioed to Viesturs and Fischer below them in Camp III, who reported that Alexei had made it into camp around 11:00 P.M. "We're going to come up and help you with Chantal," Fischer assured him.

But Thor wanted to get the hell off the mountain, fast. Having only one short length of rope, he began belaying Chantal 2,000 feet down to Camp III, 30 feet at a time. Using his ice ax as an anchor, he sat down as deep in the snow as he could get and belayed her down the 45-degree slope, time after time. As he did, he watched the slope above them with increasing dread. It was the perfect angle for a catastrophic slide, and he could see that it hadn't let loose since their last storm on ascent. Although the good weather was a godsend, the hot sun on the loaded slopes was a disaster waiting to happen. He was dancing on the edge of death, the adrenaline pumping through him like heroin. Everything tingled—his face, his hands, even his frozen feet as he sat in belay after belay. He had never felt so alive realizing that at any minute, without any warning, they could be swept off the East Face. And it wouldn't take much. With each belay, Thor and Chantal knocked small sloughs of unstable snow loose; if any of those had been above them, it would have been enough to pull his pathetic ax anchor and take them into the abyss.

Thor watched Chantal struggle with each movement down the perilous slope, and he felt the urge to wish her a final farewell. He felt death was that close. But he didn't say a word beyond those of encouragement.

Moving up toward them, Viesturs and Fischer didn't like the look of the slope any better than Thor did and opted to rope together for safety, even though the slope was relatively easy. Only a short distance out of camp, Viesturs also felt the hair rise on the back of his neck with impending mortal danger, and he began digging a snow hole, hoping to get below the avalanche before it hit. Fischer, watching him from above, never saw it coming. Without warning, he was hit by the wall of ice and snow and catapulted down the slope.

Viesturs heard the *crack* of the slab break loose and looked up in time to see Fischer get hit by the full force of the avalanche before he dove into his hole, almost jubilant that his plan seemed to be working; the slide was passing over him. His glee turned to terror when the rope between them became taut and he was plucked out of his hole like a fish on a line and carried hundreds of feet down the slope. Struggling desperately to anchor his ax underneath him, Viesturs finally felt its steel teeth dig into the slope. They were only feet from the edge of the abyss. He saved both their lives. Shaken but alive, they assessed their bumps and bruises. Since neither had sustained major damage, they continued up the slope to help Thor bring Chantal off the mountain.

Meanwhile, foot by foot, belay by belay, Thor and Chantal continued their terrifying descent. After many hours they made it through the worst of the avalanche danger and found the top of the fixed ropes near Camp III, where they encountered Viesturs and Fischer. Chantal lay down on the slope, exhausted and relieved that more help had come. Viesturs immediately tore off his pack and fell to his knees by her body, telling her he'd brought drops for her eyes. Gently, he lifted the dark goggles off her face and saw that her eyes were swollen and red with broken blood vessels. Squinting against the painful light, she opened each long enough for Viesturs to drip a few of the analgesic drops into her raw sockets. He hoped it would bring some measure of relief.

The embattled climbers continued down to Camp III at 24,000 feet for the night. The next morning they made it down to Camp II, and although Chantal was still exhausted and her eyes were swollen shut, every day brought her greater strength; by the last morning of her descent she was able to rappel by herself. As they approached Camp I, American expedition leader Dan Mazur and Charley Mace ascended from Base Camp to help get her through the last tricky sections, finally relieving Viesturs, Fischer, and Thor. Between them the five men had saved her life.

For her part, Chantal made very little mention of her collapse or rescue, instead referring briefly to her "blurred vision" and "sore eyes," her happiness at seeing Viesturs and Fischer, and her hero's welcome at Base Camp: "Charley arrives with tea and cookies, I fall into his arms, the Mexicans congratulate me, a sweet warmth of human bonding fills me." After a Russian doctor put tea bags on her sore eyes, a Spanish friend gave her a jewel, and Alexei fed her vodka-laced jam on bread, she finally "savored the victory." The person she didn't mention, or thank, was Thor.

Nevertheless, the two left Base Camp together, even sharing hotel rooms in Skardu and getting drunk together in Rawalpindi before leaving Pakistan, but they were never again lovers. Afraid of her continuing power over him, Thor feared that if he made any kind of amorous move, he would feel the bitter sting of rejection and that the humiliation and self-hatred would be more than he could bear.

Before she was allowed to leave Pakistan, Chantal was called before the Ministry of Tourism to answer for her insult in disobeying the law and not staying on her original team.

Chantal sat in the dingy ministry while a gaggle of men talked in excited Urdu about what they should do to make an example out of her. If other climbers decided the rules were there to ignore, the Pakistani military would lose all control over who was traipsing around their mountains, mountains that sat in ground zero of their border war with India. *Besides, who is this girl to decide she can do as she pleases? Our women would never dare show such disrespect.* Chantal looked from face to face, boredom rather than concern growing as the chatter continued. Finally, one official turned from the group and sat at the desk.

"So, you decide to stay by yourself at Base Camp. We hear you stay to fuck all the men."

Chantal, stunned at his language and his rudeness, stared at his angry face.

"No, I stay because I want to climb and my team—"

"No, my liaison officers on the mountain say you stay to fuck the men."

It was true that she had slept with Viesturs and then tented with Thor and Alexei on the mountain, so she didn't know what the LOs had told him.

"Climbers must share tents and I—"

"No, I think you enjoy the fucking, yes? So, why don't you fuck me too?" The men behind him giggled nervously.

Chantal decided her best option was to keep her mouth shut. She felt like she had come down from her sanctuary in the clouds only to land in a pile of *merde!*

Finally, in the face of her silence, the official told her she had to pay a $3,000 fine, an exorbitant amount of money for a woman who regularly lived on little more than $200 a month. As she left the building she tore up the fine and threw it across the pavement, muttering to herself, "Realité musulmane, Pakistan. Putain de cons de muslims. . . . Partir de ce pays vite!!" (This is the real Muslim faith, Pakistan: Fucking muslims . . . [all I want to do is] get out of this country fast!)

When the wheels of her jet finally lifted off the parched airstrip in Karachi, she and a group of trekkers cracked the first of many bottles of champagne on her victory flight home. Attributing much of her persecution to Pakistani men not liking her independence and visible beauty, she wrote of a notice she saw posted along the road from Skardu, along with the speed limits and stop signs: "Women should not show their beauty—The Koran." For Chantal, that just about summed up Pakistan.

Chantal was now the only surviving female summiteer of K2. She returned to France the newest heroine of that country's rich tradition of climbing superstars. She had it all, beauty, strength, talent, and, apparently, survivability. But outside of the French media's myopic reporting, criticism of Chantal, even ridicule, continued among the climbers: she carried small, child-like packs adorned with stuffed animals; she preferred writing poetry to actually preparing the route for an ascent; she used men to get her up, and now off, the mountains; and most scandalously of all, she didn't seem to care that people noticed. The gossip didn't seem to interest her; all she wanted was to be in the mountains. "It's a quest, not an escape. In the beginning, when I started climbing, I thought that all climbers shared this quest," Chantal laughed as she spoke to a reporter in 1997. "Later I understood that most of them, especially the men, associate mountains with a virile image that blocks their analysis."

And men were her biggest critics, claiming that she was out of her league and endangering other climbers around her. Dan Mazur is forthright about why she was condemned: "Chantal was the antithesis of the climbing mafia bullshit of big sponsorship and tons of Sherpa support. She just loved the mountains; she just wanted to climb, and all these guys trashing her, they all wanted to sleep with her. She did use her body to influence men, and why not? She had a winning personality. Sometimes she would fall apart, sure, everybody does. She had bad knees; she wasn't always in good shape. But she was extremely strong, and sometimes she pushed herself too far."

After K2 she realized a new ability to raise real expedition monies and went on a string of nearly twenty expeditions over the next six years. Part of the adventure was the travel itself: "I'm in heaven when I have to speak a foreign language all the time; it's like a voyage within a voyage." For Chantal, language was a fascinating game of discovery, intimacy, and infectious fun. She and her mostly non-French teammates played with their different languages, laughing at their combined mangling of the mixed dialects. While the growing trend in the mid 1990s was "expeditions by Internet," Chantal staunchly refused to bring any electronic connection with the outside world to the mountains—no satellite phone and definitely no website dispatches—preferring to fill her tent with books on philosophy and poetry: Baudelaire, Rimbaud, Whitman, Neruda. For Chantal, the mountains provided a spiritual path she could not walk at home. "To live a sensory experience, extreme yes, but extraordinary."

In the spring of 1993 she returned to her first love, Everest, with a boisterous New Zealand team whose mess tent was "transformed into the local discotheque," with Chantal's table dancing a favorite attraction. Although the team had nine climbers and eight high-altitude Sherpas, she said she climbed alone and "far more rapidly than my friends." It was another comment that would raise eyebrows and ire among the climbers around her. She reached 8,400 meters (27,500 feet) but was moving slowly and lacked the proper clothes for the extreme cold. Wisely, she turned back, "preferring a long life with my toes rather than irreversible frostbite."

She returned to the Nepalese side of Everest in the fall with her Spanish friends, a stuffed duck, and a flag of Bob Marley. She and the duck reached 8,000 meters, but no more. Lacking the legal and expensive permits, she and her climbing friend, Pemba Sherpa, decided before leaving

Nepal, to poach nearby 8,000-meter giants Shisha Pangma and Cho Oyu, reaching the summits of both in October. Although she seemed to be involved in more of a race than a spiritual quest, she insisted that, for her, "the mountains are living things; they are not just rock and stones stuck together covered with snow, they have a soul. When you climb to the top, you are in open space and you are space itself."

When she came down into Kathmandu, she again faced legal action for climbing without the proper permits, this time from both Tibet and Nepal, because the mountains straddle both countries. Instead of quietly paying her fines, Chantal returned to France and spoke out against the bureaucracy strangling Himalayan climbing. Upset with their high-profile and outspoken climber, the French Alpine Club denounced her as a disgrace but quietly withdrew its censure when it saw how much support her remarks generated.

Quite apart from her Himalayan pursuits, Chantal accepted an invitation to climb Mount Williams in Antarctica because it was an "impossible invitation to refuse." She departed Paris in January 1994. On the trip she met Denis Ducroz, who was on board to film the team's climb of the 6,000-foot mountain direct from sea level. Chantal had no idea where she was going or for how long. A day, a month, a year, it simply didn't matter to her. Because she had no concept of the goal in front of her, she flew blindly into its embrace, the vagueness part of the joy. Although she was impetuous and carefree in signing on, it nonetheless became a pivotal trip when Ducroz cracked the facade of the beautiful, charismatic climber to reveal the vulnerable woman beneath. But it took some finessing.

When Ducroz began filming, he was increasingly frustrated with the cartoon image Chantal presented; pretty, flamboyant, and shallow. She seemed unwilling to let him or his camera anywhere near her soul. Ducroz asked her to take a walk with him on the cold beach. He tried to explain that if she didn't allow people to know who she was, give them some hint of her heart and mind, they would create their own image. All that the world knew of her, Ducroz explained, was that she was a pretty party girl who also climbed. If she didn't tell them who she really was, their image of her as "bird-brained" would persist. As they walked Ducroz saw that she was crying. They returned to camp, and he resumed filming. Thereafter, whether passing bottles between the boats in a blinding storm or happily eating while the rest of the crew leaned over the gunnels seasick, she seemed more genuine, more open, as he shot the scenes. But in the end he wasn't sure if he hadn't been seduced along with the rest of the world at her feet. Maybe he too was part of a lie. He didn't know, and he didn't care. She had won at least one heart: his.

Fresh off the boat from Antarctica, Chantal joined another Everest expedition, this time via its then-unclimbed Northeast Ridge in Tibet, a demanding route that involved a 1,000-meter (3,300-foot) climb between Base Camp and Camp I alone. As a client on Russell Brice's guided expedition, Chantal remained in Base Camp as guide Marty Schmidt spent six days fixing 3,200 feet of rope to the first camp. After the route was prepared, Schmidt told Chantal to get her load of personal gear ready for the climb to Camp I.

She looked at him as if he had instructed her to strap a refrigerator on her back.

"No," she told Schmidt, "I've paid as a client to have my equipment taken up for me!"

Schmidt looked at her in disbelief, thinking, *Come on, lady! Would you just be a real climber for a couple of days?! I set the whole damn route. Now you put the damn pack on your back and move!* But as her hired help, he had to use more political language.

"Yes, Chantal, you are a client, but even a client must carry her own water and personal items, right? You don't really want to climb this mountain if someone else has to carry your toothbrush, do you?"

She looked at him coolly, then turned and shouldered her pack, but it was as tiny a pack as Schmidt had ever seen in his years of guiding clients up the largest mountains in the Himalayas. Later, when he tried to set a schedule for the team to climb and descend, preparing their bodies and blood for the final assault on the summit, after one trip above Advanced Base Camp, Chantal said, "No more."

"No, I am a professional climber," she said to Schmidt. "I do not need to acclimatize more. Once Camp II is established, I will go to Camp II."

Schmidt, bridling at her dependence on Sherpas to do the heavy lifting, told her it was high time she started behaving like a mountaineer. Chantal ignored him and retreated to her tent, waiting for the route to be established. When it was, she joined the team on the mountain, but an avalanche soon forced them back off the mountain. At that point, Chantal and Schmidt's other clients simply ran out of steam on the demanding route.

Knowing there was a strong team on the nearby North Ridge, Schmidt asked to buy into the tents, lines, and support of American guide Eric Simonson, who agreed. But even on the less arduous North Ridge, Chantal and most of the team just seemed to deflate, and the expedition packed for home.

Meanwhile, Schmidt, who was taking his last client to the summit, was called into service to rescue two stranded climbers, Michael Rheinberger of Australia, who perished, and Kiwi Mark Whetu, whom Schmidt was able to get off the mountain safely. Chantal watched the drama from Base Camp, "overwhelmed by a contemptuous Himalaya," and fled the "horrific battlefield to rejoin the sun, life, flowers, summer, and leave the monsoon to wash clean the mountain dirtied by Himalayan inhumanity." Simonson watched her leave, unimpressed.

"Her strategy was to hang out at Base Camp and Advanced Base Camp," Simonson said. He felt that she avoided the arduous work of acclimatizing to the thin air. While in camp, she spent her time talking to her sponsors on the [borrowed] satellite phone and giving interviews before she gave the summit only one shot. Predictably, "she got spanked and went home . . . her climb struck me as being completely unrealistic for her to accomplish."

When she wasn't planning and going on expeditions, Chantal was home paying for them, making public appearances for her sponsor, Sector watches, as well as guiding clients through the alpine playground surrounding Chamonix. Her training included skiing and long-distance biking. On one occasion, a reporter in the south of France called to see whether she could come down for an interview. She said she could, but it might take her a few hours; she would be biking the 100 kilometers (62 miles) to his office. She was also a regular feature on the Chamonix club scene, drinking and dancing her nights away with a dizzying array of handsome attendants. In the winter of 1995 she was skiing above Chamonix when she fell. As she went down she felt the now-familiar pain of her knee ligaments tearing. But when the clinic doctor asked her when she wanted to schedule her surgery to mend the damaged ligaments, she told him no, she had a mountain to climb first.

She left for Everest only weeks later as a member of Rob Hall's Adventure Consultants expedition attempting the popular Southeast Ridge route. Remarkably, she nearly made it, reaching the South Summit at 8,750 meters before turning back, or rather, being turned back. Chantal had been the slowest of Hall's clients the entire climb, and when she stopped at the South Summit, Rob put his hand on her shoulder, urging her to turn around. She looked at him, her lips blue and unfeeling, her eyes unfocused. She nodded quietly, unwilling to protest, unable to speak. She turned from the summit, but only 100 feet into her descent she collapsed onto the slope, drifting in and out of consciousness.

Hall and Guy Cotter, one of his guides, knelt next to her. "Chantal! Do you know where you are?"

Their voices sounded like they were talking through water, but she answered, *Yes, I am climbing Everest.* She struggled to stay awake against the heavy desire to sleep. Suddenly the world came into sharp, immediate focus, and she blinked rapidly, feeling the blood course through her head, making her eyes feel too large for their sockets, her heart pounding in her chest. She reached up and felt that someone had put an oxygen mask on her mouth. She dragged deep on its rich elixir, feeling it reach deep into her body, warming her feet and hands, tingling in her lips. She blinked her eyes again and sat up, trying to shake her head clear. Someone asked her if she could stand, and she nodded yes, her words muffled behind the mask. Hands came under her armpits to help her up, but as soon as she stood the world lost its edges and she fell onto the snow again.

Hall knew they would have to carry her down. He slung a rope through her harness and wrapped it around his body for leverage. Cotter got in front of her and lifted her legs on either side of his back, holding onto them under his arms as he climbed down, supporting her like a wheelbarrow down a hill. It was a dangerous and arduous descent, and different teams of men traded off to help with the backbreaking work. Again, Ed Viesturs was among them.

When she was finally examined by a doctor at Camp IV, he thought she might have suffered a stroke. Stroke or no stroke, the next morning Cotter was amazed when "she bounced up and flittered on back to Base Camp."

Rob Hall reportedly came off the mountain irate and told other climbers that they had "hauled her off the mountain like a sack of potatoes"—a quote made famous when Jon Krakauer reported it in *Outside* magazine—and that she was forever banned from his future expeditions. Oddly, Hall never told Guy Cotter of his edict. Even more curious, three years before it had been he and his best friend and partner, Gary Ball, who had both needed rescuing off of K2 in what would be a far more dangerous descent than that of Chantal off of Everest, where there were fixed ropes and Sherpas through the worst of the job. Charley Mace, who along with Ed Viesturs and Scott Fischer, was part of the 1992 K2 rescue, recalled it as one of his most desperate episodes in the mountains. While Hall got stronger as they descended, Ball further deteriorated, and "all of the sudden we're in a snowstorm dragging somebody down, putting them on the ropes, tying knots and clipping them in. Each one of us [Mace, Viesturs, and Fischer] at some point thought, 'To heck with this, let's just leave him, let's go, I gotta worry about myself, let's get out of here,' and then we'd sit down and the other two would step up to the plate and start carrying and dragging. So it's lucky there were three of us and we could rotate through and take turns and let that pass. And we did save his life and got him down to Base Camp." Viesturs remembered having to yell at Gary to keep him moving, while Rob Hall called doctors in New Zealand for help with his worsening condition; eventually the crippled Ball had to be carried down the lower sections of the mountain. "It was all very surreal," Viesturs said. Gary Ball died on Dhaulagiri in 1993 from the same pulmonary edema that had felled him on K2 the year before.

But in 1995 it was Hall who was called into action to rescue Chantal, and even though she was one of his clients, he didn't much appreciate it. Hall died on Everest in 1996, so it will never be clear why her rescue was so egregious to him while his own rescue, with Ball, off of K2 was less so. Perhaps Hall was angry in part because he and his guiding company, Adventure Consultants, had begun counting his Everest ascents, which brought in big business in the professional guiding business. In 1994 his website noted that he had become the first Westerner to summit Everest four times. But 1995 was a bust year: neither he nor any of his clients made it to the summit, and he didn't like it.

Another reason for the ill will was that Chantal always seemed to need rescuing. Men would gather around the different Base Camp tents comparing their histories, and Chantal's name would invariably come up. Beautiful women were always a topic of conversation at Base Camps, particularly when they were sleeping nearby. Suddenly two or three of the men would realize that they had all been involved in one rescue or another, jeopardizing their summit bids and lives. If Chantal had been a man, they knew she probably wouldn't have gotten a lot of the help she got. Not that a man would have been left for dead, but he wouldn't have been helped *up* past the point of his own power. Expedition gossip that Chantal was reckless spread through the climbing world, and her reputation in it continued to spiral downward.

From the beginning of her career, Chantal told the world she was climbing in an ethic of mountaineering purity similar to that of Reinhold Messner, Jerzy Kukuczka, and Christophe Profit. She told her friends and family that she would never use oxygen to reach a summit; she wanted to realize the mountains on her own physical terms, even though with oxygen she might have been able to climb Everest. But having sold herself as an alpine climber, she could never be seen using it.

"Can you imagine," Ducroz said, "she was that close [to the summit] and she refused? But it would have been the end of her career. There were people just waiting for that." But perhaps they were simply waiting for her to admit that she did not have the strength of a Messner or Profit at altitude.

Many thought her problem was that she believed she needed to climb in the purest style in order to garner media attention but just didn't have the strength or talent for its demands. Others believed that Chantal was simply bred in the French "fast and light" style of climbing mountains. Leaving for their summit bids with little more than a bottle of water and a candy bar, they found that sometimes it worked, as with Benoit Chamoux's record twenty-three-hour ascent of K2, and sometimes it didn't, as with Maurice and Liliane Barrard's exhausted and eventually fatal climb in 1986. A quick, clean ascent was how Chantal wanted to approach the mountain, and with plenty of able-bodied help at the ready, she never seemed to question her right to do so. Even so, she had a magic mark, somewhere around 8,700 meters, above which she couldn't function without the aid of supplemental oxygen. "The writing was on the wall, but Chantal just wouldn't read it," Cotter said.

Another problem with her climbing was a weak and persistently injured knee, a result of her earliest skiing accident when she was five. When she walked, some thought she looked like she was in pain. In 1994 Niels Friisbøl, the president of Valandré clothing in the French Pyrenees, followed her up a flight of stairs and noticed that she had trouble placing her legs and looked to him like someone with a handicap.

"Chantal didn't take care of herself," Thor said, remembering a few bacchanals at K2 Base Camp where she ended up blind drunk. "She wasn't a safe climber," he said, but he was painfully honest about why he, an accomplished high-altitude climber and guide, would trust his life to her. "I climbed with Chantal because I was in love with Chantal, not because I thought she was safe."

After K2 he never climbed with her again, trying to heal his battered ego and heart. Nonetheless, over ten years later Kieser spoke with awe of the love he felt.

"Chantal was Helen of Troy: the face that launched a thousand ships. The face that launched a thousand climbers."

CHAPTER 9

OF MOTHERS AND MOUNTAINS

Great things are done when men and mountains meet.

—WILLIAM BLAKE

Instead of being neatly tucked into her scheduled seat aboard the Pakistan International Airlines flight from Islamabad to London, Alison Hargreaves was standing on top of the world's second-highest mountain. Three weeks earlier she had written to Jim and their children back in Scotland that she would be leaving Base Camp on August 6 in time to catch her flight on the 13th. But she hadn't. Instead, she had gone for one last try at the summit.

And why not? She was feeling lucky. Three months earlier, to the day, she had made history as the first woman to climb Everest without supplemental oxygen or assistance, a distinction she guarded fiercely, refusing even a cup of tea from another team on the mountain lest she be accused of taking "support." She knew people would not call it a purely solo climb because there were other teams on the route whose fixed lines she could grab if she ran into trouble. But she hadn't run into trouble, and she hadn't used their ropes. She had done it alone, without support or gas, and when she had come off the mountain, she had been an instant star, chased through airports by reporters and hounded for interviews. From struggling to pay the mortgage and put food on the table for young Tom and Kate, Alison was suddenly calling the shots, deciding on the interviews, picking her sponsors. It was a heady time, far from her calm childhood in bucolic Belper, England.

. . .

One of Alison's earliest memories was of sitting atop Bunster Hill in Derbyshire. Her face was round like a pie, and her short legs with their wool stockings and black Mary Janes stuck straight out in front of her on the rocky knoll. She was five, and she had just climbed her first mountain. What she remembered most was not the mountain but her fierce pride at having climbed it. Her parents had doubted whether she would be able to make it, and her father had assured her he would carry her the minute it looked like she was too tired. But she hadn't faltered, not once. She had barely even tripped. Her parents had beamed proudly at her, and she had beamed right back.

And that was just the beginning. When she was seven, she climbed Ben Nevis, the tallest mountain in the British Isles, and by thirteen she had scaled her first rock wall. At first intimidated by the vertical stone and lacking confidence that the rope would hold, Alison soon learned to trust the belay and herself, climbing ever harder and longer routes. Her father, John, looked on, his sense of pride and love nearly bursting from his chest. Looking at her, he thought she just seemed to flow like water up the rock.

Soon her whole life was centered on climbing. Her weekdays were spent trying to find out where the club was climbing that weekend. When she learned that the climbers met at a pub on Wednesday nights at 10:30, she stole out of the house to attend. Standing in the smoky, dark bar surrounded by some of the area's strongest climbers, all clutching frothy mugs of brackish beer, Alison held back, hiding in the shadows. She felt unwelcome in their very male circle. Once she heard what crag they were gathering at that Sunday, she immediately ducked out the door and ran back home, smarting at feeling so unwelcome. Maybe it was a British thing, she thought, or maybe it was her age. Whatever the cause, she felt a predominant sexism in the climbing community and knew she would have to climb despite it.

A couple of years later she was proudly attending a club dinner as one of its members when suddenly a respected climber approached her. She looked up at the famous face, blushing at his taking notice of her sitting quietly at the table.

"Are you a groupie?" he asked, referring to the girls who clustered around the male climbers, often sleeping with them for the fame-by-association.

Her eager and still childishly round face fell. No, she told the man, shaking her head slowly, she climbed with the group.

The man walked away. Alison squared her shoulders and tried to focus on the food in front of her, hoping she wouldn't cry.

Despite feeling like an intruder in the group, she kept at it, and her sheer determination and increasing skill eventually forced many to notice her talent. At sixteen, she impressed the likes of the legendary climber Paul Nunn, who suggested that she take the next step to advance her climbing: the Alps. He was right.

Alison's first sight of the Alps set off a sea change in her climbing and in her soul. When the train pulled out of Innsbruck, returning the family to England after a summer holiday, Alison burst into tears as she watched the majestic peaks through the train window. She felt as if she had found her true home, her home of the heart, in the mountains.

As Alison matured she found the transition from girl to woman a troubled one. Stubborn, strong-willed, and now with a new passion found on rock walls rather than in schoolrooms, she shut herself off from her family, who were hurt and confused by her isolation. She and her father, always great companions, began to argue with increasing frequency and intensity over her single-minded attention to climbing. As a child, she had been prone to scene-stealing tantrums, but as she got older she channeled that iron will into climbing with a ferocious focus. It was becoming clear that Alison, unlike her older sister Susan, would not be following in their parents' academic footsteps leading toward Oxford. Most nights Alison ended up behind her closed bedroom door, writing passionately in her diary. *They don't understand me, don't get me at all. Why can't they understand how much I love the feel of the rock under my fingers, how absolutely brilliant it feels to dance up the smooth limestone, my toes and fingertips finding the merest of holds, balancing on the air between each move? Both Dad and Susan climb, why do they question my passion? How could they not want to spend every free moment suspended above the earth, channeling their aggression and mental agility, totally in charge of their own destiny, responsible for their every move, successful as well as failed? Hadn't they felt the sheer ecstasy of pulling their bodies over that last hold, and standing on top of the rock, reliving each powerful and precise move that brought them there? No matter what, I know I wouldn't be able to handle leaving the nearby rock walls to go to Oxford, where I'd be stuck in claustrophobic libraries with dusty books. No way could I handle that. Besides, climbing is where I feel best about myself, not sitting in some classroom parroting lessons. I will never be as good at studies as I am at climbing, never feel as good about myself counting numbers as I do counting rope lengths. When I push myself climbing, I get somewhere; when I push myself academically, all I get is frustrated and bored.*

Hoping to channel their daughter's climbing energies into something productive, John and Joyce Hargreaves suggested that Alison take a weekend job at a local climbing shop where the family had shopped for years. Alison agreed, and soon the sixteen-year-old was spending a lot more than Saturdays at the Bivouac, stocking shelves with the latest in ropes, carabiners, and pitons and sitting at the feet of its owner, Jim Ballard, while he regaled his customers and young employee with colorful as well as off-color stories. Ballard, with a fireplug of a body and a full, bushy beard, held court in his crammed shop, peppering his tales with sardonic bite and, in Alison's mind, hilarious sarcasm. A self-professed "blunt Yorkshireman," Ballard was proud of his frank, salty take on life. His was the kind of cynicism that with just a raised eyebrow or rolled eyes could reduce Alison to wild giggles. Everything about him was in stark contrast to her self-controlled parents, and even though at thirty-two he was exactly twice her age, Alison was attracted.

On February 17, 1980, Alison's eighteenth birthday, Joyce was up early in her small but efficient kitchen frosting a cake for the family celebration later in the day. She looked up from the mixing bowl to see her daughter, suitcase in hand, standing in the doorway. "I'm moving in with Jim," Alison announced. And that was it. Jim and his wife Jean had split up, and although he was not yet divorced, Alison was to be the lady of his modest manor, Meerbrook Lea. John and Joyce, shattered and ashamed, sat on the couch and cried.

For a while life was exactly as Alison had planned. She loved having her own house, her own kitchen, and freedom. She also loved the gifts that Jim constantly bought for her. Showing off to Susan, Alison proudly laid out Christian Dior face creams, designer clothes, and expensive trinkets. Neither girl had ever had anything even remotely flashy, and suddenly here was Alison strutting around like a queen. Susan felt an ugly twinge of jealousy.

What Alison didn't show Susan was any deep emotion for Jim. In fact, she rarely spoke of love, at least not to her sister, mother, or Bev England, her best climbing buddy whom she'd known since they were eight years old. What she did speak of was freedom, the ability to come and go as she pleased and, most importantly, to climb. Jim, she felt, was the man who could give her the keys to that independence.

In the early days Alison relished her new "grown-up" life, tending to Meerbrook Lea's gardens, cleaning her house, and cooking for Jim. She even began a line of climbing clothing and accessories that she called Faces, sewing the hats, chalk bags, and rucksacks herself. But as with many girls' fantasies of life with an older, wiser, and wickedly funny man, reality soon set in. Within months she found herself working all day at the shop, then sewing for Faces, then cooking and cleaning for Jim. Her life of mature freedom began to feel like one of droning duty, particularly when Jim used his sharp tongue on her, often berating her in front of customers and friends at the store. But with the same tenacity she demonstrated leading difficult climbs up sheer cliff walls, she seemed determined to make it work. If she had learned anything from her "upright" parents, it was that one never, ever quit a task once undertaken.

The one thing that didn't change was her love for climbing, her emotional and physical escape. As she progressed, even the truculent male climbing community began to recognize that this child-faced woman had a bold style and tolerance of risk far greater than that of the average bloke on the wall. She trusted her own moves and decisions with an unflappable calm that others found startling. Jim had been one of her climbing tutors, but she soon surpassed his ability and daring.

For generations, climbing had been a sport whose defining characteristics were grunge and poverty. But as Alison read her climbing magazines she saw that a new chic was emerging, urged on by the French press and its newest star, Catherine Destivelle. Here was a beautiful woman who could stay up most of the night throwing back shots of tequila while holding court over the roulette tables and only hours later don her Lycra tights and bra and scale one of the toughest routes in the area, a crowd of admirers watching her every move. Alison observed Destivelle's fame but found herself unable to match the Parisienne's ability to flirt, play, and climb with equal measures of grace and skill. At a time when Destivelle was the most recognized woman in France, her face plastered on posters in the subways around Paris, Alison was little known outside the climbing crags of Derbyshire. One reason for her lack of recognition was the male-centeredness of British climbing, but another was her own unwillingness to use her femininity to gain respect or notice. She had been brought up to think of herself as a person first, not a girl or woman. To pull the flirt card now seemed a little unseemly to her. But the wild popularity of Destivelle rankled her, and she decided she would just have to become the better climber to gain fame herself.

At a climbing competition in Verdon, Alison finally met Destivelle and climbed with her most of the day, scaling the canyon's shorter routes. The beautiful and famous French climbing star didn't remember the encounter, but Alison never forgot it. She watched Destivelle, judging her climbing and her success, and knew that she and this French icon were in the same game, working for the same legacy. She also considered herself every inch the climber that Destivelle was. But she knew that Destivelle had something she could never learn or charm her way into: her body type.

Rock climbing demands a body shape and size that allow the climber to hang off cliff walls by no more than a knuckle width of a finger: strong arms and torso, spindly legs, and not an extra ounce of fat. Destivelle had just such a wiry body. Alison, by contrast, was only five-foot-four and, depending on her fitness, weighed anywhere from 120 to 135 pounds, a lot of it in her heavily muscled legs. She was far from wiry and knew she never would be. She could hone her skills and experience on rock for the rest of her life, but she would never have the innate ability of someone born to it physically. Although she was quick and bold and had learned the technical skills needed to climb, she decided her future lay in the alpine world high above the rock and ice walls. There her body's natural insulation against the cold and its pure physical power were assets that were essential to success, not barriers working against it. If she couldn't beat Destivelle on rock, maybe she could in the harsher environs of the high mountains.

In early 1983 she made her first trip to the French and Swiss Alps. Walking through Chamonix like an art student at the Louvre, her body spinning around and around, face turned toward the peaks, she took in the cathedral that contains some of the world's most picturesque mountains. She climbed with her friend Ian Parsons, a man so laid-back she thought him horizontal. She practically had to kick him into action; nonetheless, they climbed route after route, she becoming the first woman on many, the first British woman on most, her fame growing with each new successful summit. Her attempts were so bold and strong that her reputation grew even when she failed to make the top of the routes, the approaches had been that strong. She suffered little more than occasional frostnip—a less severe chilling of the extremities—even though they were sometimes forced to spend the night clipped to an ice wall wearing only their climbing shells. She reveled in being known as a tough and fearless climber in the group of men around her. She felt like she was finally making a name for herself.

As she entered the dangerous and often deadly world of big mountain climbing and set her sights on ever larger mountains, Alison reasoned that with proper planning and sound experience she could avoid the worst fate. Like any climbing shop, the Bivouac had had its share of lost clientele—climbers and alpinists killed while pursuing their passion in the mountains. Alison listened to the stories, even attended some of the funerals, but she believed that if she was humble and pragmatic as she approached the mountains, she would be successful and safe. "Stubbornness and pigheadedness I fear will lead to disaster. There is a lot to be learnt about, but with a good amount of care and time put in, even greater rewards can be gained." She knew death happened, just not to her.

After three years and many more trips to the challenging ice and alpine routes throughout the Alps, including the formidable North Face of the Matterhorn and the Croz Spur of the Grand Jorasses, Jim and Alison ran into American climber Jeff Lowe at a trade show in Munich in the fall of 1985. A man with perhaps the most first rock and alpine ascents of any American, the unassuming Lowe felt a bit pounced upon by Jim.

At trade shows and climbing events, Jim promoted Alison like P. T. Barnum. He was a proud salesman, and he hawked Alison almost as if she were a product—his product. But to many his aggressive pitch was over the top, and it appeared that this middle-aged man with no career of his own was betting his future on that of his girlfriend. Peter Metcalf, owner of Black Diamond Equipment, felt embarrassed as he watched Alison, a shy, unassuming young woman, look at her shoes and fiddle with her hair while Jim, overweight, disheveled, and somehow inappropriate in the ultra-fit world of climbers, accosted dealer after dealer angling for gear and sponsorship dollars. Standing in the shadow of Jim's bluster, Alison seemed to accept the inelegant sales pitch with quiet resolve. She knew exactly how much Himalayan climbing cost, and she knew they could never foot the bill without sponsors and benefactors.

"You gotta take Alison to the Himalayas," Ballard said to Lowe by way of introduction, pushing through the crowds to where Lowe stood by a display of ropes, carabiners, and slings. Insisting that she needed a springboard into the high-stakes, high-reward world of big mountain climbing, Ballard kept up his barrage while Lowe stuck his hand out to Alison. "Hello," he said, "I'm Jeff Lowe."

Alison knew who he was and told him so, adding that she thought his climbing was quite brilliant. She took his hand and smiled back at him.

Jim and Alison knew that Lowe already had a permit for an un-climbed route on Kangtega, a beautiful 22,242-foot (6,779 meter) mountain above a Buddhist monastery in Tengboche, Nepal. Alongside a climber as strong, talented, and famous as Jeff Lowe, it would be a perfect first Himalayan peak for Alison, and it was sure to put her on the fast track of alpine climbing.

Lowe looked at Alison. She seemed like a nice enough girl, and he had already heard that she was a hell of a climber on mixed routes, those with rock and ice. He smiled back at her and said, "Sure, why not?" Less than a month later she was on her way to the Himalayas.

From a distance, Kangtega and its neighboring mountains looked like a solid, doubled-masted ship from the Spanish flotilla, but as Alison neared the mountain, Kangtega began to stand alone, its summit covered by a huge hanging glacier that stretched out like the back of a white, two-humped camel. Although 7,000 feet (2,134 meters) lower than Everest, Kangtega was 7,000 feet *higher* than Alison had ever been and represented an exciting start to what she and Jim now believed was her professional future on big mountains.

In the Himalayas, Alison truly found her mettle. Lowe watched the young woman as she assessed the mountain in front of her; he could see that she was thrilled just to be among the world's greatest peaks, her eyes following its lines, clearly itching to get her hands and feet on its foreign rock and ice. The sole woman on a four-person team, Alison never hesitated in loading her pack with as much gear as Lowe and the other three men were carrying, and whenever it was offered by her teammates, she took the lead, guiding the men, who then followed her chosen path up the demanding route.

"One of the things about Alison is that she wasn't just strong for a woman, she was just strong," Lowe said. "She did absolutely every bit as much work as anybody else on the climb. She led a couple of harder pitches, she led them very well, very safely. She was probably one of the strongest of the partners I had on the mountain, and technically the best too." High praise considering Lowe had climbed with some of the world's strongest rock and alpine climbers in history, among them Alex Lowe, Mark Twight, Renato Casarotto, and Catherine Destivelle.

In camp, Alison and Jeff sat for hours talking about climbing. She felt as if she had finally made it. No one here was asking her if she was a groupie or a roadie hitchhiking along for the fame. As they stared up at Kangtega, plotting their alpine ascent of its beautiful pillars and buttresses, Alison realized that this was the kind of climbing she craved, rather than the fixed-rope, assault-style expeditions with hired porters or Sherpas doing the heavy work and load-carrying. She loved the sense of driving an anchor into the ice with her own back muscles aching against the effort. She felt nothing but joy descending from a day's climb, having earned the exhaustion. She couldn't imagine just slogging up fixed ropes, sucking on bottled oxygen, following a trail of other climbers up a nondescript slope, made even more so by an obstructive gas mask covering her face. If she was going to get into this high alpine game, she was going to do it on her terms, and the mountains'. If she climbed a 7,000- or 8,000-meter peak, she was going to climb the peak. She wanted the pure experience and pure reward of doing it right. And if she couldn't do it, at least she would have tried without the fakery of supplemental oxygen or someone else doing the real work.

The team was enormously impressed with Alison's easy adjustment to the thin air. Many climbers' first experience at high altitude makes them feel like a fish out of water desperately learning how to live and work in the increasingly thin air, but Alison acclimatized quickly to the drop in atmospheric oxygen. Even more remarkable, in an environment where the body is burning thousands of calories more than normal and eating becomes an exercise in sheer will as the higher altitude suppresses the appetite, Alison cheerfully continued to cook and eat, actually gaining rather than losing weight. When she stood atop Kangtega after weeks of hard work, technical climbing, and difficult conditions, she felt an exhilaration known to only the rarest of souls who have shared the experience of blazing an unclimbed route on one of the world's highest technical climbs. For Alison, Kangtega was a brilliant achievement and a passion realized. When she and the team parted in Kathmandu for their different flights home, Alison cried. The trip had been everything she thought her life should be—surrounded by supportive mates and beautiful mountains.

Her return to Meerbrook Lea was anything but. As Alison gained more and more confidence from her climbing, the Pygmalion-like imbalance of power between her and Jim seemed to be shifting. Where once she might have quietly accepted his verbal tirades, her back and will became stronger with every ascent. The resulting rows were heard by customers and workers in the Bivouac. In her journal Alison wrote of being despondent and lost, "any enthusiasm I had, too has been battered out of me; it's easier not to bother." But her relationship with Jim, as with most relationships, was more complex than what others observed as simply his verbal abuse and her acquiescence. With her family down the road, she could easily have left. But a strong connection kept bringing her back to him. Social scientists have commented that the mistreated partner feels imprisoned by the aggressor's control, but Alison had what very few allegedly victimized partners do: freedom. She could and did leave for months at a time. Her decision to stay in the relationship was entirely hers.

Later that summer she followed a tragedy unfolding in the Karakoram Mountains of Pakistan, a region she knew little about: three women had finally made the summit of the world's second-highest mountain, K2, but the second, Julie Tullis, died along with four others after being trapped in a storm high on the mountain. Tullis and Alan Rouse, who also died, were the first Brits to climb K2, so the story was front-page news for nearly a week. Every day Alison read new details of their harsh deaths in her morning paper. Julie had left two children, and Rouse's girlfriend was expecting their baby in a matter of weeks. Alison read every story, horrified, but she hadn't known either Tullis or Rouse, and their deaths seemed remote, far from her own experience. She knew herself and her climbing better than that; she would never find herself in the same situation, so why be frightened by their demise?

It was the death of her friend and mentor Catherine Freer, while climbing in Canada in 1987, that rocked Alison's foundation. She had met Freer at a climbing exhibition in 1982, and only weeks before Freer's death the women had happily chatted about taking a trip to the Himalayas together. The impact of her death was similar to that of Kukuczka's death on Wanda Rutkiewicz; Alison realized as she never had before that if this strong, careful, experienced climber could die, so could she.

Instead of pulling back, Alison dove headlong into her plans for her next adventure: Nepal's 6,856-meter (22,494-foot) Ama Dablam, a beautiful mountain with a sharp summit cone reminiscent of the Matterhorn but 8,000 feet higher. This time Susan and Susan's husband Steve trekked into the mountain with her, and Alison loved having someone so close and familiar beside her every step. When it was time for Susan and Steve to leave Base Camp and continue their trek through the region, the sisters held each other in a tearful embrace.

After a long, drawn-out expedition in which fierce weather kept them all but off the mountain, Alison returned to England feeling better about her life than she had in years, writing breathlessly of the Bivouac's strong Christmas season and of Jim's divorce finally being final, nine years after his wife had left Meerbrook Lea.

In early 1988 she began vomiting in the morning. After taking a pregnancy test, she drove to her parents' house and landed two bomb-shells: after eight years of living with Jim, they were finally getting married, and John and Joyce were to be grandparents by the end of October. Now her life had all the purpose and direction she could ever have hoped for. If the relationship had been rocky, the marriage would be firmly rooted in family.

Wearing a stylish pink suit, the new Mrs. James Ballard posed proudly between Jim and her parents in the Hargreaves' backyard garden on April 23, 1988. Then she set about preparing for the baby with all the energy and organization she brought to packing her ropes and barrels for a climb. She also remained active climbing on the local crags, but as she got bigger and her climbing clothes tighter, she longed for one major climb before her bulk became too cumbersome and before it was too dangerous for the baby. She decided on the notorious North Face of the Eiger.

The "Ogre Nordwand" has a particularly heinous place in mountaineering legend and is better known for its sixty grizzly deaths than for the achievement of those who actually climbed it. With a 6,000-foot concave face of flaking limestone and ice, a brutal weather system all its own, and sections that earned the names "Traverse of the Gods," "Death Bivouac," and "the Murder Wall," it was thought for over a century to be unclimbable. It was the route that Wanda Rutkiewicz and her women's team had taken one look at in 1973 before deciding on the slightly less lethal North Buttress instead.

But Alison wanted the North Face. And she got it, becoming the first British woman to climb the most notorious route in the Alps. But it wasn't easy, and Alison suffered as she never had before, vomiting several times her first night on the rock, as well as developing horribly painful and swollen legs. Her harness pulled tighter and tighter across her belly as she climbed, and she spent three miserable, frigid nights bivouacking high above the valley floor, preparing liquids for dinner with the stove perched between her knees on the narrow ledge. As she lay in her sleeping bag, the baby kicked furiously, making sleep all the more impossible. When she finally descended back to the valley after reaching the summit, she ran to the nearest bathroom, peeled off her pants, and massaged her aching calves, swollen to twice their normal size.

The British press both praised her achievement and condemned what it considered the endangerment of the life of her unborn child. If she ever second-guessed her decision to climb while nearly six months pregnant, she never expressed it publicly; instead, she dismissed the criticism with ironic correctness: "I think I was being quite conservative. I had planned a trip up Denali, but my physician said it wouldn't be wise to go above 12,000 feet, so I went to the Alps instead." Three and a half months later her water broke while climbing with Jim on a crag near their home. Alison calmly waited for him to finish the pitch before proposing they head to the hospital.

Thomas John Ballard was born October 16, 1988, with white-blond hair, clear blue eyes, and the enormously round cheeks of his mother.

Alison savored motherhood and was awed by how she could be content to just sit and watch "TJ" for hours. She and Jim had decided that she would give up her full time work to be home with Tom while Jim, who moved into a spare room so his sleep wouldn't be disturbed by Tom's night feedings, took primary control of the business. Alison's days became a blur of dirty diapers, spit-up, and ear-splitting wails. After one particularly difficult night with a fussy Tom, Jim complained that he was kept awake by the noise. As much as she loved Tom, she began to feel isolated and alone in the consuming vacuum of his care. Whenever the weather allowed, she tucked Tom into his car seat and headed for the local bouldering area. After she got him situated at the bottom of the rock and made sure he was safe and content, she turned to the gritstone, instantly losing herself in the climb, once again free and focused. It was an escape she cherished and needed. But as he got older and began to crawl out of his seat and around the base of the rock, she wasn't able to concentrate on her climb; after that, she would leave him with her mother in Belper on the days she was able to get out and climb.

Meanwhile, Jim was struggling to keep the business afloat. Not only did the economic recession of the late 1980s hit the climbing world hard, but his tendency to delay payment until collectors literally were pounding at their door caused many suppliers to shut him off. For the first time in their ten years together, Alison realized that her life of leisure might not be guaranteed.

In the best of times their life had never included a large circle of friends, and now she found herself all but sequestered in Meerbrook without the support of girlfriends and other young mothers sharing the daily exhilarations, confusions, and frustrations of babies. Instead of devising a method of escape, Alison longed for more anchorage, eventually convincing Jim to have a second baby.

Katherine Marjorie Ballard was born March 28, 1991, a startling mirror image of her mother with a round cherubic face framed by a curly mop of blond hair. But the new baby did nothing to improve the marriage or the finances, and Susan began to watch her sister with growing alarm. Alison suffered a lot of colds and ailments and seemed less and less happy and more and more frustrated with her role of wife and mother. Climbing had always been her emotional and physical escape and reward, and that was now an afterthought to nappies, dinner, and money worries. Every month seemed to bring them closer to bankruptcy as creditors multiplied and suppliers and customers disappeared. Jim, exhausted and depressed, offered little salvation. Alison felt like her world was crumbling.

To make matters worse, Alison's nemesis, Catherine Destivelle, had become an international film and climbing star after her ascent of a new route on the Petit Dru in Chamonix was recorded by a bevy of helicopters and film crews. Adding salt to the wound, Destivelle showed up at a mountaineering event in nearby Buxton, England, with her current boyfriend, Jeff Lowe, whom Alison had known and climbed with first. It was all Alison could do to contain her jealousy as she watched the beautiful Frenchwoman win over the climbing press, a group Alison had been trying to cultivate for years. Lowe wished the two women could work together. They both had their strengths and weaknesses and were talented climbers. But there was just so much ink on women in the climbing press, and Catherine seemed to get it all.

Meanwhile, Alison had two young children to raise while Catherine did not, and Tom and Kate demanded the majority of her time and energies. When Alison found the time to climb, she often did so alone, stealing away at the last minute for a few hours of scrambling up and down the local crags without a partner to belay her. She found that she loved it. The utter freedom of strapping on just a pair of climbing shoes and a bag of chalk before heading up the rock thrilled Alison as no other style of climbing did. No ropes, no carabiners, and more importantly, no partner with whom to negotiate the climb. The only thing that mattered was the gritstone under her fingers and her rubber-tipped toes. And she was good at it. She could make her own decisions with accuracy and assuredness, choosing difficult routes with cool calculation. Not many people found the peace and power she did in solo climbing, and she reasoned that her best chance of putting herself on the map would be to exploit that strength.

She and Jim decided that a solo winter ascent of one of the six classic North Faces would put her squarely on the mountaineering world's map and gain her the attention she so sorely desired. They chose the great Matterhorn. Few women had climbed its North Face, and even fewer had done it in winter, but no one had done it alone. She and Jim began talking up her plans and flouting her achievements, but in the process they talked a big game and criticized other climbers. It was talk that angered many, including Jeff Lowe.

"[Alison] was trying to leave the impression that nothing would have happened without her [on Kangtega]," Lowe said. "And it just wasn't true. Why did she say that? Partly I think it's because Jim pushed her. But she didn't need to. She was brilliant in her own right. Climbing is like art, and she was a great artist." But for Alison, climbing was becoming less of an art and more of a career, and she was dogged in her pursuit of its rewards.

She left England in late February 1992 and drove south to Chamonix, where she planned on acclimatizing for the 4,478-meter (14,691-foot)

Matterhorn. With barely two francs to rub together, she traveled alone
and on a shoestring, living on the food she'd packed. While rejoicing in
again finding herself independent and teetering thousands of feet above
the valley floor, negotiating life-and-death moves on the rock walls and
being responsible to no one but herself, she was also lonely. She called
Catherine Destivelle's number in nearby Les Houches, trying to reach
Jeff Lowe. She left several messages with Destivelle and her business
partner, sadly hanging up the house phone each time, feeling more and
more alone. One evening, as she sat in the lobby of her cheap hotel, she
saw two children scamper across the room and tears immediately filled
her eyes. She missed Tom and Kate with a physical ache. Her curious
and outgoing children would have loved to share this adventure and the
intrigue of a hotel with its long dark corridors and staircases and to gaze
through the cheerful windows of the shops and bakeries of Chamonix.
She wiped her eyes and told the concierge she would be checking out
that afternoon.

She drove out of Chamonix, the late sunshine beautiful against the
west-facing peaks as she navigated the serpentine road through the valley. Less than two hours later she arrived in Zermatt. In the morning she
began climbing, her gloom and loneliness forgotten as she found peace
in the strength and stillness of her movement up the mixed terrain of
the North Face. But when she got into the teeth of the climb, Alison was
frustrated by the unstable ice and rock and decided to retreat while she
still could. Once she reached bottom safely, with the sun warming her,
she couldn't help but look back up to the top. *Hell,* she thought, *as long
as I'm here I might as well climb the easier Hornli Ridge route,* a less technical switchback sort of a climb to the left of the Face. Setting off again,
she climbed easily and happily in the warm sun and reached the summit in less than five hours. There she stood smiling into Italy and
Switzerland and toward distant Mont Blanc. The sun was low in the sky,
and the quality of light spilling across the peaks around her made her
glad to be alive.

Thinking herself only hours from a hot tub and meal, she began her
descent, but a few hundred meters below the summit she ran into a
group of climbers struggling to get down. They lacked the proper

descending equipment and were unable to navigate the now-icy route, which had frozen over once the sun set. With no one else around to ensure their safe descent, Alison stayed with them, belaying them length by length down the ridge that had claimed well over 400 lives in similar circumstances. The temperature sank below freezing, and Alison, barely moving as she stood in belay position, was soon shivering convulsively and her feet went completely numb. Terrified of suffering frostbite, she thought she'd lose her mind waiting for her inexperienced charges as their belays became slower and slower. Eight hours after she had left the summit, Alison and the climbers crowded into the Hornli hut near the base of the mountain, safe for the night but still hours from the bottom of the climb. After peeling off her boots, her stomach clenched in fear. Her toes were encased in ice: the sweat and melted snow from the warm day had soaked her socks and then frozen in the hours-long descent. She tried to massage life back into them, but they remained cold, white, and numb. In the morning, although desperate to get medical attention, Alison stayed with the men, shepherding them through the last tricky sections off the mountain until they were safely down. Then and only then did she rush for the cable car back to town.

Alison knew almost no one in Zermatt, so she quickly changed her clothes and jumped in her car to return to Chamonix. Once there, she drove straight to the hospital, and as her adrenaline gave way to exhaustion she sat and quietly cried, waiting to be examined. A passing nurse noticed her soaked socks, took one look at her alabaster toes, and started chattering in French to nearby orderlies. Within minutes Alison was admitted, hooked up to an IV, and given her first real meal since leaving England. *It may be hospital food, but at least it's free,* she thought. Feeling even lonelier than when she'd left Chamonix several days before, she tried calling Lowe again, but no one answered the phone. Across town, Lowe had been receiving her messages but decided not to return the calls. Living with one ambitious woman and meeting with her competition was more intrigue than Lowe could handle. Years later the guilt of that choice and its cold inevitability haunted him.

Alison lay in her hospital bed alone and scared, not knowing whether she would lose her heavily bandaged toes. The doctors had said they wouldn't know for days if the tissue was irreparably damaged and would have to be amputated before gangrene set in, or if it would naturally regenerate. The fear of frostbite haunted her. Having seen its horrible results in another climber's grotesque stumps, she lived in dread of losing her own digits. The thought of holding Tom and Kate without fingers sent shivers of fear down her back.

On her fourth day in the hospital a doctor came in and cut off the last of the dead skin peeling from her toes. The tissue had healed well; she would keep all ten toes. But the good news was tempered by the day's headline news in the *Paris Match* that lay on her tray with breakfast: Catherine Destivelle had soloed the North Face of the Eiger. Alison threw the magazine across the room with one angry flick of her wrist and immediately began rooting around for her clothes. *Enough lying around in bed waiting for a blasted toe to heal! She stole my chance at becoming the first woman to solo a major North Face in winter; she sure as hell isn't going to steal another.* But Alison's anger soon dissolved into despair and pity as the reality of yet another Destivelle triumph mirrored another of her own failures. "I want to hide away forever," she wrote. "I feel terrible, shallow, useless . . . I just fail at everything."

She returned home in a deep depression, wondering if she had any passion left to climb. If she had been hoping for a sympathetic ear in Jim, she was sorely mistaken. Conditions at home were even worse than she had left them, as employee after employee, unpaid and with little to do, quit the deserted Bivouac. As the business began to implode and Jim became more withdrawn and troubled, she wrote about her issues with her marriage in her diary but never spoke of it with her family or friends, and the marriage limped along, now bolstered by Tom and Kate. With the businesses no longer supporting the family, a plan was hatched for Alison to do what no man or woman had ever done: solo each of the classic North Faces in Europe, in the process becoming England's only professional "lady" mountaineer.

Raising the necessary gear and sponsorship funds was arduous, but they managed to cobble together much of what they needed. Then in

December 1992, Alison went before an English outdoor clothier, Spray-way, asking for equipment and financial sponsorship. The venerable and all-male board was instantly impressed with her easy charm and cool confidence. They signed the contract on the spot. And because she aimed to do all six routes in a combined time of twenty-four hours, she found a publisher willing to pay an advance for a book she was going to call "A Hard Day's Summer."

They had done it: Alison was now a professional climber, paid to do what she loved most.

By early 1993, the Bivouac and its satellite shops were gone. With few options, creditors demanding payment, and Meerbrook Lea about to be repossessed by the bank, Jim and Alison bought an ancient Land Rover, loaded themselves, the children, and their newly acquired gear into it, and disappeared into the Alps. They left under a cloud of debt, a mess that Joyce and John Hargreaves and former business associates were generous enough to help clean up, including removing boxes of their personal items from Meerbrook Lea while they still had a key. In some of those boxes were Alison's diaries she'd been keeping since she was six, diaries that otherwise would have gone into the incinerator behind the bank.

For Jim and Alison, the trip was a last resort, but it nonetheless gave Alison the two things she craved the most: unfettered climbing opportunities and quality time with her children. What she worried about was months of living, breathing, eating, and sleeping only inches from Jim. Could they survive the claustrophobic confines for the indefinite future? *Well, we'll just have to* was her ever-pragmatic answer, and they headed south.

Once again her PR timing couldn't have been worse. As she embarked on the journey she learned that fellow Briton Rebecca Stephens was aiming to become the first British woman to climb Everest. While Alison's goal was arguably the more daring and difficult, Everest was Everest, and she knew that if Stephens made it to the summit, she would garner the British media's limited mountain attention, particularly as she aimed to take advantage of the fortieth anniversary of the first ascent by Sir Edmund Hillary. Stephens summited Everest on May 17, 1993.

Meanwhile, Alison climbed her six Faces, one after the other, alone and unsupported as Jim and the children waited at the bases, living out of the shabby Land Rover and eating little more than porridge, pasta, and tins of cheap food. The region suffered some of the worst weather on record, and while most climbers had long since headed to the warm walls in the south of France, Alison repeatedly fought deep snow and unstable ice on the mountains while Jim and the children spent their days trying to stay dry in the soggy valleys.

She'd walk out of their dismal campsites in the predawn quiet and head for the nearby walls. But once she was out of sight and earshot of the children, Alison was able to completely shut them and their squalor out and turn her attention to the climb. She had always been able to do that, to close out the world, and now was no different. She knew it was a selfish devotion, but she loved it, needed it, nonetheless. After her climbs, she would return to the valley below, take tepid showers in dank public bathrooms, eat pounds of pasta with canned fish, and fall into an exhausted sleep.

As much as she loved the climbing, with the weather so horrid and their living so meager, the five months were grim and allowed Alison few moments of delight in her accomplishments. One of those rare celebrations came with her first ascent, the Shroud on the Grand Jorasses. Hoping to stick to her solo claim, she let a group of French guides head out before her in the dark morning. But even with a few hours lead time, she caught up with the three men well below the top and was able to set a new speed record on her ascent as well as make the first solo climb by a woman. She returned to the valley that night exhilarated but exhausted and allowed herself the luxury of being taken care of by Jim—hot meal, plenty of liquids, even a sponge bath. Only a few days later she became the first woman to solo the North Face of the Matterhorn, a route that had eluded her three times before. When she was asked to add her signature to a book in Zermatt that contained many of her childhood heroes, she had to first stop and wipe the nervous sweat from her palms so as not to risk damage to the historic ink on the pages in front of her.

But the summer provided many more moments of sadness and despair, most poignantly when she climbed the Eiger. As she descended from the summit she came upon what she thought was a discarded blue anorak. She had to laugh as she shoved it in her rucksack: of all the things she needed, a jacket was not one of them; still, a jacket was a jacket. As she continued she came upon an empty box of biscuits, a headlamp, and then a waistbag containing a wallet full of Spanish pesetas. She knew suddenly, with a rising fear gripping her stomach, that these items had not merely been discarded but had fallen off a climber. She scanned the route above and below where she stood, gingerly resting on her crampons, but saw no one. As she continued down the litter of gear increased: a brand-new harness, a single crampon, a pair of Gore-Tex bibs. Then, with a sickening jolt, she found an ice ax embedded in the wall, a glove still holding its shaft. It was possible for a climber to drop his rucksack or waistbelt by accident and continue down safely, but an abandoned ice ax meant only one thing: this climber lay somewhere beneath her. She gathered still more scattered gear and continued down.

As she took the final steps off the wall and onto flatter ground she started to sing happily out loud. She had done it! *No, not yet,* she admonished herself, *don't get ahead of yourself.*

Then she found him, his contorted and half-naked body twisted grotesquely before her, lifeless. She sat down on the rocks near the body and wept, her sobs echoing out over the jagged wall. She cried and cried, as if some well of sorrow had erupted deep within her, spilling all the sadness and pain she had felt since time began. She let the tears come until finally there were no more and she stood up. *Time to figure out what to do.* She knew she couldn't get the body down by herself, but she felt wrong in leaving him alone on his death perch to go and get help. Hoping she was close enough to the Eiergletscher train station at the bottom of the wall where someone might hear her, she began waving and yelling, but got no response. Again she collapsed on the rock in tears. Exhaustion, fear, and sorrow washed over her, and she once more let the grief come. Finally, she heard an approaching helicopter and was soon nose to nose with the pilot. A mountain guide lowered himself down a rope from the hovering craft. When he landed next to her, he immediately embraced her. Alison, feeling emotionally shattered, allowed herself the comfort of a stranger's embrace, but suddenly the man was clapping her on the back exclaiming, "Wunderbar! Wunderbar!" Confused, she realized he was far more interested in her ascent than the dead body at their feet.

After they flew her to Eigergletscher, she watched the helicopter fly to the mountain and then return, a single body bag swirling slowly beneath it.

Hours later, when she was finally nestled between Tom and Kate, silent tears slipped down her cheeks, and she fell into a heavy sleep.

In late August, she descended from the last of her historic six ascents, all accomplished within a total climbing time of twenty-three hours and forty-five minutes, but instead of acclaim she faced criticism for taking unnecessary risks as well as charges of fraud. The ever-critical climbing community was quick to challenge her ascents, beginning with the fact that she had not climbed the true North Face of the Eiger, a route that took Destivelle seventeen hours to solo, choosing instead an alternate route that she called "a new variation on the Lauper Face," and that took her five and a half hours. Her time-keeping was also scorned. Alison had calculated only the time she was actually moving, turning off her watch to rest and eat, and the climbing community pounced on this tactic. What she had done was impressive and unprecedented, and she didn't need to exaggerate her achievement. But she did, and the climbing world never let her forget it.

Even Alison's friends denied her unqualified congratulations. "The risk she took on her solo climbs was just ridiculous and unnecessary," Jeff Lowe said, suggesting it was all about her need to prove something. On Kangtega she had been motivated by the pure love of the sport and the mountains, he said, but now she seemed to be on a different, desperate, and dangerous track, climbing for commercial rather than personal reasons. There was also the thought in the climbing community that Jim's efforts at promoting his "superstar" were actually limiting her positive publicity because the media tended to have excellent radar for self-serving and overblown promotion.

After returning from the Alps in the autumn of 1993, the Ballards were homeless and went to live with John and Joyce. It was an unhappy situation made impossible when, with Alison's apparent blessing, Joyce read Jim the riot act about his "obnoxious" behavior and threw him out of the house. Ballard retreated to Wales, where the Hargreaves owned a vacation cottage, and Alison found herself shuttling between the two houses for months, unable or unwilling to let it be the beginning of the end of the marriage.

As Christmas 1993 approached, Alison tried to cheer the cottage up, but somehow her heart wasn't in it. She knew she had to do it for the children, but the weight of her life hung around her neck. She picked up the phone and called Bev England in Belper. Suddenly she was sobbing. Bev begged her to tell her what had happened, but Alison wouldn't say much, just that it had been a particularly hard holiday and that all she wanted to do was sit and talk like they had in the old days, no worries, no pain, no sadness. Just climbing and cute boys and their future. Bev had never felt so powerless. It wasn't like the old days when the girls lived only minutes away from each other; now Alison lived hundreds of miles north in rural and isolated Wales. Even if Bev got on a plane or in a car right that minute, she wouldn't be at Alison's for hours. She knew not to ask about the marriage. That had been forbidden territory for some time between them. Once, feeling an awful intuition about her friend, Bev had stopped by the Ballard house to make sure Alison was all right. As she approached the house she thought she saw the curtains move in the front window, but when she knocked, no one answered. She knocked again, her hand lingering on the wood; she could almost feel Alison on the other side of the door. But the door never opened. Bev turned and left. If Alison needed her privacy, Bev loved her too much not to give it. She knew that Alison was too proud to admit that her impetuous move out of her parents' house many years before was perhaps not very well thought out. She was a "make your bed and lie in it" kind of girl, and Bev knew she was going to stick it out. Make it better. Fix it and fix it herself. Alison had never looked to anyone for help before, and she wasn't going to start now.

Alison wished Bev a Merry Christmas and hung up the phone. *Just get on with it, girl,* she chided herself for her self-pity and turned her energies toward planning another bold and hopefully lucrative ascent. If Rebecca Stephens had been the first British woman to climb Everest, *she* would be the first to do so without bottled oxygen *and* unassisted, without the support of Sherpas or teammates.

While New Zealander Lydia Bradey had climbed the mountain without oxygen in 1988, controversy continued to swirl around her claim, owing mostly to Rob Hall's public denunciation of her. Unable to secure a permit for the Southeast Ridge, Hall settled for a permit for the much more difficult Southwest Face. But when that climb eluded him and his team, he decided to poach the nearby and somewhat easier South Pillar. Finally he and his partner Gary Ball were driven off the mountain by a storm, while Lydia, feeling strong and confident, continued climbing alone. Figuring many men before her had poached the Southeast Route and caring more for the climbing than the officialdom, Lydia tagged onto a French team as it left the South Col at 2:00 A.M. headed for the summit. Feeling slightly drunk from lack of oxygen but nonetheless capable of making the summit, Lydia continued up, lagging behind the other climbers until she found herself alone on the vast expanses of Everest. She took out her camera to capture the incredible ripple of peaks below her. The shutter was frozen.

When Hall and Ball heard over the radio that she had made it to the South Summit, within spitting distance of the true summit, they were outraged. If she made it, Hall feared he and his team could be fined and banished from Nepal for up to ten years, a disastrous sentence for his plans to begin a professional mountain guiding company. With Lydia still on the mountain, Hall and Ball did something that many climbers considered not only unethical and cruel but dangerous: they packed up and left Base Camp, abandoning her. American climber Geoff Tabin asked them how they could leave her. What if she got into some trouble and needed help or a rescue? Hall responded, "It's not our responsibility. If she gets into trouble, it's her fault." As they left Base Camp and walked back to civilization they were already plotting their damage control.

After making the summit, Lydia returned to Base Camp and found it deserted, her tent alone in the rubble of what was once their team's camp. Hurt but not surprised, she started her sad trek back to Kathmandu, where she was greeted with the news that Hall had told the Ministry of Tourism that she was guilty of "misconduct on Mount Everest" and that he did not believe her claim of making the summit. Once back in New Zealand, he told any newspaper that would listen that "it was simply not possible that she made it to the summit." Lydia, eager to avoid sanction for herself and for Hall, stayed quiet. In her silence, others were all too eager to believe that it was impossible for a woman to accomplish such a feat. In addition, because she sported bleached blond dreadlocks and a sapphire stud in her nose and claimed that she "dropped boyfriends like books," Lydia was seen as a party girl, more focused on her socializing than the mountain. When she not only climbed the mountain but did it without oxygen and virtually without support above Camp II, many in the climbing world believed Hall.

Alison originally bought into the doubt, in part because an attempt as the first woman to climb Everest without oxygen was an easier sell. But after asking many esteemed climbers, including Greg Child, for their opinion, she believed that Bradley had made the summit and that Bradley had been made to suffer for being a strong woman, a rebel, in a man's world. Alison was thereafter careful to state that she was going to be the first woman to climb without oxygen *and* unsupported. It was an important distinction that Alison well understood. The British media, however, was not so careful and began to trumpet her attempt as the first woman, period, to climb Everest without oxygen. Whether or not Alison tried to correct the error, the image of the determined young mother setting off to climb the world's highest mountain as no other woman had ever done before sold well, and she reaped the rewards of the notoriety. Once she was approached by a young woman who told her that she was an inspiration, a role model. Alison felt redeemed, as if all the years of her single-minded devotion to climbing had meant something more than merely a string of peaks on her belt.

In July 1994, she and her photogenic family set off for Everest Base Camp, and their attractive, smiling faces were splashed across many newsstands. Again, with no place to live and nothing to live on in

England, the entire family was part of Alison's climbing adventure, even three-year-old Kate. While nearly six-year-old Tom adapted easily to the ever-decreasing oxygen in the air as they trekked through the villages toward Everest's 18,000-foot (5,500-meter) Base Camp, Kate developed a headache and began vomiting. Alison, fearing it was altitude sickness and knowing that the only cure was immediate descent to "thicker" air, threw her young daughter on her back and ran five hours through the rainy night back down the trail, talking and singing to Kate until they reached a teahouse in the lower village of Pheriche. "I could have walked for days," Alison said, her fear and adrenaline fueling her on.

As the family trekked on, they were joined by Richard Celsi, a climber from California who told Alison he was headed for K2 the following May—did she have any designs on number two? She hadn't before, but suddenly the idea of knocking off not only the first but the second-highest mountain as well, both without bottled oxygen or high-altitude support, appealed to her. But first she'd have to see how she fared in the Death Zone, a place she had yet to visit.

When Alison went for her summit bid, she got to 8,400 meters (27,500 feet), but the bitterly cold day and climbing without oxygen took their toll. She had bought onto the team's permit, agreeing to pay just the $10,000 additional climber fee because she planned to climb without any Sherpa support above Base Camp. After days fighting the severe cold and altitude, her fingers and toes began to go numb, and nothing she could do warmed them. Her first experience in the Death Zone pretty much kicked her in the teeth, at one point forcing her to crawl across the South Col to her tent for fear of falling off. With the wind continuing to blow at gale force and the temperature hovering in the −30 degree Fahrenheit range, she feared she might lose her toes and fingers to frostbite if she continued, so she turned back and descended to base. When she got there, Jim openly and loudly berated her for quitting. The trip had not offered the embattled family any respite from their financial and emotional problems, beginning with hassles over paying her fee and ending with her failure to make the summit. Many at Base

Camp noted the tension between Alison and Jim, who at times ignored each other with an icy disdain. It was a humiliating trip for Alison, and one that left her feeling once again depressed and worthless.

She returned to England as low as she had ever been. Although she had been thinking of K2, she didn't have anything planned, and not having a clear goal in front of her scared her more than the actual mountains. Adding to that anxiety was that after twelve years of living with Jim, the relationship seemed to be over. The delicate balance of power in their relationship had shifted, and Alison was as close as she had ever been to leaving, even confiding to Susan and Bev England that she had fallen in love with one of the other team members. Because she and the man were both married, they seemed to know it would not progress much beyond Base Camp. Nonetheless, perhaps the relationship gave Alison a glimpse of what her life could be without the heavy weight of her unhappy marriage.

For a time Bev felt that she had the old Alison back, the impetuous, strong-willed girl of twenty years before. On a whim, Alison would bike up to Bev's house, where the old friends would sit and laugh for hours, talking about old flames and current gossip, giggling at their naughtiness. Even so, at the end of October she and Jim moved to Spean Bridge, Scotland, far from the strength and security of Bev and her family.

In December 1994, Susan remarried, and she and Alison spent hours on the phone planning the wedding. As they discussed the endless details, Alison talked about coming down for the ceremony and never returning. But in the end she did go back, and she never again talked to Susan about leaving. But she did talk to Bev, claiming that her reluctance to leave suddenly would unfavorably affect her ability to gain custody of the children in a divorce. She also spoke to Alison Osius of *Climbing* magazine, telling her that the marriage was over and that she and Jim had simply "grown apart." But whether she was too busy, scared, or conflicted to make the move, Alison stayed in the marriage, even though she realized her early climbing confidence had all but disappeared as soon as she moved in with Jim in 1980. It had taken her the better part of twelve years to regain her sense of self, and she wasn't about to give it back.

· · ·

Two weeks after returning from Everest, Alison traveled to Canada to attend the Banff Mountain Book and Film Festival, where she gave a standing-room-only slide show that was replete with image after image of Tom and Kate. After the program, many in the audience milled around expressing their shock that she was willing to take such huge risks with two small children. Others defended her, asking, "Don't we have to condemn the fathers who leave children behind if we are going to condemn Alison?" But somehow the spectacle of *this* mother climbing *these* dangerous routes outraged some and concerned many.

The next day she spoke on a panel discussion about the risks of high-altitude climbing with some of climbing's most famous women, including Arlene Blum, Nancy Feagin, and Sharon Wood. With her curly hair held back with a headband and her ascot tied neatly at her throat, Alison looked more like a schoolgirl on her way to the library than a seasoned mountaineer. She spoke of how she minimized the risk to realize her passion, but many thought she sounded more defensive than joyous when asked to answer criticism about leaving her children to pursue what many perceived to be selfish goals.

"Perhaps I do have a chip on my shoulder," she said, admitting she felt at times like she wasn't the best mother because she could simply "turn off the kids" and climb.

Arlene Blum commented that once she had become a mother, she couldn't imagine exposing herself to the objective dangers of Himalayan climbing, like falling seracs. Alison added quickly, "I would argue if something falls on you, then you shouldn't be there, and you've actually made the wrong decision. Everybody says to me there's all these objective dangers, but as far as I'm concerned, 99 percent of objective dangers you can actually be in control of, because if a serac falls on you, there is a very small chance you were in the wrong place at the wrong time, but generally it's your decision to be there, and if you're [there] when it's dangerous, you're wrong." Many in the audience looked at each other with raised eyebrows. Not wanting to be rude, they kept the obvious to themselves: the very definition of climbing involved objective risks. The only way to climb without risk was not to climb at all.

A poignant moment came when Sharon Wood, the first North American woman to summit Mount Everest, spoke of the time when she realized that her fear of death had overwhelmed her passion to climb; having lost her nerve for high-altitude climbing, she redirected that passion to less lethal pursuits. Again, Alison responded with a bit of an edge.

"For *me* the passion is still there. I would hope I'm rational enough to make the right decisions at the right time. I don't think I'm reckless in the slightest. As far as I'm concerned, there's loads more climbs I want to do, and the last thing I want to do is be killed on one of them. I've got two small children, and I dearly love being with them, and I don't want to leave them without a mum."

Alison returned from Banff empowered by being accepted by the likes of climbing legends Chris Bonnington and Joe Simpson, and she began thinking about a return to Everest. Even though her first trip had been devastating, she itched to give it another go. She knew she could climb the mountain. She had been almost as high as the summit of K2 on it, and she had felt pretty good, notwithstanding her frozen fingers and toes. If she had had better clothing and better weather, she definitely would have made the top. She had practically been able to touch it from where she turned around.

She called around looking for a trip going to Everest, but all the expedition leaders she contacted gave her different excuses to say no. *Sod them*, she thought, smarting at their rejection but knowing in her heart of hearts that she was as yet unproven at altitude and could prove to be a liability up high. Then Richard Celsi called, reminding her of his American expedition to K2 that summer. *It isn't Everest, but hell,* she thought, *it's a damn good second,* so she accepted and started planning for a summer in the Karakoram. Suddenly the phone rang again. This time it was Russell Brice, telling her he had a space for one more climber on his expedition heading to the North Ridge of Everest in Tibet. With the climbing season on Everest finished by May 31, and K2's starting the first week of June, she could actually do both. Again, she accepted. *The two tallest mountains in the world in a single season, both without oxygen! Only one climber has ever done it, and here I am signing up.*

She threw herself into planning the back-to-back expeditions with a flurry of lists, her favorite thing to do besides the climbing itself. She had never been happier. Knowing what she would be doing for the next six to eight months gave her a sense of peace and strength she hadn't felt in a while.

As she packed an outrageous plan began to foment: why not go for all three? Everest, K2, and Kangchenjunga? Weeks before George Band, a veteran British climber who made the first ascent of Kangchenjunga in 1955, had told her he was returning to the mountain that spring with an anniversary expedition. Why didn't she come along and make a stab at being the first woman to climb the mountain, particularly in the anniversary year, the same way Rebecca Stephens had climbed Everest in 1993? But try as Alison did, she couldn't see how she could get from the Tibetan side of Everest to Kanch in Nepal before going to K2 by the middle of June. So why not go for it *after*, in the post-monsoon climbing season in October? If Everest and K2 went well and she was home from them by early August, she would have two months to rest before heading to Kangchenjunga. She thought about what it would mean to do all three, in a single season, without high-altitude support or supplemental oxygen, and she knew it would be huge. No woman had climbed the three highest mountains in the world, and even Wanda Rutkiewicz, who had climbed number one and two but perished on number three, used oxygen and Sherpas on Everest. Alison thrilled at the prospect of setting her name so firmly in the climbing stone; she would surpass even Wanda Rutkiewicz! She wouldn't ever again have to worry about paying the mortgage or putting food on the table. After years of squeezing every penny out of a pound, she knew she could easily cobble together a living the same way some of the girls on the Banff panel had told her they were making their living years after retiring from climbing: through sponsorships, book deals, and motivational speaking for big corporations. Hell, if she got all three mountains, maybe there'd even be a movie deal.

Most importantly, if she pulled off her trilogy, she would never ever have to look in the rearview mirror for Destivelle or Stephens or any other woman climber ever again.

CHAPTER 10

ONE DAY AS A TIGER

It is better to live one day as a tiger
than one thousand years as a sheep.

—TIBETAN PROVERB

Alison organized every detail of her trips to Everest and then K2 with a growing sense of autonomy from Jim, even asking another man to handle her PR while she was on the expedition and not to share any specific information about it with Jim. Later, at Everest Base Camp, she learned that the new man had in fact asked Jim to help out when media interest in her climbs became overwhelming. She railed against Jim's intrusion and control, but thousands of miles away on Everest she was powerless to stop it.

Unlike her early attempt among hundreds on the Southeast Route, she would climb independently on the less traveled Northeast Ridge, and though not alone, she would not use any of the fixed lines of other climbers. Jeeps would bring her gear into Base Camp, then yaks a bit closer, but above Advance Base Camp she would be totally self-sufficient. Most notably, she would not use any oxygen. If she made it, she would put herself well above every other female alpinist, living or dead, and in the rare company of only one man, the great Reinhold Messner, whose feat had not been repeated since his 1988 solo, oxygenless ascent.

It was by all accounts a perfect ascent. Even taciturn climbers not prone to lavishing praise on others called Alison's ascent "quintessentially the finest piece of high-altitude mountaineering" they'd ever seen. She spent weeks ferrying a series of loads to her high camps, carrying and preparing her own meals, and building tent platforms—one of them on her hands and knees at 27,250 feet, scratching a narrow ledge out of the 45-degree ice and rock with her ice ax. Even she admitted that she wanted "to make Everest as difficult as possible. I'm really narrowing the chances of success down to an absolute tiny percentage. But for me, that's what's interesting. If I could guarantee an ascent, then I wouldn't be interested." After a month of acclimatizing and camp-setting, she was ready for her summit bid and left Base Camp on May 11, 1995.

In a series of remarkably lucid, even relaxed radio conversations back to Base Camp as she climbed, Alison provided a step-by-step travelogue of her ascent, giggling playfully as men from other teams invited her to their tents for tea and responding in articulate and cheerful detail about how she was doing physically and emotionally. Nowhere in her voice was there a hint of bravado or arrogance as she attempted, and eventually accomplished, what no other woman and only one of the strongest of men ever have: climbing the highest mountain in the world without supplemental oxygen or assistance. Rather, she thanked those at Base Camp for their support, poked good-natured fun at the snoring climbers in nearby tents, and frankly admitted that she hadn't done the most basic mountain research and was therefore unfamiliar with and confused by the route's benchmarks.

She neared the summit and viewed what looked like a giant meringue arcing out above her, smooth, white, and incredibly beautiful. She took the last step and found herself higher than any other creature on the face of the Earth, and she reacted as many have but few have admitted: she cried. Simple, joyous, overwhelmed tears. Her cool British reserve dissolved as she laughed and cried and hugged the climbers around her. She loved her children and her family, but nothing had reached in and grabbed her soul like standing on the top of the world, having earned every step of it on her own terms. She gave in and let the emotions wash over her. She wept as she radioed a message to her children: "To Tom and Kate, my two children, I'm standing on the highest point of the world and I love them dearly. Over." She had to say it twice because the tears choked her throat, constricting her words. At Base Camp many who were huddled around the radio were also in tears. Greg Child, a talented Australian climber famous for several first and difficult ascents, told her she was his new hero. "You sarcastic Aussie bastard," Alison laughed from the top of the world.

She always thought she could never be 100 percent happy, but she was wrong. For at least this one, precious, unparalleled moment, she was bursting with joy and she wept.

She turned from her sterling triumph for the long descent, a descent she knew was infinitely more important than the summit itself. She knew that reaching the top was only half the battle, that true victory would come only when she was safely off the mountain. Exhausted and fighting the urge to lie down and take a nap in her tent at Camp III at 27,250 feet, she continued to descend, determined not to spend another night in the Death Zone. She knew that her ascent to the edge of where man can go without oxygen put her at enormous risk every second she remained in the lethally threadbare air above 8,000 meters. After a night at Camp II, she descended to Base Camp, where climbers poured out of their tents and cheered her as she took the last steps into camp. After she'd gotten a hot tub of water from the mess tent to wash the days of sweat and effort off her body and out of her hair, she sat in front of a chocolate cake with "Congratulations Alison" scribbled across the top in chocolate icing. Leo Dickinson, a filmmaker with another team, grabbed his camera and filmed her as she cut pieces for everyone at camp.

She had done it. She was the first woman to climb the highest moun tain in the world unsupported and without oxygen. No one could ever take that from her. Surely the climbing world would finally take note of her ability and not harp on her maternal status! She laughed as she blew out the candles, making sure to look squarely into Leo's lens before she did.

Later Alison sat and talked with Mandy Dickinson, Leo's wife.

"My mum and dad will be so proud," she said, images of their beaming faces filling her mind. She couldn't wait to get home and share her triumph with them. She had done it, she felt great, and now she was going to finish off the next two mountains and get on with her life. She had left her parents in charge of cleaning up more financial mess, and she felt terrible. They had done so much for her, and she had never been able to thank them properly. But now, with Everest under her belt, she could begin to look ahead. Maybe she and her father would do some hill walking together once she was home and rested. Yes, she told Mandy, her parents had given her her first love for the mountains, and she really couldn't have done it without them. She didn't mention Jim.

Alison descended from Everest into a new world. The cameras greeted her as she entered Kathmandu and she proudly recounted her ascent. Back in England her sister Susan watched the evening news, smiling back at her smiling sister's face thousands of miles away. As she watched Alison's emotion her own eyes filled with tears.

Alison was truly the "superstar" she and Jim had worked so hard to create, but the attention came in a tidal wave rather than a ripple. As she came through customs at Heathrow, Alison was chased through the terminal by a horde of reporters eager to get the first word from their newest alpine hero. Although she said it was exciting and overwhelming, her sister Susan thought it a hideous circus, one in which Alison seemed lost and frightened. Exciting or hideous, it was undeniably a whirlwind time. In her two weeks between returning from Everest and leaving for K2, she had scores of interviews, a trip to Switzerland to meet with her sponsors, negotiations for another book and a film, keynote lectures at prestigious gatherings, and even an invitation to meet the Queen. There was only time for two precious days alone with Tom and Kate in a friend's caravan on the west coast of Scotland. Being away from them for months had been difficult, but she was the sole earner in the family and she had a job to do. Climbing, while her passion, was also her job.

She had barely unpacked from Everest before she was leaving tiny Spean Bridge again, headed for the airport. As was their routine, she and Jim made very little of her leaving, hoping to spare everyone a tearful good-bye.

"Take care of yourself, Ali" was all Jim said, and with a flash of her brilliant smile, she was gone.

On her last night before flying to Pakistan, Alison slept at Susan's house. The sisters talked late into the night, curled up in their pajamas. Alison was drained from two weeks of twenty-hour days as well as the emotionally wrenching experience of once again saying good-bye to the children. As always, she had tried to avoid an announced "last cuddle and kiss" with Kate. As soon as the little girl knew her mother was leaving, she would dissolve into heart-wrenching sobs, begging Mummy not to go. It was more than Alison could handle. Tucked under Susan's quilt, sipping tea and finally letting her exhaustion flood her body, she told Susan she was thinking of leaving Jim, but because she was the breadwinner, she had to get this Himalayan hat trick out of the way first. Then she would be able to leave. Susan wanted to believe her, but she somehow doubted that Alison would actually ever end the marriage. She had seen Alison return to Jim time and again, their bond stronger than reason might indicate.

Susan reached out and put her hand on Alison's arm. "Alison, you really do have options. You don't have to go to K2. You don't have to stay with Jim."

Alison told her sister she wanted to go, although her voice conveyed none of the excitement she had shown before leaving for Everest only months before. She had made commitments, signed contracts, and signed a lease on a house in Scotland. She had built herself up to do these three peaks, and she was going to do them. Susan thought she was overwhelmed, confused, and at a loss as to where to turn. As she had so many times before, Alison simply turned back to the mountains. The unspeakable joy she felt on the summit of Everest was calling her back, and she had to answer, she wanted to answer.

The sisters had barely said good-night before a town car was idling out front before dawn, waiting to take Alison for a spot on the BBC's popular morning show. Later that day, June 11, she said good-bye to her parents at Manchester Airport and boarded her nonstop flight for Pakistan.

Alison stepped off the PIA jet into the hot, dry, slightly rancid-smelling air of Rawalpindi, the industrial city just outside the manicured lawns and sparkling embassies of Islamabad. The airline had flown her free, and she had basked in its first-class attention. She felt like a movie star or a politician's wife as she walked down the mobile staircase to the tarmac and stifled the urge to raise her hand in an exaggerated wave to the faces in the terminal window watching her deplane.

She had never traveled to Pakistan before and was immediately assaulted by the heat and noise of Rawalpindi and the chaos of Islamabad International Airport. From the sea of faces that crushed toward her in the low-ceilinged cement terminal, she saw one emerge and head straight for her. *Hello, I am with Nazir Sabir Expeditions. Give me your luggage tags, and I will take care of everything.* Grateful, she handed the man the claim checks and let herself be ushered through the throngs and out to a waiting van. Once her barrels and duffels had been thrown on top of the car, it started moving through the thick traffic, each car, bus, and van boasting an ear-splitting horn that the driver seemed to use rather than his brakes.

Alison leaned her head against the cool window and closed her eyes. In her exhaustion she barely noticed arriving at the two-star Shalimar Hotel, being handed a key, and falling into one of the single beds in the austere but clean room. Half an hour later the phone shattered her sleep: *Could you please come down to the lobby and speak to a reporter?*

Between the endless demands of the media and parties and teas with British diplomats stationed in Islamabad, she barely had time to catch her breath, let alone get a deep, restful sleep. She had signed on to Celsi's American team that was two weeks ahead of her, already at Base Camp. With nothing official for her to do with the Ministry of Tourism, she left the arid cacophony of Rawalpindi and flew to Skardu, where she finally was able to relax in the cool shade and sweet breezes of the K2 Motel garden. She hadn't had a real vacation in years, perhaps ever, and she sat alone, doing nothing more than watching the silty, lazy waters of the Indus River glide by below her. The hotel was clean and well run, the meals simple but tasty—rice, chicken, cucumber salad, and plenty of chipattis, the warm flat bread that reminded her of tortillas. She spent her two days there taking long naps, writing letters to Tom and Kate, and walking the motel's Expedition Hallway where decades of teams had left photographs, mementos, and data on their climbs. It had become a de facto shrine to those who never returned from the Karakoram. She touched the smiling faces of Wanda Rutkiewicz, Liliane Barrard, and Julie Tullis, wondering what had gone so terribly wrong that the mountains had claimed each of them. She left the hallway and reemerged into the sun-splashed garden determined not to share their fate; as much as she loved the mountains, they weren't worth her life.

She rose hours before dawn the next morning and took a last shower, enjoying the simple pleasure of washing her hair in hot water and blowing it dry; a luxury she knew she wouldn't have for at least six weeks. Then she climbed into one of the jeeps that would take her and two other late-coming teammates, Briton Alan Hinkes and American Kevin Cooney, to Askole, a day's drive away.

After eight hours hanging onto the gunnels of the open jeep as it bounced and bumped over crumbling roads above the thundering Braldu River, the dust gritty in her teeth and hair, Alison found Askole a green emerald tucked into the rocky foothills. She was charmed by its lush gardens and meticulously planted fields where centuries of hill tribes had diverted the floodwaters to irrigate their crops of wheat, potatoes, lentils, and rice and their apricot trees. In many ways the beginning was the loveliest part of the trek. She couldn't help but note that just days before she had been fighting the crowds in the Underground from Heathrow. Now here she was in exotic, primitive Pakistan watching women in colorful head scarves with babies strapped to their backs bent double as they planted rice in the verdant fields.

Unlike her rather pleasant, even touristy approach to Everest and Kangtega through cheerful villages where cold Coca-Colas and hot pizza were available from clean teahouses, Alison found getting to K2 a bit of a shock. Once the luggage was dumped in the dust and the jeeps were headed back to Skardu, Alison and her two teammates began the week-long trek over a trail of varying degrees of rock—hot flat rock, steep crumbling rock, and wet slippery rock along the Braldu River. Still drained from her Everest climb and the two enervating weeks in England, Alison kept to herself, lagging behind the small group because she preferred to trek alone on the trail that stretched out endlessly in front of her under the unrelenting sun. The temperature hovered near 100 degrees Fahrenheit, and she found herself longing for the damp cool of Scotland. After two days of stumbling over the dusty trail, she looked far ahead and saw a thin patch of trees hugging the edge of the otherwise barren slope—Paiju.

Although once a lovely, poplar-filled oasis, Paiju was already beginning to show the signs of too much wear and tear on its fragile ecosystem. Hundreds of climbers, trekkers, and porters used it annually as a rest stop, but lacking toilets and trash facilities, the thin stand of trees fed by a trickle of freshwater from the snowfields above was rapidly being devastated. Looking around at the piles of human and animal feces, Alison thought that burning the waste would be a logical answer since decomposition was too slow at that altitude. Alison was glad to finally leave the sad camp and get on with the trek to K2.

An hour out of Paiju she saw what looked like the Hoover Dam stuck between the mountains. A vast wall of rock, sand, and ice, the snout of the great Baltoro Glacier stretched nearly two miles across and rose 150 feet above the Braldu River, which gushed out the bottom. Climbing onto the glacier, she knew the easy part was behind her. A forty-mile snake of ice, rock, rivers, sand dunes, and, worst of all, crevasses, the Baltoro was one of the world's largest and longest glaciers. She'd be on it and its offshoot, the Godwin-Austen Glacier, for the rest of the summer. It was an unsettling thought somehow. Living on this frozen river of ice, with its mournful moaning, deep, guttural cracks and timeless shifting, was not going to be restful.

Oddly enough, there was also a telephone wire threading the length of the glacier that more or less connected a half-dozen desolate Pakistani army outposts, posts designed to keep Pakistan alert to the presence of any Indian insurgents in its decades-long war with India for Kashmir. Miserable and filthy, the camps were nothing more than burlap huts and corrugated tin shacks, littered with human and donkey waste, empty kerosene cans, and weapons that looked as if they were bought at a World War I auction. As Alison made her way up the glacier, she was greeted effusively by the lonely and isolated army men in tattered and soiled clothes and often invited into their depressing smoky huts for tea. (*Why do all Pakistanis smoke?* she wondered. *Even the porters!*) She knew it was an invitation best avoided; a cup of tea could last hours and ruin any chance she had of making the next camp before night fell.

Finally, after a week of walking, she reached Concordia. As it had been most days of her trek, it was spitting hail and snow; they couldn't see much beyond the trail at their feet. She hadn't done much reading up on K2 besides learning about the disastrous Black Summer of 1986 and its heavy toll on British climbers. Beyond newspaper accounts, she had never been one to do much reading about the mountains; she simply wanted to climb them. But when she woke the next morning to a clear day and actually saw K2 before her, it mesmerized her. Standing outside her tent in the early morning chill, her sleeping bag still wrapped around her, she stared at the monolith ten miles away. Kangtega, Ama Dablam, even Everest, had been tucked away behind lesser mountains, making their appearance somehow softer, less imposing. But this mountain had no such diversion, no such minimizer. This mountain stood there naked and alone, almost daring her to approach it.

Later that day she stood at the base of K2 and felt the power of the mountain in her belly—the visceral, magnetic force of 12,000 feet of sheer ice, rock, and snow rising right out of the glacier at her feet to the summit above. It was a primeval feeling, and not an altogether good one. Peter Hillary, son of Sir Edmund, who was climbing the mountain with a Kiwi team, said he felt an evil, ominous, almost taunting energy from the mountain. Others spoke of its maleness, its purely masculine, even angry essence. And some simply felt minuscule in its shadow, like an ant scratching at its towering, frozen surface.

Alison didn't spend much time concentrating on K2's mythical image; she was too busy with its very real presence in front of her. She also missed Tom and Kate as she never had before. Every step of the weeklong trek had made her feel the distance between her and the children with a sharp ache. She hadn't spent any real time with them in months, and now, so many miles away, so many weeks really, she felt torn between her longing for the mountain and her longing for the children. The weather was also impossible, frustrating her and her team's efforts on the mountain. Already acclimatized by her ascent on Everest, she had hoped to come into K2, climb it, and get the hell out by the end of July. Instead, she sat in her tent at Base Camp while storm after storm roiled around her, listening to a 10,000 Maniacs CD she kept borrowing from Celsi, filling the pages of her journal with angst, and physically longing to "cuddle" Tom and Kate and to be there for Tom's first day of school. But there she sat, thousands of miles away, waiting for the ever-troublesome weather on K2 to give her a proper chance at the summit.

Another frustration was that Alan Hinkes had gone for the summit after only a few weeks at the mountain while she had decided to climb with the more cautious Americans, who wanted to wait another week before their attempt. Hinkes made it, while Alison and the Americans missed a rare window of good weather and were forced back to base just as Hinkes made his triumphant descent. It was a crushing blow for Alison. "She had a bit of a cry. She could have done it then, she was strong enough," Hinkes said.

By the third week of July, he was headed down the glacier and back to Heathrow while she watched him go, getting smaller and smaller as he disappeared down the moraine toward Concordia. The British press, having been primed for her success, heralded Hinkes's instead and wondered in bold typeface, what had happened to Alison? She began getting faxes from home demanding to know why Hinkes had made the summit and she hadn't. Some at Base Camp speculated that she began to get desperate to reach the summit and go home. Toward the end of July, while the rest of the team waited out yet another spate of bad weather, Alison decided to go for it alone. She climbed all the way to the Shoulder at 25,600 feet, where she bivouacked without a tent for the night, hoping the weather would hold. She talked with Celsi in Base Camp over the radio for hours, both of them with eyes trained to the thin band of lenticular clouds licking the summit. The cloud formation usually foretold bad weather. In the morning the winds were worse, and she was also suffering a particularly heavy menstrual cycle. Alison turned and headed back down the mountain.

Descending to Base Camp, she began to doubt everything, including her own career. Sitting with Matt Comeskey, one of the Kiwi climbers who wanted to interview her for a climbing magazine in New Zealand, she shared her frustrations with the lies and "bullshit" rife in the Himalayan climbing community. She told him she was so fed up with climbers bagging peaks for the sake of sponsors and fame that she was thinking of quitting "the 8,000-meter game" for a while. It was an odd statement coming from someone who was selling that very "peak bagging" image herself by collecting the three highest peaks in the world, one after the other. Perhaps she realized that the media didn't make a distinction between her immensely more difficult style of climbing—unsupported and without bottled oxygen—and the "get the peak any way you can" style she watched Alan Hinkes employ when he ducked in behind a well-equipped Dutch team, drafting their steps to the summit. To the *London Observer* and the *Daily Mail*, a summit was a summit; how someone got there was just arcane detail for which the public had no patience.

Adding to her frustration over Hinkes, the weather, and her own failed bids at the summit, she was beginning to have doubts about the entire expedition. The Americans bickered constantly about food, leadership, and cohesion, and she was sick of it. Plus, the mountain was a much tougher climb than Everest had been, the weather was fierce and unrelenting, and the very remoteness of the Karakoram bothered her, reminding her again and again of how far she was from home and the children. Even if she wanted to leave tomorrow, it would be weeks of portering, trekking, and traveling through Pakistan before she could hope to be home, whereas on Everest a helicopter flight to an international airport was only hours down the trail. She called the children on a satellite phone from Base Camp, but their voices nearly tore her apart, and she walked away from the phone wiping the tears off her cheeks. "The kids will definitely come with me to Kanch," she promised herself as she returned to her tent. "I'll never go on a long trip without them again."

Sitting at Base Camp was the worst. She had never been patient, and these days-into-weeks of waiting for the weather to clear were chipping away at her resolve. But as soon as the clouds lifted and she strapped on her harness and crampons, the darkness lifted and she climbed unfettered, cheerful even, relishing the physical work and emotional boost of being on the mountain again.

During her second summit bid in early August, she, Celsi, and team leader Rob Slater found their cache of equipment at Camp III destroyed, making further ascent suicidal. Slater, a big-talking stockbroker from Colorado, had been obsessed with climbing K2 since setting eyes on the mountain years before while climbing Gasherbrum II.

When he had left America weeks earlier, he had been asked about the risks of climbing a mountain as dangerous as K2. He had turned to the reporter and said, "Summit or die, either way I win." No one asked him what he meant. When he stood at Camp III and saw his summit bid disappear with his equipment, something must have snapped. Slater turned and told Celsi it looked as if he was suffering from the altitude, and he demanded that Celsi give him and Alison *his* food, stove, sleeping bag, down suit, and overboots. Celsi was shocked and dismayed. For him, the expedition was over. If you no longer trust your climbing partners, you get down, fast. And he did. He believed Alison and Slater had become "obsessed" and "driven," even paranoid, and that the bizarre and self-serving behavior was out of character for Alison.

"She was desperate to get the climb done and get home to her kids," said Scott Johnston, a teammate from Oregon. She also just wanted to get her teeth into K2. It stood there, taunting her. All she needed was a good weather window, and she had it.

In the end, that summit bid also failed when bad weather once again moved in and she and Slater were forced to descend to Base Camp. They were greeted by an angry team demanding that they explain their outrageous treatment of their teammate and friend. Alison's misery deepened.

The team had enjoyed climbing with her. They were amazed at her skill and raw strength and charmed when she carried perfume to the high camps just to instill a measure of feminine distinction in the overly male world. But now they were worried that she seemed to need the summit more than she wanted it. And Slater was worse, even more driven and blind to the mountain's objective dangers.

Cooney, Johnston, and Celsi decided to pack up and head for home. Their porters would arrive August 6. Slater said he was staying; Alison packed to leave, but she was still undecided about whether she would stay for another week. As she talked to her teammates she changed her mind six or seven times. Because the New Zealand team was still on the mountain, she and Rob Slater had a choice of leaving with their team or staying and climbing with the Kiwis. She wrote anxiously in her diary: should she call it quits for the year and go home to her children, or stay for one last try?

"They're young and time flies. I want—I feel—I should be with them." *But what would one more week matter, now that I've spent over a bloody month here? Don't I owe it to myself, my future, my sponsors, Tom and Kate, to give it one more chance? This mountain is so far off the radar screen, coming back would take a lot of time, money, and planning. I'm here now! All I need is a few days of clear weather.*

Alison watched the porters pack her loads onto their wooden frames for the early morning trek out of camp. She wasn't at all sure she would go with them.

Ghulam Rasool, the team's cook, walked by her tent late that night and heard her crying inside; respecting her privacy, he quietly returned to the mess tent. A couple of times that evening she came to him asking if she could have some tea, which he made, asking politely how she was. She smiled gently as she took the tea but said nothing. What was there to say?

In her tent Alison sat over her journal, wiping the tears with the back of her hand, her words blurring in the soft yellow light from her headlamp. "It eats at me—wanting the children and wanting K2." She'd been to Camp III twice, above Camp IV at 8,000 meters, and to the summit of Everest—all within just three months. She was beginning to wonder if her hat trick was such a great idea. She could feel that her repeated exposure to the thin air was taking its toll. Plus, Tom was starting school in mid-August, and she desperately wanted to be there for him. But again, the "pressure back home" kept her wrestling with her decision. She knew she would have to answer as to "why I failed, what went wrong. Personally it doesn't matter to me, but I worry how everyone else will see it." Besides, she felt like she hadn't had a fair shot at the mountain, and she wanted it. She knew she could climb it, if only the weather gave her a chance.

The morning of August 6, as the porters shouldered their loads in the predawn chill, Alison sat with Celsi drinking coffee. She had had a sleepless night, between writing, crying, and zipping and unzipping her tent to check on the weather, and in the morning she was still not sure whether to stay or go. The mountain sat impassively behind her, but its pull was nonetheless magnetic. A task once undertaken was to be completed. It was her dogma. Her self-definition. Her parents would be so proud.

Finally, she looked at Celsi: "That's it. I'm staying! I'm giving it one more go." She hugged him, thanked him for his counsel, gave him letters and a fax to send when he made it back to civilization, and ran to find the porters who had her loads. Immediately, she felt at peace.

"I'm happy my decision is the right one. . . . I feel much more content, restful, and happier now—I have a job and I will try my best to do it. . . . Surely a couple of weeks won't make any difference?"

Johnston, Cooney, and Celsi said good-bye to Rob and Alison and started their long walk home. Celsi turned one last time and saw Alison watching him leave. He raised his arm and waved. She laughed and raised her arm and waved back, her face beaming as he hadn't seen it beam in weeks. She had made her decision. She was going to climb the mountain.

Three days later, August 9, the remaining fragments of different teams whose other members had already left posed for a de facto team picture before they, as a new assemblage, made a final bid for the summit the next morning. In it were Kiwis Peter Hillary, Bruce Grant, and Kim Logan, Canadian Jeff Lakes, American Rob Slater, and Alison Hargreaves. They were holding old aluminum dinner plates that the team had used for Frisbee tournaments during the many storm days at Base Camp. Alison was a frightfully poor toss, and an equally bad loser, but the men loved playing with her just to see her tantrums when throw after throw *kerplunked* on the rocks far from the intended mark. Some hammed it up for the picture, but Alison sat primly in the front row, holding her expedition plate, as if eager to get it over with.

Before going to bed, she wrote of the golden sunset over Chogolisa, a peak down the glacier near Concordia that reflected the sun off its flat white summit like a roof. She wrote about the porters returning on August 16 to take the team out of Base Camp through the beautiful Hushe Valley. The weather had finally broken, although she worried about the "unfortunate" wind blowing to the north. "Can we possibly be offered a chance to summit? God willing."

Inshallah.

They where the last words she wrote before she ripped out a few blank pages she would take on the mountain with her and tucked them into the top of her rucksack. It weighed only ounces, but every ounce felt like a pound of bricks, and she didn't want the extra weight of her journal on the climb. Still, she always needed paper and pen to write her thoughts. She turned off her headlamp and snuggled down into her sleeping bag, hoping for a few hours' rest before Ghulam woke them at 2:00 A.M. for their early breakfast and departure for the summit.

This was it: she'd give it one more try. If she didn't make it, so be it, but she was never coming back to the Karakoram. There were so many other mountains and climbs she'd rather do than K2 in this desolate wasteland. This mountain would be a prize in her collection of achievements, and she wanted it. But who was she kidding? She knew she hadn't come to climb a mountain like K2 because it was a good arrow in her quiver or someone wanted her to do it.

"At the end of the day," she said to the dark tent walls, "it's me that wants to do this."

The ascent began well. The sky was clear with a litter of stars above them, and the wind was low as they left Base Camp and made steady, even relaxed progress up to Camp III, which they had laboriously restocked. Snow had buried many of the ropes, necessitating painstaking efforts to free them as they climbed, but they nonetheless ascended efficiently and quickly. When they reached Camp III, they found it had once again been buried by an avalanche, and after an exhausting hour spent trying to find the tents, Alison urged them to continue up to Camp IV, betting that the camp and its supplies would still be there. The bet paid off—the camp was still there—and the team hunkered down for a brew and a rest before heading up in a few hours. Getting to the summit and back to camp would take about eighteen hours; they planned to leave around midnight so as to return to camp by sunset. Although climbers had been known to make it off the summit in the dark, it was a risk that drastically decreased their survivability.

When Alison checked the weather early on August 12, it was clear and calm; despite the cold, conditions were perfect for the summit. Even though graced with a favorable weather window, the ascent had left her and the team exhausted, and they opted for a day of rest in camp. Perhaps if Alison had been a better scholar of mountaineering, and K2 in particular, she would have heard the warning bells. Almost nine years earlier to the day, Julie Tullis and six other climbers made the same decision to forgo a day of good weather for oxymoronic rest at 8,000 meters. Near Alison and her team on the Shoulder were five Spaniards who had climbed to the Shoulder via the South Southeast Ridge; although a parallel route to the Abruzzi, it was many degrees steeper, and because they were alone on it they had set all of their own ropes. Their grueling ascent also prompted them to opt for an extra day "recuperating" at Camp IV.

In hindsight, their decision seemed foolhardy to the point of cavalier. But it was a bad decision that many mountaineers have made. The late British climber Alex MacIntyre used to insist that the best training for altitude climbing is to get desperately drunk and then climb with a horrible hangover. Not only do climbers have to deal with the same physical sickness—headache, queasy stomach, dizziness—but mentally they have to overcome an absolute lack of motivation to move, never mind climb an 8,000-meter peak. Alison's desire to remain snuggled in her sleeping bag was one shared by nearly everyone who had ever climbed into the Death Zone. So, while the sun blazed and the winds remained calm, she and the rest of the team slept and tried to hydrate in preparation for their climb the next day.

Finally, at midnight on August 12–13, Peter Hillary and Jeff Lakes were the first to leave Camp IV for the summit. Two hours later Kim Logan, Bruce Grant, Rob Slater, and Alison followed, their headlamps bouncing off the windswept Shoulder, their crampons squeaking across the brittle snow. Soon after leaving the tents, Kim Logan felt ill and retreated, his summit bid over. Not long after him, another Kiwi, Matt Comeskey, called it quits. Of the Spanish, four started out, but shortly out of Camp IV, Lorenzo Ortas also felt ill and decided not to ascend any farther.

When Peter Hillary and Jeff Lakes reached the Bottleneck, they sat down in the snow trying to decide what to do. Hillary, suffering in the extreme –40 degree Fahrenheit cold, was unsure about whether to continue. He also didn't like the looks of the weather. As they deliberated the others passed them on ascent, Rob Slater looking particularly exhausted. He didn't say anything as he stumbled by Hillary and continued up the route.

When Alison reached Hillary moments later, she stopped briefly, drawing ragged breaths in the thin air. "I'm going on" was all she said, and then she turned and continued up the route.

When she and Slater reached the top of the Bottleneck, she called down to Hillary, "Come on up, use the red rope," alerting him to which was good rope from that year versus old rope left from previous expeditions. But for Hillary the day was done, his attempt on K2 over. Jeff Lakes decided he had to give it one last try.

"I'll kick myself if they get to the top and I don't give it one more try," he said to Hillary. "I've been here twice, mate, I don't want to come back." Hillary wished him well, and Lakes resumed his ascent. Hillary looked up the mountain one more time and saw only dots, still ascending, Alison's lime green and blue climbing suit still distinguishable in the line of climbers. He turned and found himself in a fight for his life as the weather closed in around him. Still on the Shoulder above the start of the fixed ropes, he was scared out of his mind that he would simply walk off the edge of the mountain. He kicked at the slope and watched where the snow fell. If it rolled and fell out of sight, he wouldn't go in that direction. If he could see where it rolled, he would progress that far down the slope and kick again. Talking out loud to himself against the panic, he inched his way toward what he hoped would be the established route. When he found the fixed ropes, he almost cried out in relief as he clipped onto them. No sooner had he clicked onto the rope than a gust of wind pushed him away from the slope, and he found himself swinging on the rope, clinging to it for his life. If he hadn't been on the fixed line, he would have sailed off into the abyss. By the time he reached the top of the Black Pyramid at 7,400 meters (24,280 feet) the storm had moved in with a fury, the wind blowing 80 to 100 miles per hour. He continued his slow retreat through the storm, feeling at times like he might lose his mind to fear at any moment. Giggling like a madman, he suddenly remembered he had a pair of hand warmers in his pocket. In his hypoxic, terrorized mind, those hand warmers became his ticket to survival, and perhaps they were. Digging them out and cracking them into life, he continued down, focusing on the warmth spreading through his mittens, smiling at the simple pleasure.

In the Himalayas, as on the open sea, there are storms so violent and so exquisitely timed that the resulting disaster is dubbed "perfect." The afternoon of August 13, 1995, warm moist monsoon air began blowing up the narrow valley toward Base Camp. From the north, a powerful anticyclone moved in from China with its counterclockwise winds. When the opposing air masses collided, the turbulence was violent, and with nowhere to go in the narrow Karakoram Valley but up, those at Base Camp felt the first gust of the hurricane while those above them climbed unaware of the maelstrom headed their way.

On nearby Broad Peak, American guide Scott Fischer was struggling to get his climbers off the mountain, fast. That much farther down the glacier and lower in altitude, the storm had hit him and his team well before it did those on K2, blasting them with bitterly cold wind. Using his telescopic lens, Fischer had been watching the progress on K2 all day, cheering them on. But as he battened down his team's tents for the night, he again looked over and what he saw stunned him. They were still moving, up.

The storm hit Hillary full force at about 5:00 P.M., while those above him were still reporting good weather at 6:00 P.M., when Lorenzo Ortiz and Bruce Grant reached the summit. Moments later Alison joined them.

At 6:17 P.M. on August 13, 1995, exactly three months to the day after her exhilarating summit of Everest, Alison Hargreaves became the fifth woman to place her boot atop the world's second-highest mountain. She had done it. After weeks of indecision at Base Camp, she had made the right choice. She had stuck it out, worked hard, used all of her skills and daring, and here she was, atop K2, where only 121 had gone before her, and only four of them women. Half of those women had died on descent, but she was going to rewrite K2's terrible history and descend to her children and her life. From now on, her life was going to be her own. She looked around her, but there wasn't much to see. The storm that was battering Hillary and the lower part of the mountain obscured everything below her. She might as well have been on the moon for the view that greeted her from atop the mountain.

She felt a similar joy to that on Everest, a joy that made her want to sing a 10,000 Maniacs song that she'd been singing along to all summer about the days being blessed and lucky and ones she'd remember, forever.

Unlike her victorious summit of Everest, where she spent time to chat with Base Camp on the radio, Alison didn't linger on the top of K2. Looking below her, she could see the clouds billowing up the mountain and swirling around her and with them a wind that hadn't been apparent only moments before, its gusts blowing in from the north and east, forcing her to stand with her back into it, looking down the south face of K2 toward Base Camp. There, two miles below her, sat her tent, her journal, her future.

Below her, Hillary was making it into Camp II, shocked that he was still alive against such unspeakable odds. He could only hope the climbers above him had also turned around and gotten back to the fixed ropes before the storm hit. But suddenly the radio crackled to life from Base Camp reporting that six of the climbers were on the summit. *Oh God,* Hillary thought, *it's blowing 100 knots down here at 21,000 feet; what the hell is it doing at 28* [thousand]?

What it was doing was plucking the climbers off the slope and tossing them into the void. Because of the air's reduced barometric pressure at 8,000 meters and corresponding lessening of air molecules, the force of 100-mile-per-hour winds is reduced so that the actual blast feels more like 30 miles per hour. One can only imagine how strong the winds were to be able to push 150-pound men and women to their deaths. With no fixed rope above the Traverse, and nothing to crouch behind or beneath on the steep ice of the summit ridge, one by one they were blown off the mountain and thrown to their deaths down the South Face like loose shingles off a roof: Rob Slater, Bruce Grant, Lorenzo Ortiz, Javier Oliver, Javier Escartin, and Alison Hargreaves.

Jeff Lakes was just reaching the tents at Camp IV as the hurricane winds hit the Shoulder. He had turned around above the Bottleneck, deciding it was too late, he was too cold, and the clouds beneath him were too menacing. He fell into his tent glad to be alive, but no sooner had he allowed himself to relax into the warm security of his sleeping bag than the wind flattened his tent, cracking the brittle poles like matchsticks. For the rest of the night he sat crouched down against the brutal cold, his back to the wind that roared like a freight train and rocked his body with every gust. The morning dawned clear and calm, and Lakes looked repeatedly toward the summit, hoping to see signs that life had survived the maelstrom. He saw nothing. No movement. Only the painfully bright white snow. Deciding there was nothing he could do, and desperate to escape the lethal air, Lakes readied for his descent, grateful for the sun's warmth. But his ice ax, crampons, harness, and a descending device—all life-or-death equipment that high on K2—were gone, lost in the winds. Without crampons or an ice ax, he crawled most of the way down to the start of the fixed lines rather than risk slipping off the smooth slope and falling thousands of feet. When he reached them, he took out his penknife, which he thankfully had put in his pocket the day before, and cut a section of old rope, wrapped it around his body, and used it in place of a harness and carabiner to strap himself to the fixed lines. Then he finally started down the mountain.

In the history of epic descents, Lakes was about to make one of the most heroic. Facing 35- to 50-degree ice slopes and unstable avalanche snowfields, slurring his words from dehydration and exposure, tying and untying his rope between anchors, he inched his way down the fixed line, his feet skittering across the glassy surface. When he found the Kiwi tent at Camp III buried by a serac avalanche, he wept in frustration. Not only was he bone-cold from the laboriously slow descent, but he had no stove, no fuel, no food, and his inner reserves were spent.

Logan, Hillary, and Comeskey talked to him by radio from Camp II, urging him to dig out the buried tents at Camp III for the night. They needed more time to recover enough to ascend with food and equipment, and they worried how he would make it through the technically demanding Black Pyramid. But Lakes couldn't bear the thought of another night in the cold. As he continued down the three men waiting in Camp II spent an agonizing night, half-expecting to hear Lakes's tortured scream as his body flew past them off the mountain. How could he possibly make it with just a piece of rope and a penknife?

But he didn't fall, he didn't make a fatal error, and he didn't even suffer frostbite. He made it down to Camp II without the most rudimentary safety devices designed to keep him attached to the ice walls. He was hypothermic and semiconscious, but alive. Comeskey, Hillary, and Logan bustled him into a sleeping bag and gave him tea. After some labored breathing, his systems calmed down and he slept. But his Herculean efforts had drained his body to a point from which it couldn't recover. In the morning Comeskey found Lakes dead.

After waiting most of August 14 at Camp IV for their teammates to descend, Lorenzo Ortas and Jose Pepe Garces finally decided it was no use: Javier Escartin, Lorenzo Ortiz, and Javier Olivar were gone. As they made their slow progress down the South Southeast Ridge, they found a trail of clothing and a boot. In the boot was a heating device shown to them only days before by its owner, Alison Hargreaves. She had told them of her close call on the Matterhorn and proudly showed how the battery-operated coils prevented her frostbite-prone toes from suffering in the extreme cold. Ortas and Garces looked up from where they found the boot and saw three bloody tracks in the snow that seemed to come straight off the summit ridge at about 8,400 meters (27,500 feet), several hundred feet above the Bottleneck. As their eyes followed the tracks down the slope, one ended at a body at approximately 7,000 meters (23,000 feet). It wore Alison's distinctive clothing. The body lay about 300 meters away from them in the middle of a huge avalanche field; even if they had had the energy to climb over to it, getting there would mean senselessly risking their own lives. Alison would stay where she fell.

· · ·

When the phone rang in Spean Bridge on the evening of August 16, Jim Ballard thought it might be Alison. He'd heard rumors that she'd made the summit; perhaps she had found a satellite phone and was ringing home with her news. It wasn't Alison. It was the Press Association's bureau chief in Scotland asking if he'd heard a very different rumor being reported on the Outside Online website: "Alison Hargreaves, a rising star in the international climbing community, was killed Sunday, August 13, 1995, shortly after reaching the summit of K2." Scott Fischer on nearby Broad Peak had spoken earlier that day to the website, which had posted the report worldwide within minutes. Because the Internet was still a fledgling medium, untried and untrusted by many, it wasn't until the rumors persisted that the PA thought there might be something to it and called Ballard to confirm the news.

Ballard stood in his low-ceilinged living room looking out toward Ben Nevis, the last of the day's light fading rapidly. As he stood there still holding the phone, numb, headlights appeared over the hill, approaching the isolated stone cottage from the main road. Before his mind absorbed what was happening, his hair stood on end. It was in that instant he knew Alison was dead. A friend had driven out from Alison's press office in town; tears streamed down her face, and in her hand she clutched a fax. Ballard called Michael Kennedy, editor of the American *Climbing* magazine, to see whether he could get any more information; Kennedy had just heard the same report over the loudspeaker at the outdoor retailer show in Reno. Kennedy told Ballard how very, very sorry he was and promised to call if he heard anything else. Ballard hung up. It was really happening. As much as he'd known how dangerous climbing was, Alison had always come back. After all of those frightfully risky solo ascents, her face had always reappeared through the dark evening, returning to their little camps. She'd almost fallen off the Croz. But she'd come back. She'd made it to the top of Everest unassisted and without oxygen, but she had made it back down. But this time she was still up there. Somewhere. And she wasn't coming back.

Ballard heard Tom and Kate upstairs, their gentle breath audible in the silent house. He walked upstairs and stood in their bedroom door, listening. How in hell was he going to tell them their mother was never coming home? Then the phone rang again, and for days it didn't stop.

The press descended on sleepy Fort William and Spean Bridge like a swarm of locusts in a feeding frenzy for information, rumor, and opinion, and Ballard held court at Alison's press office at the base of Ben Nevis. He gave scores of interviews, telling reporters that Alison "died doing what she loved best," and he offered a piece of Tibetan wisdom as her life motto: "It is better to live one day as a tiger than a thousand years as a sheep." It played worldwide, even making "quote of the week" in a couple of British newspapers. Ballard was calm and collected as he spoke nearly nonstop. Expecting, perhaps desiring, the image of a widower prostrate in grief for their cameras and instead getting a composed, even witty husband and father, the British press judged his reaction odd, calculated, even cold.

Ballard found himself defending his response to his wife's death as the result of years of preparing emotionally for "this horrible day." When people lived at the cutting edge as Alison did, he said, you had to be ready for them to fall off of it. But the press persisted, finding fault not only with the grieving husband but with Alison as well. They had built her up to be an icon in mountaineering, and now they seemed to relish tearing her back down as a bad mother.

In the weeks after her death climbers, columnists, and social scientists came out of the proverbial woodwork to opine about her "obsession" with climbing K2, about her being "blinkered" by summit fever, about her "selfishness" in choosing the mountain over motherhood. One of those throwing his criticism into the ring was Peter Hillary, who criticized Alison for ignoring the telltale signs of bad weather moving in. When the rebuke of the son of Sir Edmund ran worldwide, the firestorm began, causing Alison to suffer in death the indignity of having her morals and her mental health questioned in a way never suffered by the men who died with her or by the other fathers who have left children behind: Alex Lowe, Scott Fischer, Rob Hall, Paul Nunn, Al Rouse, Maurice Barrard, Nick Estcourt, and so many more.

After Ballard had sated the media's thirst for every detail about Alison's life and loss, he took Tom and Kate into a quiet room at the ski area out of view of the cameras and sat them down. Their attentive, intelligent faces nearly broke his heart. Ever the straightforward Yorkshireman, he didn't mince words.

"Your mummy is lost in a mountain storm, and I don't think you will ever see her again," Ballard said.

When they stopped crying and dried their tears, six-year-old Tom looked up at Ballard.

"Can we go see Mum's last mountain?" he asked.

"Yes, we can go see your mum's last mountain," Ballard told him, although he had no idea how he was going to get himself and two children under seven into some of the world's wildest territory. Somehow he knew he would. He had to. At six, Tom's fierce blue eyes and set jaw told Ballard there was no alternative.

Five weeks later they were on their way. Like their mother, the children did well in the demanding chaos of Rawalpindi and Skardu and also acclimatized well to the thin, arid air as they climbed into the foothills of K2. But when they reached Paiju, their expedition doctor came down with dysentery. Not wanting to continue without him, Ballard decided they had come far enough.

Ballard and the children climbed above the poplars where they could see K2 far off in the distance, its sharp summit poking above the smaller peaks around it. Tom and Kate busied themselves choosing the best rocks with which to build two small cairns for "Mum." In each cairn they left her their personal pictures, talismans, even little bits of food. It was as close to their mother as they would get. Kate, done with her task, trotted off, but Tom lingered and sat by his cairn, looking up at K2.

Ballard, watching nearby, felt that his heart couldn't stand much more wrenching. He too looked up at the far-off mountain in the impossibly blue sky: *I did what I thought was best, Ali: I brought your children to you so you could have one last look at them.*

Tom got up and dusted off his legs and walked over to Ballard, slipping his hand into his father's. They didn't speak. When they were ready, they turned and started back for home.

Due northeast, across the still expanse of crystal air, the South Face of K2 shone in the sun. Somewhere on it lay Alison.

The summer following Alison's death, Richard Celsi had a solid brass plaque designed and forged in California bearing a William Blake quote that he altered to reflect the feminine. He then carried it into K2 on his back and bolted it to the Gilkey Memorial. On it reads

Alison Jane Hargreaves, 1962–1995

In what distant deeps or skies
Burnt the fire of thine eyes?
On what wings dare she aspire?
What the hand dare seize the fire?

William Blake

CHAPTER 11

THE LEGACY IS
SEALED

I have an appetite for silence.

—EMILY DICKINSON

From 1992 to 1998, Chantal Mauduit remained the only surviving female summiteer of K2. As with Wanda Rutkiewicz before her, that glory would last exactly six years.

In those years Chantal continued her career in the 8,000-meter game, reaching summit after summit, but few were without controversy. There were charges that she didn't reach some of the summits she claimed, as well as the ever-present judgment that she used her wiles, not her wits, to climb mountains. In 1994 the French climbing magazine *Vertical* wrote, "The trouble with Chantal Mauduit is that her climbs seem too easy to be taken seriously," adding to the ambivalence about just how worthy her achievements were.

"I think she was dreaming all the time," Catherine Destivelle said. "She liked very much this feeling of being in high altitude, something I don't like. She liked to have this feeling of being in the clouds."

Blithely ignoring the criticism, Chantal forged on, joining eighteen expeditions in little more than ten years, but one mountain continued to elude her. When Chantal was asked in June 1995 how she felt about Alison Hargreaves finally achieving on Everest what she had tried and failed to do many times, she brushed it off as an unimportant distinction, not a motivator for her climbing.

"I'm happy for her," she told her brother François, "but I don't see mountaineering the same way Alison does; I climb to experience more than just the mountain; I like to travel and share with the people." Three months later Alison was dead, and Chantal was asked by the mountaineering press to react.

"I admired her, but you see, we are different. For one thing, I am still climbing." A charming and warmhearted person, Chantal seemed oddly unaware of or indifferent to how powerfully her words could hurt others and her own ability to exist in the community in which she chose to live.

After six consecutive failures to reach the summit of Everest, in 1996 Chantal turned to 8,516-meter (27,939-foot) Lhotse, the world's fourth-highest mountain, as she continued in her quest to reach all fourteen 8,000-meter peaks. Sitting just across the Western Cwm from Everest, it shared base and three approach camps on the Cwm before the route split above the Yellow Band for either Everest or Lhotse.

On a brilliant day in May, Chantal climbed the crowded ropes above Camp III, the last shared camp before she would veer right and onto Lhotse proper. Climbers from all over the world had descended on Everest, and she was glad for once to not be attempting the mountain. *Too many people,* she thought as she passed nearly twenty clients and sherpas from Scott Fischer's group on their way up the ropes, among them Charlotte Fox of Aspen and Sandy Hill Pittman of New York City. Fox was amazed when Chantal "just galloped by" them, even though she wasn't breathing supplemental oxygen. Pittman, in an almost reflexive show of camaraderie at seeing another woman in a world of so many men, greeted Chantal as she climbed passed. Chantal never responded, as if she hadn't heard her hello at all.

Chantal was climbing with Americans Tim Horvath and Stephen Koch, the latter known for his snowboard descents off many 8,000-meter peaks. Dan Mazur, the Seattle-based expedition leader, decided to stay lower on the mountain with his other clients and help ensure their ascent, while Chantal, Koch, and Horvath climbed to 7,900 meters on the Lhotse Face, where they established what Koch called a "shitty" Camp IV, perched on a tiny ledge that only allowed the three to sit upright in their small two-man tent while their feet dangled off the ledge. It was a miserable night as squalls hit the face, soaking the climbers and forcing Koch to repeatedly pound pitons into the ice to secure the tent. In the morning both Koch and Horvath were "wasted" and decided their summit bid was over. When asked what she was going to do, Chantal smiled at them and said she was going for it.

As she made her way up the mountain alone she looked over at Everest and saw a string of tiny black ants in a traffic jam waiting on the fixed ropes below the Hillary Step. She thought, *That's not right. There are too many people.* The wind was fierce, but she felt she was well equipped and in great shape to make the summit before anything serious hit her. Ducking her head against the ice particles spraying her face, she continued climbing, watching her feet step by step inch up the slope.

Hours later she made the summit alone and again without oxygen, becoming the first woman to climb the mountain. But the victory was muted: she realized she preferred sharing her climbing with others. Unlike her ascent of K2, she didn't have friends nearby with whom to share her victory via radio or from whom to receive blessings and energy. She took out her camera to capture the moment as well as to record her ascent, but the camera failed, apparently frozen. After giving it a few shakes, hoping to release the shutter, she gave up and shoved it back in her pack. She felt enchanted, but the experience was nothing like her mystical summit of K2, where she had come to peace with her mother's death. She tried to focus on the purity of being alone with the mountain, but all she came up with was sadness for Lhotse because it was overshadowed by its neighbor Everest. As she looked across she saw that the winds were now swirling around the mountain with an evil intensity.

Many athletes, climbers included, feel a measure of panic when they find themselves at the edge of their sport, dangling beyond the reach of its safety nets. But Chantal never felt such terror. Time and again she climbed alone, without a partner or fixed lines, reaching the pinnacles of mountains and their dangers, seemingly at peace with her proximity to death. She miraculously never suffered frostbite, and one reason may have been her fantastic calm. Frostbite is often caused by life-and-death fear that releases a catastrophic surge of adrenaline, the body's most powerful blood constrictor. Panic also causes panting, which further consumes the body's precious fluids through the lungs. Chantal's mantra-like serenity served her well. Her heartbeat remained steady, her limbs and extremities well fed by a constant blood source.

After watching the storm rage on Everest, Chantal turned and made the steep but not terribly technical descent back down the face to the start of the fixed lines above the Yellow Band. Fifteen hours after she had started her ascent, she arrived back in Camp III at 24,000 feet, where Koch and Horvath were waiting.

"Did you make it?" they asked.

"Oui," Chantal smiled. "Yes, yes, I did."

But other climbers weren't so sure, and doubt about her claim started almost immediately: she hadn't had enough time to make the summit, they charged, and she hadn't returned with any photographic proof. Her critics never answered why or where she spent over fifteen hours above 8,000 meters if it wasn't climbing the mountain. While doubt raged, many others believed her, including Elizabeth Hawley in Kathmandu, the queen mother of Himalayan record-keeping: "She absolutely made the summit. I have never heard any doubt that she didn't."

When Chantal finally made it off the mountain, she caught a ride out of Base Camp in a military helicopter sent in to get the frostbitten survivors of the infamous storm on Everest, among them Charlotte Fox.

Fox sat with her hands bandaged, shell-shocked from the carnage above her. She turned to Chantal and offered congratulations for making Lhotse.

"But of course!" Chantal replied, giving her long brown curls a toss.

Fox rolled her eyes behind her dark glacier glasses. *Typical French,* she couldn't help thinking.

Chantal's victory was lost in the aftermath of the Everest tragedy, as was the fact that she made history as the first woman to climb Lhotse, a fact unknown even to her climbing partners. Chantal never seemed to resent or even notice that the world ignored her achievement, and she went quietly on with climbing her 8,000-meter peaks.

After Lhotse she immediately traveled to the dangerous and deadly Manaslu, also reaching its summit, again without oxygen, and, after her Sherpa turned around near the summit, alone for the final pitch to the top. Chantal now had climbed five 8,000-meter peaks, something only Wanda Rutkiewicz had done before her. While many climbers stormed that she seemed to do a lot of these ascents alone and without a functioning camera, some in the French press started calling her the greatest living female alpinist. It was not an important distinction for Chantal.

"What does it matter?" she said after her ascent of Lhotse. "Such titles are unimportant to me. I only climb because it's beautiful up there." While sponsors flocked to have their gear hawked by a beautiful enchantress from the top of the world's highest mountains, she was halfhearted in her own self-promotion. When Dan Mazur planned a slide slow and lecture tour for her in America, something that would have helped put her squarely on the American mountaineering dole, she demurred. "I have to help my brother plant his garden this weekend; I cannot make it."

In the constant planning-executing-planning of her string of expeditions, Chantal found the time to write a small book of personal meditations that she called *J'habite au Paradis* (I live in Paradise), a title the publisher insisted she change or he wouldn't print the book. She refused and was about to walk away until the publisher relented and allowed her title to prevail. Available only in French, *J'habite au Paradis* is an odd rambling of poetry and prose, and while mostly opaque in its themes, it nonetheless occasionally offers poignant and revealing insights into a woman more complex than her own words would indicate.

"She wanted the world to think she was all light and laughter, but she was very complex," said Thor Kieser, the man who saved her life on K2. "She wanted to appear like a Buddhist monk, simple. But she was complex and she had her ghosts." While there are stories of her dancing on tabletops and drinking to the point of oblivion more than once, she was also driven, competitive, and often critical of others. She also toyed with the emotions of men around her.

"She had a power over men, and she used it. She used to joke, 'So many men, so little time,'" Kieser said. She also knew how to cut them to their core. On more than one occasion, if she ran into a former lover who looked at her with a bit too much wolf for the sheep, she would stare the man right in the face and say, "Oh, I'm sorry, I don't remember you. Have we met?"

Dan Mazur thought Chantal had a wonderfully wicked sense of humor and found her cunning rather than cruel, and always in control. "I saw so many guys who were getting flirty or in her face, get her famous 'Hmm, I don't remember you' line, and they would look like a little boy who's been told he's not going to get a birthday present that year," Mazur said. On another occasion she asked a particularly obnoxious climber from Athens who had refused to take her more gentle rebuff, "Is it true what I've heard, that Greek men like little boys' bottoms?" After a heated defense of Greek heterosexuality, the crimson-faced man fled. Mazur, for one, thought she enjoyed her control over men and used it with killer precision.

But apart from the playful putdowns, she also dealt with real harassment, both from rebuffed hell-hath-no-fury male climbers who condemned her as a climber after the affair dissolved and from climbing officials who would push themselves on her. During her 1992 summer on K2, she decided to visit her Spanish friends at their Broad Peak Base Camp. A Pakistani liaison officer, seeing her leaving, offered to accompany her on the two- to three-hour hike down the glacier. As soon as they were out of sight and earshot of Base Camp he grabbed her, pulling her toward him. She gave him a powerful shove that sent him stumbling across the rocks, and he fled back to Base Camp. She reported the incident to Mazur when she returned later that evening, but given her precarious position of being an outlaw climber on the wrong team, she didn't pursue any action against the liaison officer. Yet the incident fueled her already intense dislike of Pakistani men.

To her family she remained happy, energetic, and wild, like an unbroken colt. When she arrived at the house to meet her brother's in-laws visiting from America, rather than walk in the front door, she climbed up the old farmhouse's stone wall and entered through the second-story window, knocking over a shelf of cookbooks as she finally fell into the kitchen.

"Hi! I'm Chantal," she announced, laughing, her hand outstretched to the startled in-laws, brushing the hair out of her face.

"That was Chantal," her brother François said years later. "It was just fun all the time. 'Life is great, let's enjoy it.'"

Prior to one of her expeditions, friends and family threw her a good-bye party. The last of the guests finally left in the early morning. Only hours before her flight for Nepal, Chantal decided she'd better pack. She hadn't even started. She started throwing boots, clothes, books—always books—into her bags. Something that takes most climbers months of lists, organization, and careful consideration Chantal accomplished in little over ninety minutes.

Unlike a lot of women, and unlike most who have an ounce of extra flesh, Chantal was completely comfortable with her feminine, even fleshy body. Climbing in Thailand, she wore a bikini top and shorts as she climbed on the cliffs over the beaches, not in the least bit uncomfortable about revealing the cellulite on her thighs. For many around her, it was a refreshing change from the hyper-obsessed women who lived in fear of revealing the slightest flaw. She was lighthearted and fun, and people around her somehow felt happier in her presence.

Her last climb with her friend and fellow Chamonix guide Frédérique Delrieu was full of that sense of living life to the fullest; together they climbed the Byzantine Basilica of Sacre Coeur on Montmartre in Paris. They climbed at night, hoping to avoid the searchlight of patrolling police, and although many hundred feet off the ground with no safety ropes, Chantal considered getting caught the greatest danger. The year before that they had placed the Tibetan flag on the top of Notre Dame. Chantal had wanted to cover the basilica in Buddhist red.

In 1997 her energies took a more sober turn when she became involved in a very passionate and public condemnation of a Franco-Chinese Everest expedition being planned by the French Alpine Club in Chamonix because it was perceived as endorsing the Chinese presence in Tibet. Joining her fellow French climbers Christophe Profit and Jean-Christophe Lafaille, she declared it "an expedition of collaborationists" and helped to put the expedition on indefinite hold.

She also began putting more and more time into raising money for her sponsorship of Nepalese families, and in particular children. Struck by their poverty and lack of adequate health care and education, she supported several children, seeing to their physical needs and helping in their education. She also was granted a rare personal audience with the Dalai Lama, laughing casually with the spiritual leader of millions as she showed him pictures of her past expeditions and got him to sign a Tibetan flag that she took to her next summit. The Dalai Lama seemed as delighted by the beautiful, charming, energetic girl as any other man she had ever met.

In 1997, for the first time in five consecutive years, she did not travel to Nepal. Instead, she returned to Pakistan to climb Gasherbrum II, this time making little reference to the "crude" men in her path. What she did notice was the ecological disaster befalling Pakistan. In 1992 the area had still been pristine, but the five years since had seen thousands of people traveling through the valleys and glaciers, leaving their waste and garbage behind in the rivers, on the rocks and ice, and along the path. The trek into the mountain was foul. Chantal remembered why she loved Nepal, where the villagers had long since figured out that outhouses, campsites, and regulations had to be fixed and maintained to accommodate the influx of thousands of climbers and porters on the delicate land.

Filth aside, her ascent of GII was successful, her sixth 8,000-meter peak. Unlike most climbers who bring only tiny, lightweight mementos to the summits of 8,000-meter peaks because of their weight, Chantal stood atop the mountain proudly carrying the full-size Tibetan flag that she had had the Dalai Lama sign. As she posed for a photo, behind was K2, her first 8,000-meter peak. GII would be her last.

She returned to her beloved Nepal in the spring of 1998, this time to Dhaulagiri, at 8,167 meters (26,794 feet) the world's seventh-highest mountain. As she prepared to leave she gave a slide show in Chamonix that many who were there will never forget. Instead of taking the usual place by the podium, Chantal decided to talk while hanging on a rope suspended over the audience. Twirling around and around, laughing and twisting to face the screen, she described the screen images of her latest adventures. Those below her were captivated by the girl spinning above them, forgetting there was a slide show to watch.

She called her expedition to Dhaulagiri the Sunflower Expedition: she adorned Base Camp with huge yellow, plastic flowers and painted her green high-altitude tent with sunflowers, mountains, and poetry in splashes of gold paint. Some of the words on the tent read, "I call this the Sunflower Expedition; climbing to the summit, watched by the sun." Film of the expedition showed a perpetually playful Chantal, throwing rice and flour into the air during the traditional *puja* cere-mony to bless the climb, mugging for the camera with a flour-smeared smile, and performing one of the world's highest-altitude stripteases. With her was her climbing partner, Ang Tshering Sherpa, who was more of a friend, she said, than a paid load-bearer and trail-blazer.

Also at Base Camp was Ed Viesturs, her former lover who had helped rescue her off K2. Their romantic relationship had ended years before, but they remained cordial. Viesturs was chipping away at his goal to become the first American to climb all fourteen 8,000-meter peaks, all without supplemental oxygen. But the weather on Dhaulagiri was vicious that May, and he and his climbing partner, New Zealand climber Guy Cotter, were repeatedly forced back to Base Camp*.

Chantal and Tshering were undaunted by the heavy snowfall and climbed apart from the other teams on the mountain, establishing Camp II at 6,600 meters (21,000 feet) near the tents of Spanish and Ital-ian teams. Viesturs and Cotter, fearing the area's tendency to suffer heavy snowdrifts and avalanches, opted to dig a snow cave rather than lose their tent. But Chantal put up her green, gold-splattered tent so that she and Tshering could wait out the weather in the comfort of a tent rather than an icy snow cave.

On May 7, Chantal packed up and headed out of Base Camp. Guy Cotter looked over as she prepared to leave, surprised. Above them he could see a "very ugly-looking weather front coming toward us," and he called to Chantal, asking her whether she was sure she wanted to go up with the impending storm. She did. In Cotter's mind, it seemed as if

*On May 12, 2005 Viesturs successfully ascended Annapurna, becoming the first Ameri-can to climb all fourteen 8,000 meter peaks, none with supplemental oxygen.

she was out of sync with the mountains she climbed and with her own position in the grand scheme of things. Hours later Base Camp was blasted by gale-force winds and snow, and the storm became the most terrifying Cotter had ever encountered in his twenty-something years in the Himalayas, with lightning flashes through his Base Camp tent and snow blowing in the zippers.

Chantal and Tshering made it safely to Camp II late in the afternoon, before the worst of the storm hit. They passed the Italians' tent fifty meters below where their green one sat, and as they did Franco Brunello warned her of a crevasse above his tent; she thanked him and continued on up. He watched her small figure disappear into the green tent, Tshering slipping in after her, and the zipper closing behind them. Brunello would be the last man to see them alive.

On May 9, a Nepalese friend of Chantal's walked slowly through his village. Suddenly a cloud of butterflies appeared in front of him, obscuring everything with their bright fluttering.

"Putali," he said, the word floating among the colorful swarm. Chantal's love of butterflies had earned her the nickname *Putali* in Nepal: Butterfly. He looked up toward the mountains. "Putali," he said again; it was a whisper. Without any more evidence than the horde in front of him, he knew something was horribly wrong with Chantal.

Back in Base Camp the other climbers hunkered down in their tents, holding their backs to the thin nylon while the storm continued to rage. It was a long week. When the skies finally cleared, the climbers resumed their ascents. On May 14, Brunello reascended to Camp II, where he checked Chantal's tent; finding it partially buried by snow, he assumed it was empty. Viesturs, thinking Chantal and Tshering might have moved up the mountain, checked the site where he knew they were to establish their Camp III but found no sign of them or a tent. Finally, on May 15, after the mountain had been scoured and no trace of the climbers had been found, the Italians decided to properly dig out Chantal's tent, which, according to Cotter, had only a "little piece of green" left poking out of the heavy snowfall and spin drift. Franco Brunello, with a sudden panic filling him, first began digging with his hands, and then team members brought a shovel to help remove the deep snow from the side of the tent where the weight had partially collapsed it. When he finally cleared the snow, he unzipped the tent door and looked in.

He found Chantal near the door in her sleeping bag, a "peaceful" expression on her face but her jaw twisted and broken. It looked like a piece of ice had struck her head from outside the tent and killed her "in a moment." Further back in the tent he found Tshering, who had apparently been trapped by the slough of snow and ice and suffocated under the weight. Italian climber Tarcisio Bello thought an ice fall or small avalanche hit the tent, small by Himalayan standards, but "large enough to cause one huge tragedy."

News of Chantal's death hit the wires almost immediately. While the French embassy in Nepal issued a statement saying Chantal probably died as the result of an avalanche, Ed Viesturs was asked by the American press to speculate on what could have killed her inside a tent. One "possible" scenario, he told Mountainzone.com, was that she could have been asphyxiated when she left a camp stove burning during the long snowstorm. As the snow covered the tent, it was surmised, the stove consumed all the oxygen inside the tent, killing Chantal and Tshering. Because gas stoves consume oxygen as they burn, the already thin air can become lethal within minutes. It's a mistake that many climbers have made, but few have been killed by, and the story ran worldwide. Viesturs unwittingly sparked an international war of words that lingered for years and further tarnished Chantal's reputation as a talented and experienced Himalayan climber.

Adding to the controversy was speculation that Chantal and Tshering's tent could not have been hit by an avalanche. First, a Spanish team's tent stood untouched less than fifteen feet away from Chantal's, and the Spanish tent appeared to be more in the direct line of an avalanche path. Guy Cotter, a teacher of avalanche safety, said he found it virtually impossible to believe that they were hit by an avalanche because the tent was still standing, its top sticking out of the drift, while Chantal and Tshering lay dead inside.

In mid-June a report by British mountain writer Ed Douglas

appeared in the *London Guardian* stating that Chantal's and Tshering's bodies were found "intact and undisturbed," adding to the theory that they suffocated. But even Douglas admitted later that he wrote the story so soon after Chantal's death that he could have misunderstood some of the details from the Spanish and Italians who found her body. "She died. If she made a mistake, who really cares, apart from families and friends?" he said.

In late May, Frédérique Delrieu and Marco Francesconi of Sector Watches, Chantal's major sponsor, flew from France to bring her body home. When Frédérique arrived, she saw that Chantal's neck had been broken, her head twisted at a terrible angle to the body, indicating an ice slab or isolated avalanche rather than merely slipping into an "undisturbed" sleep.

But the rumors persisted, fed when the media repeated Viesturs's early assumption that the "nonchalant and carefree" Chantal had forgotten to clean the snow off her tent. Delrieu fired back in an open letter to Mountainzone, loaded for bear. "She was a very intelligent woman. For her, life was the most important thing in the world. Chantal took part in eighteen expeditions, participated in hundreds of well-known ascents throughout the world, and she had been climbing for eighteen years. Do you think you can go back eighteen times in a row to the highest altitudes and participate in many of the most demanding 'vertical trips' by climbing carelessly?" Chantal was also with a forty-five-year-old Sherpa, Delrieu reminded the world, a man with close to thirty years of climbing experience, much of that caring for climbers and their tents on high-altitude mountains. Viesturs apologized for his early remarks, but the damage was done.

When asked to comment on the cause of Chantal's death, Himalayan data-keeper Elizabeth Hawley said, "This is an easy one. An autopsy in France showed Chantal Mauduit died of a broken neck." Autopsies on climbers who die in the Himalayas are rare because recovery of the body is almost always impossible. But this time the body had not only been recovered but flown home, where an autopsy had been performed and an official cause of death declared. In the years since Chantal's death, her official cause of death was changed in Hawley's and Richard

Salisbury's Himalayan data bank from "avalanche" to "falling rock/ice."

But even with the hard evidence, doubt remains and speculation persists that Chantal asphyxiated owing to her reckless disregard for safety. Many in the climbing community still choose to believe that the woman who had been on eighteen Himalayan expeditions, climbed six 8,000-meter peaks—all of them without oxygen—and chose as her climbing partner a man with nearly thirty years of climbing experience, made a rookie error.

As Delrieu was bringing Chantal's body home to her family in France, word of her death filtered out to the world. Few who heard it were shocked.

Denis Ducroz had feared for his lovely friend, worried that she was on a "spiritual quest" with no clear agenda. "She was looking for something else, and she probably didn't know where to stop." When Ducroz heard the news that she had perished, he cried. Telling his young daughter was particularly wrenching: the girl had looked up to Chantal as a role model, a beautiful, shining hero, and losing her was like losing a dream of her own future.

"The last time I saw her, in her eyes, I saw that she had already passed. Already died," observed Niels Friisbøl, president of Valandré clothing in France. "She had an addiction to these mountains, and her need to feed that addiction took over."

"It was a shock," her brother François said, "but not a complete shock. She lived a dangerous life. And I think she had some sort of a premonition as well. She told a shopkeeper in Chamonix that she knew she would die young. But even knowing that, I don't think she would have changed [the way she was living]. She knew that she was taking chances. . . . She lived such a full life. She only lived 34 years, but in 34 years she did more than people who live 100."

Back in Colorado, Thor Kieser "wasn't the least bit surprised, because I knew it was her destiny. It was her drive, the way she was composed emotionally. It was just gonna happen. She might have been overly ambitious; but then, most of us climbers are."

Lynn Hill, America's premier woman of the rock, also had no illusions about Chantal's longevity. "She was the kind of climber that was just winging it," Hill said, "and she would just go for it. So she seemed like one of those airy characters that just seemed to float through life, and most of the time it worked out, but it's easy to see that one little error could cost her her life. I wasn't surprised to hear that she died, even though she really didn't die in a situation that was irresponsible." But still the stigma persists that somehow it was.

Chantal left strict instructions that she wanted to be cremated, and years after her death François and the family were still not done scattering her ashes. "Well, the ashes." François Mauduit laughed at the absurdity of it all. "She wanted to be spread in so many places, you see? But that's the great thing about ashes, you can put them everywhere." François and the family have been busy dispersing her to the corners of the world she loved and where she was loved. To date she resides in Germany, different areas of the French Alps, Paris, and soon in the corner of the world she loved the most: Nepal.

Chantal's funeral in Chamonix was one of poignant humor and lingering pain where many stood and shared their memories. Her friend Christophe Profit had the last word: "Above all, she showed that there was a beautiful way to get to the top."

As the mass concluded a recognizable voice suddenly floated down through the mourners where they sat in their pews. Recorded in one of her last interviews, Chantal's trilling laughter soared like a diva's aria through the crowd and embraced each person present. After several minutes it began to fade and rose through the open windows and out to the mountains above.

CHAPTER 12

A HERO IS FOUND

God gave us mountains and the strength to climb them.

—ANONYMOUS

"What's that? A tent?" Fausto de Stefani asked his teammates Silvio "Gnaro" Mondinelli and Marco Galezzi. It was the spring of 1995, and the Italian team of friends was climbing Kangchenjunga, the world's third-highest peak, when they spotted what looked like a yellow and pink tent lying to their right on the wide expanse of the mountain's Southwest Face.

"No, I don't think so," said Mondinelli, looking closer at the colorful mound on the snow. "I think I see legs."

The three men felt a cold grip deep within their bellies and bowels that all climbers feel when finding a fallen climber. Although they had witnessed a lot of death in their years of climbing these big mountains, frequency never bred nonchalance. Not only was it a glimpse at their own possible fate if they continued to challenge these deadly peaks above 8,000 meters, but after years of exposure to the UV rays at high altitude, hurricane-force winds, avalanches, rockfall, even predatory birds and snow foxes, the human body becomes a hard, baked, wrecked shell of decay with pieces broken off and scattered and its features long ruined and almost unrecognizable as man or woman.

But this body was different. This one lay on the slope undisturbed, casually, like someone taking an afternoon nap in the sun. Not until they crossed the wide snowfield did they see that the top of the head was missing, as if a giant and very sharp machete had cleanly sliced it off above the eyebrows. Either something traveling 100 miles an hour had hit the head or the head had hit something when it was traveling at freeway speeds. This climber was nearly decapitated. After years on this high-altitude gravesite, the remaining skull had been emptied of its human material by the huge black ravens that float above the 8,000-meter mountains. Instead of gray matter, it was packed tightly with snow and ice. It looked like a melon that had been cut in two and filled neatly with vanilla ice cream. The eyes, nose, and mouth were visible but barely recognizable in the ruination of what used to be a face. They decided to pull the body farther down the slope to remove it from beneath a nasty-looking serac. When they reached down to take hold of its arms, they felt that one had been ripped out of its socket, and then they saw that one of the pant legs hung loose and empty: half of the left leg was missing. But the rest of the body was oddly untouched. As violent as this climber's fall had been, the pink and yellow down suit it wore was in almost perfect condition, as though it had been taken off the rack the day before—no cuts, nicks, or tears. In fact, the down inside appeared as fluffy and new as the eiderdown quilts on their beds in Italy. On it was a Valandré label. *High-end stuff,* they thought. *This climber either had the means or the sponsors to be outfitted by the best.* The remaining leg wore an expensive Italian Scarpa boot and equally high-quality Italian Grivel crampon. What was missing was the climbing harness. Where had this climber been that he hadn't needed his harness? A climber without a harness is like a deep-sea diver without a face mask or a marathon runner without sneakers—the harness is that much a second skin. But maybe he was alone and climbing on the summit ridge, where there are no fixed lines.

All three men turned to look at the cliff above them, each visualizing the terrible fall and wondering, *Who could it be?*

Then they saw the breast. Not only are women few and far between on the Himalayan giants, but this mountain had hosted only a handful of female climbers in the forty years since it was first ascended in 1955. And while not one of those summiteers before 1995 was a woman, four had died trying: Marija Frantar of Slovenia, Yekaterina Ivanova of Russia, Jordanka Dimitrova of Bulgaria, and Wanda Rutkiewicz of Poland.

"I think it's Wanda," Fausto said simply, looking down at his friend.

As they had done with the odd assortment of bodies each had found over the years of their climbing on these killer peaks, they dragged the body to the nearest crevasse, said a silent prayer, and watched it fall out of sight into the icy depths.

When the men returned to Italy, they wrote in an Italian climbing journal that they had found the body of Wanda Rutkiewicz, but the news was met with skepticism in the larger climbing community, particularly in Poland.

"Impossible!" said Anna Czerwinska, Wanda's former climbing partner. "Wanda was too vain. She would never be caught dead in pink!"

But perhaps she had.

Of the four women who have died on Kangchenjunga, one was avalanched below 6,700 meters, and another—Marija Frantar—was discovered by Rutkiewicz herself during their 1991 attempt on the mountain. Therefore, the climber could only be either Dimitrova or Rutkiewicz.

After an exhaustive investigation involving the president of Valandré clothing, Elizabeth Hawley in Kathmandu, Simone Moro, Fausto de Stefani, Marco Galezzi, and Silvio Mondinelli in Italy, a host of people in Bulgaria and Poland, and the legendary iron horses of high-altitude climbing, Reinhold Messner in Rome, Carlos Carsolio in Mexico City, and Ed Viesturs in Seattle, the absolute truth remains elusive, as do so many truths that reside in the opaque world of 8,000-meter peaks. But a few facts have been uncovered: even though her fashion police are convinced that she would never have worn pink, Wanda ordered and received at least three high-altitude suits from Valandré, including the "dreadful" pink. While pictures from her last expedition to Kangchenjunga show her in the yellow and blue down suit, she could easily have taken the more lightweight "Combi" on the mountain for her final summit bid.

When Carsolio was asked to dig deep into the recesses of his faded memory to remember what color he last saw her wearing, he demurred. "She was wearing yellow in Base Camp, but she could have been wearing the pink in the cave. I just can't be sure." Carsolio nearly lost his own life on descent, and for the past twelve years he has been asked repeatedly to tell the story of Wanda's last moments: how he came upon her in the pitiful snow cave without a stove or sleeping bag on a particularly frigid night and how she pled for his warm clothing and water, always water. But he had nothing to give her.

Finally, and perhaps most telling, was the missing left leg. Wanda suffered a series of injuries to her left leg, including a severe compound fracture of her left femur in 1981. Although most fractures heal stronger than the original bone when set properly, Wanda's frenetic life of expedition after expedition never gave the bone the chance to heal fully. She complained of residual pain and weakness in the leg as late as October 1991. In a violent fall from the summit ridge thousands of feet above where the body was found, its weakest links would immediately have been evident, and an already compromised femur would have needed a lot less than a blow of that magnitude to rebreak, even be severed.

The body found on Kangchenjunga was almost certainly that of Wanda Rutkiewicz.

But does it really matter? We know that Wanda died on Kangchenjunga; does it matter how? Perhaps not, but knowing how she *didn't* die does matter.

Wanda was last seen high on Kangchenjunga's *Northwest* Ridge by Carsolio. He says that she was suffering from the severe cold and begged him for his down pants, a plea that suggests she was not wearing the heavier yellow suit but the more lightweight pink Valandré. She had been climbing light—no stove, no food, no extra clothing—hoping that she would summit and descend back to their high camp in a single day. But she hadn't been able to make it. Carsolio had climbed faster, made the summit at about 5:00 P.M., and started back down when he found her in the snow cave around 8:00 P.M.

"She wanted to stay, she said she wanted to try for the summit in the morning," he said years later, tears filling his eyes, still grieving for the woman he left for dead. "I had not the guts to tell her to come down. Perhaps that was all she needed, an excuse; she was so proud. She was Wanda."

For twelve years that was how history recorded Wanda Rutkiewicz's death: disappeared, probably died of exposure at 8,300 meters on Kangchenjunga's Northwest Face. But if the body found on the *Southwest* Face after a fall of thousands of feet is Wanda's, then her story and her history change. It means she didn't just curl up and die, alone and freezing to death, desperate for a drink of hot tea and another climber's clothes. She fought, even "raged against the dying of the night."

"She was very proud," Ewa Pankiewicz said. "If she was able, she would never have gone down without trying again, especially since Carlos had made the summit. He was just a kid. How could she not try again?"

And so it seems she did. After Carlos told her the route above was not very technical and therefore not roped, she left her harness in the cave, again saving herself some precious extra weight for the final summit push. Climbers on the Northwest Face of Kangchenjunga must cross over the summit ridge at about 8,450 meters onto the Southwest Face and climb through a section of rock called the Pinnacles. Ginette Harrison, a British climber with the only known female ascent of the mountain in 1998, recalled on her ascent of the Northwest Face that the last meters to the summit were "really exposed, with this awesome drop down the Southwest Face," but nothing needing a fixed line and nothing to stop Wanda from going for her ninth 8,000-meter peak. If she made it, she accomplished another milestone: first and still only woman to climb the three highest mountains on Earth.

Whether she made it to the summit is not important, mostly because it will never be known. What *is* crucial is that she died fighting. She died trying. Her pride, her toughness, her absolute refusal to give up, is indeed her legacy, not a sad and desperate frozen death in the side of a mountain, refusing her last chance at survival when she sent her climbing partner down without her. She not only survived the bitterly cold night bivouacked at 8,300 meters with nothing more than her lightweight down suit but dug herself out of that hole at first light and, rather than starting down, turned up and continued toward the summit.

Wanda Rutkiewicz, the world's finest female alpinist and the first woman to place a boot on the top of K2, was left for dead in that frozen tomb, but she refused its death grip and rose to climb at least one more day.

A plaque in her honor at the base of Kangchenjunga reads: My fear vanished, and I felt a great freedom.

Death liberates.

THE PRICE OF PASSION

What we get from the adventure is just sheer joy.

—Sir Edmund Hillary

The last time I approached K2, rounding the famous corner in Concordia and seeing it there, sitting ten miles up the glacier, I bent over my trekking poles and sobbed. I simply knew too much. I knew I was looking at the graveyard of scores of people, five of whom I had come to know tenderly, lovingly. And I knew my days would be spent in anxious worry watching Jeff Rhoads, my love and partner, inch his way up a mountain that had killed so many.

It was June 17, 2002, and we were heading into the mountain to film the attempt of Spanish climber Araceli Segarra to become the sixth woman to summit K2. Jeff would not only be filming her but climbing with her on a mountain known for its savage weather, catastrophic avalanches, and unrelenting rockfall, all of which make K2 one of the deadliest mountains on Earth. And even if our small team of four made it to the summit, their chances of dying on descent were greater than on any other mountain on Earth—one in seven.

So I knew that sitting at the base all summer and watching them climb the mountain was going to be tough, and I was right: it was two months of unrelenting worry, sadness, and strain. While my team climbed I walked the glacier, and found the heartbreaking and grotesque bits and pieces of some of the scores who've died on the mountain and then buried and crevassed their broken remains.

Finally, the day of our departure came. I woke that morning as the sun breached the Northeast Ridge of Broad Peak, and I got out of the tent feeling an odd happiness. Something was different. My nose rose high, searching the air, like a wolf looking for dinner. My body knew what it was before my brain did, and I smiled: wood smoke, that beautiful, sweet, warm smell of my childhood in Vermont. Like pied pipers, we all walked toward the source and found ourselves guests at what was probably the world's highest cremation ceremony.

Seven years before, a team of Japanese climbers had been swept off the slope while they slept in their tents, an enormous avalanche throwing them into a deep crevasse. Earlier that summer five of their bodies had been found, and two of the surviving teammates had ventured from Japan, along with 120 porter loads of special wood and kerosene, to give them a proper burial.

I sat at a distance from the flames, trying not to enjoy too much the pure visceral pleasure of a wood fire, trying to remember that it wasn't only wood that was burning. Occasionally one of the Japanese would throw a gallon-size container of kerosene on the fires, and they would explode into the thin air in a burst of red and black, the picture-postcard K2 visible through the flames. I watched the five pyres slowly dissolve, their teepee stacks falling into the centers and onto the bodies beneath. Then I saw a white cage of ribs emerge from the red coals. In another I began to make out a bent arm, in another a perfectly round skull. My selfish pleasure dissolved, and feeling numb, mute, and heavy with sadness, I watched the bodies dissolve in the fires.

I looked at the five distinct cairns. Not four, not six, but five. How odd that just five of the Japanese were found, and here I was witnessing the one and only cremation at K2 Base Camp in history. Here they were burning before my very eyes—the five lost Japanese . . . the five women of K2. How eerily ironic that five women had climbed it, and although two made it off alive, another two had died trying, so five women remained up there, down here, somewhere. None of their families were here to usurp this ceremony for their loved one, so I thought I might as well. This was also the funeral for the women of K2.

How they had lived and the facts of their deaths had consumed me for years, too many years. My fascination began as it does for most journalists: I was consumed with the compelling facts, the five lives, the five deaths, the one mountain. But as that research developed into a book and a documentary, my emotions ranged from fascination to obsession to sadness to anger. As I delved deeper and came to know the women with an intimacy not shared by some of those closest to them, I began to get mad. I felt like a parent whose emotions turn to rage after losing a child to a random murder or stupid accident: Why didn't the women see trouble coming? Why didn't they turn around? Why did they try to cheat the mountain by going to K2 before they had more experience? How could they have been so blind, driven, selfish, you name it, I had the adjective for my blame and judgment. But as I came to the end of my research I finally came to peace with their deaths. I saw that they lived heroically and that even though they died too young, they did not die senselessly. They lived in passion and died in stillness, doing what they loved in a place that fed their souls. Someone had told me that when a climber dies in the mountains, it's not a tragedy; it's fate, and it's where they wanted to be. Another climber told me that he never felt as alive as when he climbed at the edge of death, and the closer he got, the more alive he felt.

I finally realized that although I didn't celebrate living at that edge, I couldn't condemn these five women, or the mountains, when they themselves accepted the risks.

Most of us will not choose where we die. But climbers who enter their deadly arena know they are dancing on that razor's edge with every movement they make. They don't mind the risk; in fact, they embrace the risk as part of the price of such unbridled joy. If they accept their fates, so must I. I finally realized that I had to understand that, given the choice, the women of K2 would have chosen to die right where they did rather than rotting from cancer or being crushed in an automobile accident or slipping into the long dark tunnel of Alzheimer's. If they had peace, who was I to judge that quiet happiness?

Their choice to live and die in the mountains was one of passion, purpose, and talent, not idle arrogance or selfish whim. They were talented climbers, and they found their greatest purpose in the mountains.

The women of K2 were mothers and daughters, wives and lovers, sisters and aunts, rivals and friends. Their deaths are losses for all of us, but the way they lived should be a lesson for all of us. Perhaps losing so many good women in such a relatively short period of time, 1986 to 1998, has kept other women from becoming high-altitude climbers. Most women today who are becoming climbers choose to stay out of the 8,000-meter game, instead excelling on rock and ice, like Lynn Hill, Catherine Destivelle, and Nancy Feagin. Some say the commitment of a Himalayan expedition is too great; others who venture into alpine climbing in their twenties quickly retire once they've hit their childbearing years to stay close to home for their children and families. Some simply don't think the risks of high altitude and all the "macho bullshit" are worth it.

Regardless of the reasons, most women climbers just don't aspire to high altitude's risk and rewards. Today there is no Wanda Rutkiewicz, no apparent heir to her strength, determination, and sacrifice, no follower who can claim bragging rights to her legacy. Alison Hargreaves was well on her way, but fate and foul weather changed her plans.

Today there are a small handful of women within spitting distance of Rutkiewicz's record of eight 8,000-meter peaks, each apparently a strong and able climber. But their rise has been meteoric, almost too quick; one of the women achieved four of her 8,000-meter peaks in just two years, another achieved six of the mountains in just three years. On the other hand Rutkiewicz doggedly climbed her first six 8,000-meter mountains within twelve years, one every two years, learning how to temper her mind and body against the rigors before her, peak by peak. Today's 8,000-meter women seem hardly to be in the same sport, ticking off mountains like mile signs along the freeway. This trend toward quantity versus quality is a trend throughout Himalayan climbing, but it is a dangerous one. It was when Rutkiewicz started climbing in this rapid-fire fashion in her so-called "Caravan of Dreams" that she got into real trouble. She upped her ante, pushing her own scales and body beyond their limits striving to bag her remaining eight peaks in little over a year and climbed into what became her own death zone.

Edurne Pasabán and Eva Zarzuelo, both of Spain, Nives Meroi of

Italy, and Gerlinde Kaltenbrunner of Austria are among the female climbers working to reach and break Rutkiewicz's record. From all reports, these women have strength, determination, and focus. But as strong as these women are, they depend on others to prepare the routes for them and once on the mountain usually climb with strong male partners who break the trail (particularly on summit day), carry the heavier loads, and often make the crucial decisions.

Maybe that's not a bad thing, so long as those men have the strength to get them both out of trouble if it hits above 8,000 meters. But such dependence can prove deadly, as it did for Liliane Barrard and Julie Tullis, both capable but not very experienced altitude climbers who found themselves on the summit of K2 after only a few years climbing 8,000-meter mountains. In the end those partners led them into the Death Zone, but were unable to bring them safely out of it.

As I sat in the incongruous warmth of the funeral pyres, I looked through the flames as they flicked at the summit of K2 miles above. As I had done intermittently all summer, I bent my head onto my knees and wept.

A few weeks later Jeff and I were finally home. With my mountain research finished, I dove into the personal. And if I thought the mountain's cold, impassive cruelty had been tough on my psyche, I was in for a dose of reality.

Five women have many people in their lives: husbands and lovers, children and siblings, mothers and fathers, friends and adversaries, supporters and detractors. The five women of K2 were no exception. One of my joys in being a writer and a journalist is the privilege I have had to meet and interview people who most interest me. Over the years I have been amazed and disappointed, shocked and chagrined, enraptured and disgusted, bored and enthralled, but nothing prepared me for getting to know the people the women of K2 left behind. With every new person I found, every fact I learned, every controversy I unearthed, I scratched away at the veneer of their lives, learning things I sometimes had no right to learn, talking with people who hadn't spoken since the woman's death, or since their love affair with her had ended. I spoke with families who hadn't yet found closure, siblings who never had a chance to say good-bye, lovers who were unacknowledged, and children who were sad and confused at having played second fiddle to a monolith of rock and ice.

The women of K2 left a tapestry of grief behind them because even though each climber and her family knew the risks involved, when someone is actually lost, the hole they leave is raw with unsaid words, unlived potential, and unrealized dreams.

I watched the tears pool in Carlos Carsolio's eyes as he told the story of saying his last good-bye to Wanda Rutkiewicz. I realized he would carry a survivor's guilt for the rest of his life for not insisting that she descend Kangchenjunga with him.

"But she was the great Wanda, and I had not the guts to tell her to come down," he said, remembering himself as a young kid on one of his first Himalayan expeditions. Looking up at an invisible spot on the ceiling, he continued in a whisper, "Perhaps that was all she needed, for me to tell her to come down. She was so proud."

I listened to Alain Bontemps's voice break over the phone from Paris. No one had asked him to speak of his sister, Liliane Barrard, in the seventeen years since her death on K2. Alain lost not only his sole sibling that day but one of his best friends, Maurice Barrard, as well. The three had climbed together, and Alain had shared their lives for months at a time, even summiting Gasherbrum II with them as a joyous trio.

"Madame Barrard called to tell me that her son and Liliane were lost," Alain said, "and I remember thinking, 'Oh God, not now, *not now.*'" The still-grieving brother was crushed by emotion, and I could hear him patting his chest, trying to regain his composure for the journalist calling from America asking about Liliane. The three had been planning to climb Everest after K2; he was helping the "World's Highest Couple" pursue their dreams. The dreams were now over, and the sister was gone.

I sat facing Terry Tullis in the living room of the crowded Bothy, his oddly shaped shoebox of a house filled with Himalayan artifacts, comfortable, worn furniture, and a pair of wiry boxers that happily sniffed at the guests. Above us on the mantel sat a black-and-white photograph in a dusty frame. In it a thirty-something Julie stands in the lee of a white horse's broad neck, her long hair and the horse's blowing in the wind. Julie had loved the cramped Bothy, the excitable boxers, and her gentle husband. Terry's composure was steady; he'd had more experience talking about his loss than Alain Bontemps had had. But then I asked him about Kurt Diemberger.

As soon as news of the 1986 tragedy reached Tunbridge Wells, Terry had flown to Vienna to where Diemberger lay in a hospital bed recovering from the amputations of his fingers and toes. Terry had been sitting by the bed when Diemberger opened his eyes. "Oh, Terry, you've come," Diemberger cried in anguish and relief, extending his bandaged hands.

"He didn't know if I'd come with a handshake or a shotgun," Terry chuckled. It wasn't a happy sound. As he retold the story Terry's sharp blue eyes became wet with tears, his voice cracked. It was hard to say whether he was remembering Diemberger's pain or his own. Today Terry Tullis struggles to recover from a series of strokes that have left him physically and mentally weak.

Jeff and I traveled through the French Alps speaking with the men Chantal left behind, and there were many: her brother and father, her climbing partners and friends, and her lovers, her many lovers. Regardless of the degree of the relationship they shared with Chantal, each wept at remembering the woman. But none could reveal the enigma beneath the image. Chantal had guarded her soul fiercely, filling page after page of her journal with poetry and travelogue but no revelation. She kept who she was deeply inside, far from even the lovers and friends.

Denis Ducroz struggled to hold his mouth from sobbing, his eyes from pouring tears, but he was only somewhat successful, and for a long moment he couldn't speak. He looked on the shelf above him where an enormous photograph of Chantal occupied an entire shelf in the low-ceilinged office overlooking Mont Blanc. She, of course, is smiling and unbelievably gorgeous in the summer sun, her fingers part of her storytelling, her hair in a curly cascade around her face.

John Hargreaves sat next to his wife in their neat-as-a-pin home in Belper, his hands tucked under his thighs, his feet crossing and uncrossing under his chair. Upstairs, Alison's room remained a daily reminder of the twenty-five years since she left it to live with Jim Ballard. Hargreaves looked as if he'd rather be anywhere else. It wasn't that he didn't want to talk about his admittedly favorite child—it was that he didn't know how. And then the father put his head in his hands and wept for the lost daughter, giving in to the pain, letting it bend him double and sit heavily on his shoulders. When he was able, he blew his nose, removed his oversized wire-rimmed glasses to wipe his eyes, placed them carefully back on his nose, and then continued politely answering questions.

And finally, there were the children. Today Tom and Kate Ballard are beautiful, charming, fun, funny, and talented teenagers. The world judged their mother as selfish, unbalanced, and irrationally driven to climb mountains rather than stay home with them. But Tom and Kate seem to know what the world isn't able to accept: Alison Hargreaves didn't abandon her children. Not only did she leave them in the loving care of a dedicated father, but she gave them a gift many other children lack: she showed them how to live with passion, dedication, and heart. They live an austere life in Scotland; there are no Game Boys or titanium mountain bikes cluttering the Ballard home. What does fill it are shoes—climbing shoes, hiking shoes, running shoes, mud shoes, snow shoes, ski boots. It is the cluttered hallway of a life lived outdoors. As we drove away Tom stood behind Jim Ballard, but at fifteen he already poked above his father's head, and Kate was to their left, her head bent against the setting sun in her eyes; all of them waved and smiled. Then they turned and resumed climbing a wall of their stone cottage.

As we drove south, passing lochs scattered like lapis gemstones through the impossibly green, gray, and wet Scottish Highlands, I thought of Wanda on faraway Kangchenjunga, fallen off its summit ridge and now deep in one of its crevasses. I wondered whether she had realized another 8,000-meter triumph, nine in all, and whether her last moments were filled with fierce pride at having done what no other woman ever would—become the first to climb the three highest mountains in the world.

I thought of Liliane who lay above the Gilkey, her broken body tucked into the rocks. Had she witnessed her love's death or had Maurice watched hers? Either way, one watched the other go and then soon followed down the unforgiving mountain.

Straightforward, strong Julie, was she floating in the glacier's effluvium or had she become entombed on the Shoulder? I prayed her last thoughts were ones of pleasure and peace at having finally climbed the mountain of her dreams.

Beautiful Chantal, she made it home, sweet girl, and her family was still celebrating the fact of her life by sharing her ashes with the places she loved, spreading her thin and laughing all the way.

Finally, dear, determined Alison. I wondered whether Tom and Kate would ever go to K2, suspecting they probably would. What could keep them away? They were already gifted climbers, and their mother was part of the landscape. They had lost her so young and been told so much about her life and death. Surely they would have to see it for themselves?

And finally I thought of the two unheralded women of K2 who paid for their passion for the mountain without having reached its summit: Halina, the tiny woman with a huge personality, a pipe clenched between her teeth, telling a string of foul jokes just to shock her more reserved teammates, and Mrowka, who spent all of her energy helping save another climber's life but in the end didn't have enough to save herself.

The women of K2. I finally had my book.

AUTHOR'S NOTE

"Mountaineers climb because they love the mountains, yes; but they climb too because climbing prepares them boldly and tenaciously for death, then guides them faithfully to the edge of another world, a world I now recognize as the world of the dead, and there allows them to dance, mountain after mountain, year after year, as close to death as it is possible to dance, which is to say, within a single step."

—ROBERT LEONARD REID

Just as we were going to press with the publication of *Savage Summit*, halfway around the world a tall, lanky woman from the Basque country of Spain made history.

July 26, 2004. It had been nine years since a woman had stood atop K2, and over six since K2's last surviving female summiter had perished on her attempt of Dhaulagiri. In a matter of moments, as long as it takes to move your foot from there to there, the dark history changed; at 4:30 P.M. Pakistan time, Edurne Pasabán became the sixth woman to place her boot in the airy snow on the world's second highest peak.

Pasabán, thirty-one, has had an impressive rise through the climbing world, faster than any woman and most men in history. She's climbed seven 8,000-meter peaks in just four years, three of those mountains in a miraculous eight-week period during the summer of 2003. It took Rutkiewicz over three times as long to accomplish the same number, thirteen years from 1978 to 1991. Pasabán now has more 8,000-meter peaks than any woman alive and is the only woman to have climbed four of the five highest mountains. Number three, Kangchenjunga, eludes her. If her track record continues, she could well be the first woman to climb all fourteen 8,000-meter peaks.

Before leaving for the K2 in May of 2004, Pasabán acknowledged having some healthy fear of the mountain, but reasoned that she would be climbing with a strong team of experienced men. She wasn't wrong. She climbed every step of her ascent with Juanito Oiarzábal, a man who has already climbed all of the 8,000-meter peaks a stunning total of twenty-one times. K2 is now among those he has climbed twice. In fact, he is one of only three men to have ever "repeated" on K2.

Pasabán also knew as she approached K2 this summer it would be overcrowded with nearly 150 climbers who came to the mountain to be part of the fiftieth anniversary of its first ascent. And so it was. Among the fifteen teams clustered at Base Camp was an enormous Italian national team as well as a commercial group with "client" climbers paying for someone else to do the heavy work, "tourists" as they were facetiously called by more seasoned climbers. The growing trend in high-altitude climbing of relying on Sherpas, bottled oxygen, and other teams' men and equipment is a change many alpinists watch with fear and loathing, particularly on K2, which demands, as no other mountain does, that climbers have the strength and expertise to get themselves up and off its treacherous slopes. The resulting tensions tore through Base Camp in June and July and some bitterly complained on websites that certain teams were misrepresenting their climbing style as barebones "alpine" when it was anything but, and that the inexperienced "tourists" were making it dangerous for everybody.

Meanwhile, Pasabán and Oiarzábal quietly climbed, inexorably inching up K2, ascending and descending as foul weather continually forced them off the mountain. Until the last days of July it looked like the mountain and its infamous weather might repel all would-be ascenders for yet another season, making it unclimbed for three straight years. Then, suddenly, there was a break in the wind and snow and dozens of climbers made a run for the mountain. Within two days the summits had started.

Five Italians made the summit first, followed closely by Pasabán and Oiarzábal, who were triumphant and awed that they were among the first in three years to lay claim to the near-impossible. But their triumph soon turned to calamity when Oiarzábal collapsed on descent, exhausted and most likely suffering from high-altitude sickness. Their pace slowed to inches per hour, the blood in their veins running like glue in the thin air and frigid temperature, frostbite chewing at their toes and turning their down-climbing into a dangerous agony. Their descent was frighteningly similar to that of Liliane and Maurice Barrard's, with Maurice spending every ounce of his energy to get them both up the mountain. But unlike the Barrards who, alone and exhausted, fell to their deaths on descent, Pasabán and Oiarzábal had plenty of company on the crowded mountain and dozens of strong rescuers who risked their own lives and forfeited their attempts at the summit to bring the stricken climbers all the way down to Base Camp. (In an ironic twist, one of the men who helped get them off the mountain, Italian climber Tarcisio Bello, helped dig out Chantal Mauduit's body from her ruined tent on Dhaulagiri in 1998. With the rescue of Pasabán, his connection to the dark history of the women of K2 is now sewn even tighter.)

By the time the Spaniards made it back down, they had been on the mountain for over five days and Oiarzábal was a shadow of the man who has the 8,000-meter record and Pasabán, with black toes and IV tubes in her arms, sobbed that "never, ever, am I going to climb again." Twenty-four hours later she was once again talking about her love of the mountains and how she might consider Dhaulagiri in the fall, but Oiarzábal was admitting they had gone too far, underestimating the mountain and overestimating their abilities against it. They had pushed their envelope and survived, he said, but barely. Without the willing and able climbers who helped save their lives, he knew their histories on K2 could have been fatal rather than merely mortal.

Although they lived to talk about it, Pasabán and Oiarzábal were unable to walk out of Base Camp and were flown by helicopter all the way to Islamabad, at a reported cost of $25,000, where they caught the next flight to Spain. As of mid-August, Pasabán was reporting that she will lose two of her toes, Oiarzábal all of his. They were lucky to get away so cheap.

K2 had stood impassively for three years without a single climber and nine years without a woman reaching the top when suddenly history was made: forty-three climbers touched the summit in three days as the rare weather window remained miraculously open. Pasabán was among them, and she now joins the select club of women who made it off K2 alive. But she is its only living member, and many observers wonder why the Savage Mountain seems so hard to survive, even once you are safely off it.

K2 has always been a mystical mountain, and one of its earliest explorers and climbers, Aleister Crowley, was a self-proclaimed worshiper of the devil whom he called "the Beast 666." While unsuccessful in his 1902 summit bid, his climbing skills, antics, and oddities were legend and became woven into the tantalizing fabric of the "Savage Mountain."

And indeed it is an oddly enticing lore. Even more eerily interesting is the chronology of the women's history on K2. In 1986 Wanda Rutkiewicz became the first woman to climb K2. Six years later she perished while climbing Kangchenjunga. That same year, 1992, Chantal Mauduit became the first woman since Rutkiewicz to climb K2 and make it down alive. Then six years later, *she* died while attempting Dhaulagiri. Now in 2004, six years after Mauduit died, there is finally a sixth female summiter.

With only slight apology to the realists in the crowd, one can make a case for there being, in the very least, an uncomfortable coincidence with the numbers and perhaps even make the suggestion that Pasabán would be wise to choose a sea-level excursion in the year 2010.

Jennifer Jordan
August 17, 2004
Salt Lake City, Utah

SPECIAL THANKS

In each of the chapters of this book resides the work of hundreds, through their excellent written accounts as well as the untold hours many spent with me over the phone and in e-mails, sharing their thoughts, memories, opinions, research, and data. Without them, a book containing five biographies would have been utterly impossible, and I am indebted to each and every one for the energy and intellect they shared so generously:

The families and friends of the women of K2: John and Joyce Hargreaves, Alain Bontemps, Tom, Kate and Jim Ballard, Nicholas Blaszkiewicz, Susan Hargreaves Stokes, François and Stacey Mauduit, Chris and Julie Tullis, Terry Tullis, Zita Latham, Bev England Marshall, Ewa Matuszewska, Michal Blaszkiewicz, Mick Renier, Sylvie Borelli, Anna Pietraszeu, Pierre Barrard, Claire Barrard, and Miss Elizabeth Hawley.

Mountaineers: Jeff Rhoads, Carlos Carsolio, Ed Viesturs, Reinhold Messner, Peter Hillary, Jeff Lowe, Nazir Sabir, Carlos Buhler, Greg Child, Thor Kieser, Richard Celsi, Ewa Pankiewicz, Denis Ducroz, Dan Mazur, Krystyna Palmowska, David Breashears, Eduard Loretan, Ferran Latorre Torres, Anna Okopinska, Frédérique Delrieu, Anna Czerwinska, Fabien Ibarra, Dianne Roberts, Kim Logan, Pierre Neyret, Jim Whittaker, Lynn Hill, Catherine Destivelle, David Rose, Edward Douglas, Simone Moro, Silvio Mondinelli, Fausto de Stefani, Marco Galezzi, Tarcisio Bello, Pete Athans, Jozek Nyka, Dee Molenaar, Eric Simonson,

Guy Cotter, Alison Osius, Sharon Wood, Edurne Pasabán, Lydia Bradey, Adrian Burgess, Alan Burgess, Stephen Koch, Peter Metcalf, Sandy Hill, Charley Mace, Geoff Tabin, Anna Keeling, Greg Mortenson, Charlotte Fox, Andres Delgado, Arlene Blum, Barbara Washburn, Sher Khan, Henry Todd, Gary Neptune, Mike Bearzi (whom we all lost in 2002), Charley Shimanski and the entire staff of the American Alpine Club, Lisa and Terry Austin and all the wild women of Wild Women Outfitters, and my fellow teammates on the mountain in 2002, Araceli Segarra, Armando Dattoli de la Vega, Hector Ponce de Leon Gomes, Jeff Cunningham, Fida Hussain, Muhammed Hussain, and Ghulam Mohammad of Blue Sky Tours–Pakistan.

My friends and interpreters: Dr. Ewa Wasilewska, Mike Reinne, Niels-Henrik Friisbøl, Jean Mi Asselin, Anne Badalado, Chelsea Webber, Cy Park, Doug Wortham, Zainab Omar, and Abbas Khan.

And the valued work of those talented chroniclers of K2 who never stopped answering my questions: Charlie Houston, Jim Curran, Jim Wickwire, Rick Ridgeway, Kurt Diemberger, Richard Salisbury, Xavier Eguskitza, Ray Huey, and Eberhard Jurgalski.

In addition to those who provided intellectual gold are those who supported the entire messy process, from a hot meal to a cold martini to a well-bent ear. Without them, book-writing would be an even lonelier task: Alice Webber, Nan Inskeep, Charlie and Nancy Gear, Jeff Gear, Marcie Saganov and Susan Maclure, Maria Coffey, Rolf Glessner-Gates, my agent Jill Kneerim, and the women of HarperCollins who put it all together: my editor, Maureen O'Brien; her incredibly able right hand, Lindsey Moore; and my copyeditor, Cindy Buck, whose every change made the book better.

And mostly to Jeff, who has the patience of a saint and always made room for the mess.

CHAPTER NOTES

CHAPTER 1

In addition to interviews with Dianne Roberts, Jim Whittaker, Rick Ridgeway, Arlene Blum, and Jim Wickwire, I turned to several written accounts of the 1975 and 1978 American expeditions to K2 to try to understand the circumstances of those troubled and yet triumphant teams, including but not limited to Rick Ridgeway's *The Last Step*, Cherie Bremer Kamp's *Living on the Edge*, Galen Rowell's *In the Throne Room of the Mountain Gods*, and Jim Whittaker's *A Life on the Edge*.

CHAPTERS 2 AND 3

In the last years of her life, when not on an expedition, Wanda Rutkiewicz spent the lion's share of her time working on her biography with Ewa Matuszewska, a journalist, writer, and friend. I've based most of Wanda's thoughts and quotes on the resulting book, *Uciec jak Najwyzej: Nie dokonczone zycie Wanda Rutkiewicz* (Escaping to the Highest: The Unfinished Life of Wanda Rutkiewicz). The original Polish was translated for me by Dr. Ewa Wasilewska, an anthropologist at the University of Utah, Salt Lake City. In addition, an Austrian journalist, Gertrude Reinisch, published a biography, *Wanda Rutkiewicz: Caravan of Dreams*, which was translated from German into English in 2000. I have tried, whenever possible, to rely on Matuszewska's book, as I consider the book and the author closer to Wanda and her life and thoughts.

CHAPTER 4

Liliane Barrard lived a very quiet life with only one sibling and few friends outside of her marriage; her life and energy were devoted to her husband Maurice. No biography has been written of her life, and the few magazine and newspaper articles that mention her do so in relation to her husband. As a result, ferreting out information about Liliane's innermost thoughts and emotions was an enormous challenge. It took me years to discover that she even *had* a brother, and several more months of Internet searching to find the man himself. While her brother, Alain Bontemps, could offer me very few clues to his sister's early and most private thoughts, he did send me three films about her climbing. One, *Lettres du Karakoram,* was made after her death and contains the narrated journal entries she made on her three major Himalayan climbs: Gasherbrum II, Nanga Parbat, and K2. It is from these letters that I was able to get my first real glimpse of the woman behind the man, and from them I gleaned what her thoughts, fears, anxieties, and joys were in the last years of her life.

CHAPTERS 4 AND 5

The agonies of the Black Summer of 1986 live to this day. In yet another heart-breaking epilogue, soon after losing his mother on K2, Mrowka Wolf's five-year-old son also lost his father in a climbing accident in the Tetra Mountains of Poland. In addition to Jim Curran's outstanding chronicle of the 1986 climbing season, *K2: Triumph and Tragedy,* I am indebted to Kurt Diemberger for providing insight into Julie's experience that fateful summer, both in several conversations as well as his book *Endless Knot.*

CHAPTER 7

There have been several published reports that doctors warned Wanda Rutkiewicz to avoid climbing because her liver and kidneys had been severely damaged over the years. But these reports are without corroboration. Each of her closest friends, climbing partners, and family members only knew her to be in excellent health. In fact, her Kangchenjunga teammates commented on her remarkable circulation and noted that she was one of the few members not to suffer frostbite in the extreme cold.

Seven years after Alison Hargreaves died on K2, I found the body of Lorenzo Ortiz on the glacier mauled and mangled from his 12,000-foot fall off the Savage Mountain. In 2003, Jeff and I described the clothing to climber Ferran Latorre of Barcelona, who was able to identify the body as that of Ortiz. He still wore his climbing harness but lay alone on the ice; none of his climbing partners lay near, but farther out on the ice I found Bruce Grant's blue parka and what I surmised was Rob Slater's red Patagonia climbing suit. Thankfully, no one has ever found a trace of Alison. Seeing the ravaged state of the bodies I had found, I lived in fear of discovering her remains or Julie Tullis's. I never did.

SELECTED BIBLIOGRAPHY
AND SOURCE MATERIALS

BOOKS

Auerbach, Paul S., ed. *Wilderness Medicine*. St. Louis: Mosby Publications, 2001.

Ballard, James. *One and Two Halves to K2*. Auckland, N.Z.: Penguin Books, 1996.

Birkett, Bill, and Bill Peascod. *Women Climbing: 200 Years of Achievement*. Seattle: Mountaineers, 1990.

Blum, Arlene. *Annapurna: A Woman's Place*. San Francisco: Sierra Club Books, 1980.

Bremer-Kamp, Cherie. *Living on the Edge: The Winter Ascent of Kanchenjunga*. Perregrine Smith Books, 1987.

Brown, Rebecca A. *Women on High: Pioneers of Mountaineering*. Boston: Appalachian Mountain Club Books, 2002.

Burgess, Adrian, and Alan Burgess. *The Burgess Book of Lies*. Seattle: Mountaineers, 1998.

Child, Greg. *Thin Air: Encounters in the Himalayas*. Salt Lake City: Peregrine Smith Books, 1988.

———. *Mixed Emotions*. Seattle. Mountaineers, 1993.

Coffey, Maria. *Fragile Edge: A Personal Portrait of Loss on Everest*. Seattle: Mountaineers, 2000.

———. *Where the Mountain Casts Its Shadow: The Dark Side of Extreme Adventure*. New York: St. Martin's Press, 2003.

Craig, Robert W. *Storm and Sorrow in the High Pamirs*. New York: Simon & Schuster, 1977.

Curran, Jim. *K2: Triumph and Tragedy*. Boston: Houghton Mifflin, 1989.

———. *K2: The Story of the Savage Mountain*. Seattle: Mountaineers, 1995.

Da Silva, Rachel. *Leading Out: Women Climbers Reaching for the Top*. Seattle: Seal Press, 1992.

Diemberger, Kurt. *The Endless Knot: K2, Mountain of Dreams and Destiny*. Seattle: Mountaineers, 1991.

Diemberger, Kurt, and Roberto Mantovani. *K2: Challenging the Sky.* Seattle: Mountaineers, 1997.

Fay, Charles Ernest, Allen Herbert Bent, Howard Palmer, James Monroe Thorington, Andrew John Kauffman and William Lowell Putman, eds. *A Century of American Alpinism: 2002.* Boulder, Colo.: American Alpine Club, 2002.

Hargreaves, Alison. *A Hard Day's Summer: Six Classic North Faces—Solo.* London: Hodder & Stoughton, 1994.

Herzog, Maurice. *Annapurna.* North Salem, N.Y.: Adventure Library, 1995.

Houston, Charles S. *Going High: The Story of Man and Altitude.* New York: American Alpine Club, 1980.

Houston, Charles S. *Going Higher, The Story of Man and Altitude,* rev. ed. Boston: Little, Brown & Company, 1987.

Houston, Charles S. *High Altitude, Illness and Wellness: The Prevention of a Killer,* Globe Pequot, 1998.

Houston, Charles S., and Robert Bates. *Five Miles High.* New York: Dodd, Mead and Co., 1939.

———. *K2: The Savage Mountain.* Seattle: Mountaineers, 1954, 1979.

Houston, Charles S., and Geoffrey Coates. *Hypoxia and Mountain Medicine.* Lake Louise, Can.: International Hypoxia Symposium, 1991, 1993.

Kauffman, Andrew, and William Putnam. *K2: The 1939 Tragedy.* Seattle: Mountaineers, 1992.

King, John, and Bradley Mayhew. *Karakoram Highway: The High Road to China: A Travel Survival Kit.* Berkeley, Calif.: Lonely Planet Books, 1993.

Matuszewska, Ewa. *Uciec jak Najwyzej: Nie dokonczone zycie Wanda Rutkiewicz* (Escaping to the Highest: The Unfinished Life of Wanda Rutkiewicz). Translated by Dr. Ewa Wasilewska. Iskry, Warsaw, Pol.: 1999.

Mauduit, Chantal. *J'habite au Paradis.* Paris: Lattes, 1997.

Mazel, David, *Mountaineering Women: Stories by Early Climbers.* College Station: Texas A&M University Press, 1994.

McDonald, Bernadette, and John Amatt, eds. *Voices from the Summit: The World's Great Mountaineers on the Future of Climbing.* Washington, D.C.: Adventure Press/National Geographic, 2000.

Miller, Luree. *On Top of the World: Five Women Explorers in Tibet.* Seattle: Mountaineers, 1984.

O'Connell, Nicholas. *Beyond Risk: Conversations with Climbers.* Seattle: Mountaineers, 1993.

Ornter, Sherry B. *Making Gender: The Politics and Erotics of Culture.* Boston: Beacon Press, 1996.

Polk, Milbry, and Mary Tiegreen. *Women of Discovery: A Celebration of Intrepid Women Who Explored the World.* New York: Clarkson Potter, 2001.

Potterfield, Peter. *In the Zone: Epic Survival Stories from the Mountaineering World.* Seattle: Mountaineers Books, 1996.

Reinisch, Gertrude. *Wanda Rutkiewicz: A Caravan of Dreams*. Ross-on-Wye, Hereford, UK: Carreg Publishers, 2000.

Ridgeway, Rick. *The Last Step: The American Ascent of K2*. Seattle: Mountaineers, 1980.

Roberts, David. *Escape Routes*. Seattle: Mountaineers, 1997.

———. *True Summit: What Really Happened on the Legendary Ascent of Annapurna*. New York: Simon & Schuster, 2000.

Rose, David, and Edward Douglas. *Regions of the Heart: The Triumph and Tragedy of Alison Hargreaves*. Washington, D.C.: National Geographic, 2000.

Roskelley, John. *Stories Off the Wall*. Seattle: Mountaineers, 1993.

Rowell, Galen A. *In the Throne Room of the Mountain Gods*. San Francisco: Sierra Club Books, 1986.

Saunders, Victor. *Elusive Summits*. London: Sphere Books, 1991.

Schoene, Robert B. *Limits of Human Lung Function at High Altitude*. Seattle: Department of Medicine, Division of Respiratory and Critical Care Medicine, University of Washington, 2001.

Schoene, Robert B., Peter Hackett, and Thomas Hornbein. "High Attitude." In *Textbook of Respiratory Medicine*, edited by T.F. Murray and J.A. Nadel. Philadelphia: Saunders, 2001.

Simpson, Joe. *Touching the Void*. New York: HarperCollins, 1988.

Tullis, Julie. *Clouds from Both Sides*. San Francisco: Sierra Club Books, 1987.

Washburn, Barbara. *The Accidental Adventurer: Memoirs of the First Woman to Climb Mount McKinley*. Kenmore, Wash.: Epicenter Press, 2001.

Whittaker, Jim. *A Life on the Edge: Memoirs of Everest and Beyond*. Seattle: Mountaineers, 1999.

Wickwire, Jim, and Dorothy Bullitt. *Addicted to Danger*. New York: Pocket Books, 1998.

Willis, Clint, ed. *High: Stories of Survival from Everest and K2*. New York: Balliett & Fitzgerald, 1999.

Workman, Fanny Bullock, and William Hunter Workman. *The Ice World of the Himalaya*. First published 1900.

FILMS

Lettres du Karakoram, Alain Bontemps, director (1987)

Un Homme, Une Femme, Un 8000 : Gasherbrum II, Alain Bontemps, director (1983)

K2: Death and Destiny, Kurt Diemberger, director (1989)

K2: Triumph and Tragedy, Jim Curran, director (1987)

Women of K2, Jeff Rhoads, director (2003)

Requiem, Wanda Rutkiewicz, director (1988)

In the Shadow of Everest, Anna Pietraszeu, director (1999)

Namasté, Viva Productions and M6 (1998)